D0021324

THE WAY
UP FROM
DOWN

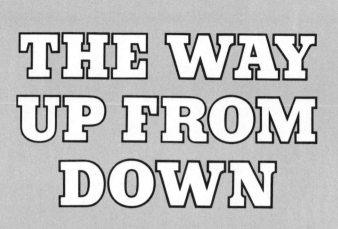

THE WAY UP FROM DOWN

A Safe New Program
That Relieves Low Moods
and Depression with
Amino Acids and
Vitamin Supplements

PRISCILLA SLAGLE, M.D.

RANDOM HOUSE
New York

Library of Congress Cataloging-in-Publication Data

Slagle, Priscilla.
　The way up from down.

　Includes bibliographies.
　1. Depression, Mental—Chemotherapy. 2. Depression, Mental—Nutritional aspects. 3. Amino acids—Therapeutic use. 4. Vitamin therapy. I. Title.
[DNLM: 1. Amino Acids—therapeutic use—popular works. 2. Depression—drug therapy—popular works. 3. Vitamins—therapeutic use—
popular works.
WM 171 S631w]
RC537.S575 1987　616.85′27061　86-28062
ISBN 0-394-55194-X

Book design by Charlotte Staub
Manufactured in the United States of America
24689753
First Edition

This book
is dedicated to
KEIRAN BREEDEN
whose enthusiasm
and love helped
to make it
possible.

Acknowledgments

My particular gratitude is extended to:

- My patients who were willing to trust and who have taught me so much
- Dr. Rita Scherrei, assistant university librarian of UCLA, who was invaluable in obtaining all necessary research materials and in compiling the bibliography
- Jay Allen, who provided me with initial tangible encouragement
- Reid Boates, my agent, whose suggestions were always helpful as well as being agreeable
- Linda Alexine, who faithfully transcribed my handwriting
- And to my family, who taught me hope and optimism

Contents

Introduction xi

PART I: AMINO ACIDS AND LOW MOODS 1

1 The Horror of Depression 5
2 How to Recognize Depression 16
3 The Brain Amine Theory of Depression 29
4 The Amino Acid Treatment Program 40
5 Amino Acids, Brain Amines and Precursor Loading 63
6 Program Adjustments for Special Circumstances 72

PART II: EVERYDAY CONTRIBUTORS TO CHEMICAL IMBALANCE
    AND LOW MOODS 83

7 Nutrient Deficiencies 87
8 Other Food-Mood Connections 104
9 Life Habits and Exposures 115
10 Specific Physical Illnesses and Low Moods 124
11 Stress and Traumatic Life Events 134
12 Psychological Stressors 144

PART III: SPECIAL ATTENTION FOR SPECIAL PEOPLE 151

13 The Young: Special Attention for Special People 155
14 The Old: Special Attention for Special People 163

PART IV: A MOOD-BALANCING WAY OF LIFE 171

15 Improving Mental Habits and Life-styles 175

Appendixes 185
Bibliography 221

Introduction

This book presents a safe, effective treatment for depression and low moods—a nutritional approach. It is completely natural, virtually free of side effects and scientifically based. I have seen it work in my own practice and there are more and more reports from around the country of its effectiveness.

Here is a list of what I hope to convey:

- Proof that depression is biochemically induced and treatable
- Why and how certain nutrients—chiefly amino acids and vitamin-mineral supplements—bring relief
- How to start your own program of nutritional supplements—and when to turn to a physician for help
- How the program can help you when you're not actually depressed but suffer only from occasional low moods
- A self-rating scale to help you discover whether you are depressed
- How to identify depression in yourself or someone close to you and how to recognize its psychological and physical symptoms

THE MONOAMINE THEORY OF DEPRESSION

The brain needs certain chemicals—the neurotransmitters—to function properly. When these chemicals are in short supply, depression sets in. That, in a nutshell, is the biochemical theory of depression—the monoamine theory, named for the brain chemicals that control our moods, and thus the very quality of our lives.

The monoamine theory of depression is the theoretical basis for the various types of antidepressant prescription drugs on the market today. But there are better ways to increase the brain's store of these important chemicals, better because side effects are minimal to nonexistent, and because of decided positive effects on the depression as well as on overall general health.

THE NUTRITIONAL APPROACH

Brain amines are manufactured from amino acids. In this book, we will examine the principle of "precursor loading," a dietary technique that includes supplementary amino acids which produce an increase in certain brain amines. The program also describes in detail the "support" supplements, chiefly vitamins and minerals, that go along with the treatment. There is emphasis throughout on how the reader can personalize the program to specific symptoms and needs.

THE PROMISE

Depression is temporary and treatable. That is the stark, simple truth.

It is treatable through a nutritional approach that is more natural than drugs, and far cheaper and more effective than psychotherapy alone. Anyone with low moods or mild to moderate depression can try it in her own home. Those with more severe depression can try it in cooperation with their physicians. The required amino acids are available in pharmacies and health food stores—without a prescription.

Depression is a national health crisis. This book contains the theory, the program, the answer. There is hope for the millions of people who suffer mood pain.

Part I

AMINO ACIDS AND LOW MOODS

I live on hope
and that, I think, do all who
come into this world.

—Robert Bridges, Sonnet 63

I can remember how, when I was growing up, my siblings and I would carefully monitor our mother's mood. As soon as we saw her, we would try to read her and then adjust our behavior accordingly; either to have a wonderful time or to lay low and keep out of her way. My mother was intense, powerful and changeable—at times delightful and at other times very difficult.

Having to react to her may have been the beginning of my own focus on moods, but most of us hear about moods all our lives. So and so is in a bad mood or a good mood, a happy mood or a sad mood, a rosy, black or blue mood. In my opinion mood is the most consistent determinant of the quality of our lives. No matter what's going on, we can handle it if our mood is good. Some people seem blessed with a pretty consistent good mood. They remain buoyant and optimistic even in the face of seemingly insurmountable external odds. This explains how a limbless thalidomide baby can grow into an active, swimming, wheelchair-racing, "normal" teenager; or why a fifty-year-old woman fired from her job has been able to use the trouble as an opportunity to find a rewarding new career. People like these seem to have the indwelling presence of an optimistic and positive mood.

Conversely, there are those who externally seem to have all that life can offer, yet are pessimistic and filled with worry most of the time. They endure a miserable life, so depressed, anxious and angry that they are blinded to the good in and around them. Such people use the trials of life not as learning experiences but as fuel to create even greater pain. They don't seem to have the wherewithal for emotional, physical and spiritual growth. It is my

3

belief, and the thesis of this book, that what they lack are certain simple nutrients, substances I (and other physicians) have recommended for many years. They have been helpful to people who have severe depression, to those with occasional mood swings, and to those who are temporarily facing very difficult life situations.

In essence, what I hope this book will do is lead you to a safe, healthy method for promoting mood control and thus enriching and empowering your life.

1 The Horror of Depression

Hello, Dr. Slagle."

The woman's voice on the telephone is tense, determined, resigned. "I'm tired of fighting. Tired of trying to make life work when it never does anyway. I'm in my apartment; all the windows are closed and the gas has been on for a while. I just wanted to say goodbye to you. I don't want you to be upset. Everyone has tried very hard to help me, but I'm too tired to care anymore."

This same woman had twice tried to kill herself before we ever met. She had once slashed her wrists severely, not feeling the slightest pain, and had almost bled to death on the lawn of the prestigious university where she was a straight "A" student.

She had only recently become my patient and still felt too hopeless and despairing to cooperate with the treatment program. Fortunately, I was able to contact her mother and the police on that potentially fatal night, and they rushed her to the hospital in time to save her. Still more fortunately, she became a willing patient over the next several months.

A year and a half after that phone call, this witty, beautiful young woman visited my office, beaming with pride. She had come to introduce me to her new baby daughter. I can't express what that visit meant to me. I can tell you, though, that she is one of many patients who have been treated successfully with a nutritional approach for alleviating depression and low moods. This method has proven to be 70 to 80 percent effective during the nine years I've been prescribing it in my practice, both for patients in real trouble as this woman was and for those with temporary mood swings.

Luckily most people only experience brief mood swings that

may be annoying but are not overwhelming. For such people this program can be almost 100 percent effective. It can also help on those crucial days we all face, when we want to perform optimally and not be at the mercy of a "down" period. A striking example of this situation is that of an attorney who came to my office with the complaint that she never knew how to arrange her court schedule because her performance was so influenced by her moods. She was not consistently down, but some mornings she woke up feeling "off," vague and slightly fuzzy-headed. On other days she was a dynamo charged with energy and focused intensity. On the good days she was a star performer, on the bad days she struck out. Once this lawyer was able to gain biochemical control of her moods by taking the proper nutrients, she was able to score consistently and to create an important position for herself.

Even though the majority of us only experience occasional blue days or low periods, it's important to understand how bad depression can be and to know how to avoid it. The sad fact is that, unfortunately, most of us will, at some time, have to deal with other depressed people even if we ourselves do not succumb.

When low feelings come and go, the periods of relief can bring a much needed respite, and allow the person to continue functioning normally in society. But when depression is continuous and severe, it can squeeze every last drop of color and vitality out of life, pressing relentlessly down on its victim until despair alone survives. There is then no need to think or worry about punishment in the hereafter. The torture is here and now. John Milton must have known something about this state when he penned those famous lines in *Paradise Lost:*

> The mind is its own place, and in itself
> Can make a Heav'n of Hell, or a Hell of Heav'n.

With severe depression, the world is colored black and blue. There are psychological, spiritual and physical bruises. The pervasive pain can seep into every compartment of life. No matter what the religious beliefs, faith and hope are lost, there is little or no ability to feel enjoyment, the ability to give and receive love fades or entirely disappears, and guilt and anguish set in. Only someone who has suffered from this illness can understand the utter devastation it can inflict.

The mental pain of depression is sometimes so great it erases physical pain. I remember being called upon to treat a depressed woman who had slashed both wrists, both sides of her neck and both ankles, and had stabbed herself in the liver, and lived through it feeling no physical pain. The degree of desperation involved in such self-attack was difficult to comprehend. It was as if she had entered a "trance-like" or altered state of consciousness without the aid of drugs or alcohol to dull the feelings.

Incidents like this left their mark on me. I was in my psychiatry residency at the time. Young. Impressionable. Most doctors can tell you the training years at major university hospitals are the times when they see the most exotic, extreme and various kinds of illnesses. They are confronted with the most difficult when they are the least experienced. My training was no exception. I was assigned a variety of fascinating but hard-to-treat patients, and I learned a lot—fast!

During this same intensely difficult first year of psychiatry residency, something else happened that stunned all of us with the profound suffering in depression. One of my co-residents was particularly brilliant, an exceedingly hard worker, who gave his patients considerable attention. The brightest of us paled in comparison to him in his thoroughness and attention to detail. He was handsome and, by all outward appearances, had his life together.

One Monday morning the director of the residency program called us for a special meeting. There was no way he could have prepared us for the news that this brilliant young man had been found dead in a motel room over the weekend. He had left a suicide note, and had died from an overdose of sleeping pills.

Many years have passed and though I still believe depression is hell, I now know it is not eternal and everlasting, as some feel.

On the contrary, *I know that depression is treatable and temporary.* I know it professionally, through my practice. And I know it personally.

MY OWN STORY

I suffered from intermittent but intense depression from the ages of fifteen to thirty-five. Though I always functioned, depression colored my attitude and thoughts, and caused me unnecessary suffering for nearly twenty years.

As a teenager, I came very close to taking an aspirin overdose. Usually, aspirin isn't fatal. Fortunately, many suicide attempts made by the young are unsuccessful because young people lack the knowledge of what kills.

One part of the residency in psychiatry requires that the young doctor undergo a personal psychoanalysis, as well as sampling various other kinds of therapy. Five years of psychoanalysis three to five times a week, and seventeen thousand dollars later, I was still running into those same moments of intense depression. Also, I sampled many other forms of therapy: individual Gestalt, Reichian, Jungian, reality and behavior therapy as well as encounter, sensitivity and Tavistock group therapy. Through it all my insight, awareness and coping mechanisms increased, but the depression was still there. I was especially worried because depression surrounds my profession. The suicide rates of doctors and dentists are higher than any other profession, and those of female physicians are higher than of male physicians.

Just as psychoanalysis wasn't the answer for me, neither were drugs. My depression was not constant enough to make me want to experience the side effects of antidepressant medication. But the desperate times continued. I remember some of them very clearly. One time, I was sitting on the edge of a cliff at Sea Ranch, California, looking down a few hundred feet to where the blue light of the full moon shimmered and danced on the restless sea. It was so inviting and I wanted very much to jump, to end it all. And on another occasion, while sitting on the warm sand at twilight, watching the endless waves curl into the earth, I wanted to walk slowly out to sea, never to return.

There were no psychological precipitants for such feelings, so I began to wonder if my depression had more to do with the state of my body chemistry than with my mental attitude. I noticed that the time of day had something to do with my moods. Whenever I awakened at three or four in the morning, I felt horrible, in complete despair. When I went back to sleep and awakened later in the morning, I would often feel fine.

Food seemed to be connected, too, as I would feel much worse after eating certain foods. I began to look for some kind of biochemical way to change my feelings and was rewarded in my search by learning about specific nutrient substances that could directly influence certain mood-elevating brain chemicals. From then on, I applied to myself the kind of nutritional treatment I'm now recommending in this book. Almost unbelievably, it worked, and the day came when I knew I would never again feel so much pain as to want to die. That was ten years ago and I have been depression-free since that time.

It rarely happens any more these days, but if I ever awaken in the morning feeling slightly low, I take several tyrosine capsules and put a few sublingual vitamin B_{12}'s under my tongue. Within an hour my mood and outlook will have completely improved. I don't have to waste unnecessary time and energy on an unwanted, unneeded state of being, and I experience no side effects whatsoever.

THE PROMISE

This book offers you the same proven, safe method of treating depression and temporary low moods that has worked so well with me and with many of my patients. It is a completely natural, scientifically based approach backed up by some impressive research. It makes sound, theoretical sense. An increasing number of doctors are using it, with dramatic results.

By reading this book, you can discover whether you are in fact depressed. If you are, you will discover some of the answers you've been seeking. You will learn what to do to free yourself from this burden—one that may very well be the result of a simple nutritional imbalance in the first place!

For the depressed person, the light at the end of the tunnel isn't an oncoming train: it is daylight, because there is hope. The right treatment for you exists. Medical science already has a variety of possible approaches and the revolutionary nutritional procedures described in this book may well prove to be the safest and most effective of them all.

What you can learn in *The Way Up from Down* will allow you to take control of your own moods by making sure your brain has enough of its essential amino acid nutrients. If you try to confront life's problems while your chemistry is off, you are already at a disadvantage because you will perceive everything as harder and more complicated than it is.

Once you achieve the proper chemical balance in your brain, your whole outlook will change. You will no longer feel stuck, you will be better able to cope with your problems, and you will perhaps have the strength to work with and resolve seemingly impossible situations. You will also have more physical and psychological energy and endurance.

Even if you are not actually depressed, this book will help you deal with your psychological processes and mood swings as you react to different life events. All of us are especially stressed when faced with disappointments, loss and grief. This program will fortify you by promoting "optimum" brain chemistry and decreasing the negative impact of stress reactions.

THE GUILT HOOK

Who wants to deal with depression if he can avoid it? If you haven't experienced it, it's very hard to understand what it's like to feel out of control of one's mood and thoughts and persistently able to perceive only the darker side of life. Such pessimism, gloom and immobility seem a perverse quirk that can easily be corrected, if one "really" tried to rise above it. A great impatience develops in the "up" ones who don't want to be bothered by this aspect of life—unless someone near becomes afflicted. When this happens, it is usually experienced as *self-inflicted* by both the sufferer and observers alike.

In my experience depressed people and their families have great difficulty accepting the biochemical origins of low moods. They doubt mood disorders can be successfully treated with nutrition or medications. They think depression is only a state of mind, and therefore must have a purely psychological cause for which a psychological remedy must be found.

Depressed people feel acute sensations of guilt and remorse. These symptoms—for they should be considered symptoms— actually encourage the victims to blame themselves for their condition. Somehow, the idea that depression might have a biochemical cause looks as if it's going to let the patient off some kind of hook—the guilt hook, the hook of despair and self-accusation. A depressed person is not at all sure that she should be allowed to get off that hook.

The family of the depressive, too, is liable, inadvertently, to encourage the patient in this way of thinking. Family members often tell their depressed relatives they'd feel better if they "only took a more positive attitude," or "looked on the bright side," or "would only stop thinking about themselves and quit complaining." "Just look at all you have to be grateful for." The depressed person cannot comprehend this. "How can I feel thankful and grateful when everything is wrong?"

When you pressure a depressed person to think positively, it's almost as if you're insisting he speak to you in Latin, and he becomes even more guilt-ridden and helpless. "I can't think any of the positive thoughts other people are talking about. Something terrible is wrong with me. I am bad. I am hopeless." And the cycle continues.

Who wants to be around someone like this? Since family members cannot very well avoid contact, relationships can deteriorate from the strain. Impatience, anger and alienation may set in. Marriages may be ruined. Parent-child relationships are disrupted. Friendships are dropped. And the guilt hook digs deeper.

All of us need to understand the true nature and causes of depression in order to minimize or even to eliminate the suffering it can produce. It's all well and good to say depression does have a psychological side, that it is related to attitude and will. Certainly, attitude and will have their parts to play, as we shall see in the chapters on the psychological aspects of depression and the power of expectations. But, believe me, I'm a psychiatrist, and I'm telling you that psychology is only part of the question—and it's the *second* part!

What we are discovering is that depression is caused by biochemical imbalances which in turn create both psychological and physical symptoms.

YOUR MIND IN THE HEALING OF DEPRESSION

What part does your mind have to play in all of this? After all, depression does have a major effect on the way you think and feel about life. And your thoughts and feelings seem to have some very important connection with your becoming depressed in the first place.

Even if depression does contain a biochemical component, what about thoughts and feelings? Do they play a part in creating depression? Have they any part to play in healing?

When you are thinking pleasant thoughts, even when you are daydreaming, the chemistry of your brain is likely to be in balance, and nothing needs to be done about it. But there are other patterns of thought that we all sometimes slip into, which directly tie in with depression. We need to be aware of them, in order to do something about them.

All of us occasionally have thoughts we don't like or want. For some of us, these thoughts occupy our minds much of the time. It's simply no fun to be worrying about questions like, "Do I have cancer?" "Will my home be robbed while I'm away on vacation?" or "Will we have enough money to pay the bills?"

Thoughts like these become more than mere concerns when they repeat themselves over and over to the point of being worrisome or becoming obsessions.

When there is constructive action you can take, take it. If you are worried you might have cancer, for instance, you need to ask yourself whether you've noticed any change in your health, and if so, go to your doctor to have the appropriate checkup. There are a number of routine exams for cancer, chest X rays, rectal exams, PAP smears, breast exams and so on. Do what needs to be done, and if you still can't release the thought, face up to it as a possible sign of depression.

Once a thought becomes obsessive, once the mind starts running away, it becomes more and more difficult to control. The thoughts are like a rudderless ship in a storm, tossed about with no pattern or direction, creating feelings of helplessness, panic or worse. When you lose your ability to focus and concentrate, any kind of self-directed thinking is almost absent, or even impossible.

We need to be able to control our thoughts. I don't mean that we should avoid ever entertaining a passing worry, nor that we should be so controlled that we never daydream or allow our thoughts to wander. But it is important to be able to dismiss worries from our minds when there is nothing we can do about them, before they destroy our peace, our mood and even our lives.

It's difficult to appreciate that unbalanced *brain chemistry* may be making it far harder for you to direct your own thoughts. When your brain chemistry is right, your thoughts will automatically be more positive and balanced, and easier to direct. If you are going through a hard time, or have been around others who are pessimistic, you still may need to work to steer your thoughts in a positive, creative, stress-free direction. But when you make this effort, you will be able to think more positively. In time, you can literally retrain your thought patterns.

So the mind does have an important part to play in all of this. Yet, if you are already depressed, getting your brain chemistry back in balance is the first step. Steering your thoughts in a positive creative direction will become much more manageable once that first task has been accomplished.

THE NUTRITIONAL APPROACH

What does the nutritional approach to depression really mean? What is it all about? Let's look at the idea briefly, before going into more depth in the coming chapters.

Medical science now understands a great deal about the specific chemicals that exist in our brains. In particular, certain chemicals known as the brain amines seem to be directly connected with the way we feel about life. We have discovered that people who suffer from depression often have an insufficient amount of these amines in their brains.

The nutritional approach to depression proposes that if the brain's balance of these chemicals can be restored, the depression itself is likely to lift. If you are not enjoying life, a simple chemical imbalance may be largely responsible for causing your suffering.

Fortunately, the brain chemicals in question can be created by increasing the amount of certain nutrients—vitamins, minerals and amino acids—in your diet. These nutrients, readily available in any good health food store or pharmacy, really can lift depression.

This book will teach you about the nutritional approach and give you enough information either to try it for yourself or, if you have severe depression, to work on this approach in conjunction with your own doctor.

The comprehensive chemistry and psychology of depression is beyond the scope of this book. What we are presenting is the basic biochemical theory of depression, which in turn underlies this new and effective alternative therapeutic program.

AN IMPORTANT WARNING

The nutritional approach discussed in this book is *not* a replacement for consulting with your own personal physician, nor is it intended to replace any psychotherapy you may currently be engaged in. If you are severely depressed, or are seriously considering suicide, you should certainly be under the care of a psychiatrist, and perhaps should even be hospitalized.

Regardless of whether your depression is mild and occasional or persistent and severe, however, you can try this nutritional approach. It is so new that your doctor may not be familiar with this type of treatment and therefore may not even encourage it at first.

If you are under a doctor's care, I would suggest you show your physician the paragraphs that follow, and indicate that you would like to try this approach.

A WORD TO MY COLLEAGUES

The nutritional approach to the treatment of depression that I am recommending in this book has been used safely and successfully by myself and by many other physicians for several years with predominantly favorable results. An explanation of the brain amine theory on which this treatment modality is based is found in Chapter 3, and my recommendations regarding which depressions qualify for this modality are to be found in Chapters Four and Six.

Just as some depressions will not respond to such orthodox psychiatric treatments as the use of antidepressants, psychotherapy or electroshock treatment, some depressions may not respond to this approach. The range of causes involved in the initiation and continuation of depression is extensive; depressions may exist that in no way relate to the biochemical imbalances mentioned in this book. In cases where the nutritional supplements suggested have little or no impact within a month, I recommend a more intensive examination of such contributing factors as thyroid disease, sugar, caffeine and alcohol abuse, possible allergies, etc.

I myself have been surprised and gratified to observe the effectiveness of this approach with patients who have been unsuccessfully treated with other therapeutic modalities. I would urge my medical colleagues to try this approach initially with a sufficient number of patients to provide a first-order impression of its potential. Besides clinical impressions, you may want to substantiate and monitor the effectiveness of the therapy through amino acid analysis (ion exchange chromatography). My own and my colleagues' findings suggest that above 70 percent of patients respond favorably to this therapy, and can therefore in most cases be spared the potential side effects of antidepressants.

As Michael Oliver suggested recently in *The New England Journal of Medicine*, "The risks involved in correcting risk must be compared with the risk of the disease in question." Non-invasive, nutritional approaches are, I suggest, to be preferred to equivalent pharmacological approaches where possible.

I trust that this book will be of service in introducing this treatment possibility to my fellow physicians and to the wider lay public that is now beginning to recognize the importance of the patient's role in recovery. For your convenience, I have included at the end of the book an extensive bibliography of relevant publications.

How to Recognize Depression

Are you depressed? If you answer with a clear yes, you are closer to finding relief than the many who are depressed and don't even know it. It's sad but true that even those seeking psychiatric help can be totally unaware of the depression which underlies their symptoms.

For example, a twenty-seven-year-old man told me, "I just can't get going in the morning and there's not much to do when I get up anyway." When I suggested he sounded depressed, he vehemently denied it and presented many reasons for his apathy. "I'm just upset because I don't like where I'm living, but I don't have a job, so I can't do anything about it. I'm not looking for a job because I'm waiting to settle a workman's comp case, and besides, I don't know what I want to do." He was surprised when his responses to a questionnaire I gave him indicated the presence of moderate depression. With further interviewing that very day, he was able to recognize and acknowledge the source of his complaints.

DEPRESSION IS NOT ALL IN OUR MINDS

Most of us think that to qualify as "depressed" our symptoms have to be severe: extreme pessimism, sadness and negativity, with a low mood and outlook. Yet depression can exist without the presence of these elements. Some symptoms may be so subtle that we're not even aware of them individually. Put enough of these symptoms together, and the result is a mystifying "change in mood." That change can be persistent and take over your life or it can come and go, giving you "up" days and "down" ones.

Sometimes we don't recognize depression because it comes disguised as physical illness. People complain of backaches, headaches, muscle tension, constipation, fatigue, weight changes or sleep problems, and they naturally go to their family doctor, who may or may not be trained in recognizing the subtler symptoms of low mood and depression. Two different studies have found that only a third of patients later diagnosed as depressed initially sought attention from a mental health professional.

The evidence tells us that depression *is* a physical disorder. Even though there may be accompanying psychological symptoms, we are finding that depression is first and foremost associated with changes in brain chemistry, and that these changes can cause other physical alterations in the body as well. Still, to be properly treated, the specific psychiatric diagnosis of depression must be made.

DIAGNOSIS MAY BE ELUSIVE

It is difficult even for the most skilled professionals and psychiatrists to identify certain kinds of low mood or depression. Though it is the most common disorder seen in non-psychiatric medical practices—one in five of us will experience this illness at some time in our lives—half of all depressions are undiagnosed and untreated. Just look at the list of obstacles in the way of a clear diagnosis.

1. Depression is often veiled by physical complaints and confused with physical illnesses.
2. It may be "masked" by or coexist with other illnesses. For example, a person with heart disease may also be suffering from a separate biochemical depression.
3. Despite overwhelming evidence to the contrary, many people still consider it a purely psychological disorder. They think the depressed person with heart disease is "only" having an emotional response to his medical illness.
4. There is a stigma to the admission of depression.
5. It may be hidden by other psychological problems. For in-

stance, those with schizophrenia may also have a depression; those with eating disorders may be preoccupied by their binging and fasting behaviors and ignore their depression.
6. It can be confused with grieving or reactions to other stressful life events. We blame our depressed feelings on the severity of what is happening and fail to recognize when our reactions have progressed beyond what could be called "normal."
7. It's such a "personalized" illness. There is a tremendous range of symptoms and severity in the way depression manifests itself in each of us.

Most people in whom depression is eventually diagnosed have visited their doctor several times within that year. If you have been seen by your physician and are experiencing no improvement in your symptoms, at least consider the possibility of an associated low mood or depression. Generally, it is best to obtain at least two separate opinions when you aren't making any progress or when you are trying to decide whether or not to undertake any major treatment such as surgery or a potentially harmful medication.

Don't be afraid to search out other opinions when your doctor isn't helping you or isn't sure about your diagnosis or treatment, or when you yourself just aren't sure what's happening or what your doctor is telling you. It's amazing to me how afraid people are to question their doctors. Remember, a good doctor will welcome questions, will be receptive to other opinions, and will want you to be as educated as possible about your health. If this is not the case with your physician, you might consider a replacement.

When physicians miss the diagnosis of depression, they either aren't thinking in these terms or they explore only superficially, to the extent of asking the patient, "Are you depressed? Do you feel sad and blue?" If the answer is "no," the doctor often accepts that, with the result of further delaying the proper recognition and treatment.

Often when there are obvious emotional symptoms they are only viewed as anxiety or insomnia. Such patients are then inappropriately given tranquilizers such as Valium, Librium, Serax, Centrax or sleeping pills. One study revealed that 82 percent of those who killed themselves had seen their physician within one month of their death and 55 percent died of an overdose of tranquilizing and sleep medication supplied by that doctor. It's my belief that doctors would be wise to clearly consider depression in all those with sleeping problems or anxiety and to treat them more appropriately for their depression.

FAMILY HISTORY

In obtaining a family history, I generally want to know the medical and emotional backgrounds of parents, grandparents, aunts, uncles and siblings. Is there any history of suicide, depression, anxiety, psychiatric treatment, eating disorders, alcoholism or drug abuse?

If so, this raises the index of suspicion for depression. Are the relatives living or dead? How have they spent their lives? What are their attitudes and activities? What is their general health and history of medical treatment? What is the level of their vocational and interpersonal functioning?

This exploration can yield valuable material when the patient knows the information. But correct and complete family history is not always easy to obtain. Family members may have been depressed but not identified as such, so no one ever knew. Sometimes when I ask my depressed patients if anyone in their family was depressed, they say no. Then when I ask the specific questions listed above, a clear picture of depression emerges. Having denied that her mother was depressed, one patient went on to say, "My mother stayed home most of the time and didn't have many friends. She didn't like us to go out very much either, because she was afraid something would happen to us. She was always worrying."

PHYSICAL PAIN

A woman came to me with long-standing abdominal and back pain. She was afraid she was dying of cancer and kept saying, "Doctor, tell me the truth, you know something terrible is wrong with me." Though she had been to numerous specialists and had undergone exhaustive, expensive medical work-ups and hospitalizations, nothing had been found. Yet she remained convinced of imminent death and would not accept any reassurances. Her focus on death was a tipoff, though no one had previously considered depression. Once this diagnosis was established, she was placed on the nutrient antidepressant treatment which this book is about. She recovered from her anxiety and pain, and from the underlying depression.

Many people are more comfortable focusing on their bodies than on their emotions or on psychological symptoms. For them physical pain is more understandable and therefore more acceptable than psychological pain. They go to a disastrous business meeting and feel its effects as a headache. They call chronic digestive problems "a food allergy" to avoid dealing with the emotional basis. They tend to engage in a process known as somatizing, converting mental states into bodily symptoms. For this and also for biochemical reasons, depression can create chronic physical pain. In certain ways, such people may be fortunate compared to those with extreme forms of *mood* pain. You can only make a comparison if you have fully experienced both.

Dr. Humphrey Osmond studied thirty patients hospitalized for depression. Each had also previously experienced severe physical pain from illness, injury or surgery. When they were asked to compare the mood pain with the physical pain, all but one "preferred" physical pain—and the one exception said he "didn't know."

There is, in fact, such an overlap between the two that many chronic pain clinics now routinely evaluate patients for depression. Often, treating such people for depression decreases or eliminates the chronic physical pain they have suffered for years.

NOTE: Traditional medical exploration must be undertaken to rule out other causes for pain before assuming chronic pain is created by depression.

Often the diagnosis is complicated by the coexistence of depression with other mental or physical disorders such as high blood pressure, ulcers, cancer, parkinsonism, alcoholism and so on. Doctors and patients may feel they have the answers when they have arrived at one or two diagnoses and stop looking for what else may be wrong.

Still a Stigma

Many people still feel there is a social stigma attached to the symptoms or diagnosis of depression. One of my patients was a very successful film celebrity who suffered for many years from such severe depression that she attempted suicide six times. Her last sleeping pill overdose resulted in three days of unconsciousness and ten days in a hospital intensive care unit. When she recovered from this nearly fatal attempt, she was placed in a psychiatric hospital and there first became my patient. We went on to work together very closely and successfully.

Several years later, she wrote her biography. The fascinating thing to me was that there was not a single mention in the book of her difficulty with depression or of her suicide attempts! Shame and guilt obviously kept her from sharing this information though it might have made a human and interesting story and helped others to acknowledge depression in themselves.

Usually, we hear about depression in well-known people only when it results in the tragic end of suicide under circumstances difficult to keep secret. I have seen in my practice that there are many more suicides of prominent people, and, of course, of private individuals, than we have ever dreamed. For example, the twenty-five-year-old daughter of a famous film star killed herself, and then, one year later, his wife followed with a similar overdose. The bereft man hired attorneys and, in essence, almost forced everybody who knew to sign documents declaring they would never, ever reveal the suicides.

In our current culture, it seems easier to admit a problem with drinking than a problem with depression. Witness the alcoholism declarations of Betty Ford, Dick Van Dyke, Mary Tyler Moore, Liza Minnelli, Richard Burton, Elizabeth Taylor and so on. Their honesty has been an inspiration to drinkers and has, no doubt, helped others to obtain necessary treatment. If only depression would find its way into the celebrity spotlight!

Symptoms

Generally speaking, if your blue days come and go with one or two accompanying symptoms, you are suffering from only brief low moods. If the symptoms multiply, or if they come and go often enough to cause you significant pain or to interfere with your fully partaking of life's pleasures and bounties, you may be undergoing a *sustained mood change.* If you have a combination of at least four of the following symptoms, which have lasted for two or more weeks, you may be suffering from the *illness of depression.*

The symptoms are:

Fatigue

You may have a general loss of energy, may tire easily and lack ambition for getting things done.

Insomnia—or the Reverse, *Excessive Sleep*

If you have an anxious type of depression, you may have trouble falling asleep, or have a very restless sleep with frequent awakening. If you are more severely depressed, you may awaken very early in the morning, around two or three o'clock, feeling even worse at that time, fearful, dreading, unable to return to sleep at all. Less usually, and often with milder depressions, you may sleep much more than before—almost as an escape from life.

Indecision

You may be stressed and unable to make decisions, ranging from important to even the most simple matters.

Loss of Sexual Desire

There may be a reduction in sexual activity or total lack of interest and loss of sex drive.

Changes in Eating Patterns

You may have lost your appetite or may be eating excessively. This may be accompanied by an associated weight loss or gain. Generally, more severe depressions are accompanied by weight loss.

Anxiety

You may have generalized anxiety which comes and goes for no apparent reason. You may have restless, agitated feelings. You may have specific panic attacks. About 70 percent of persons with panic disorder, agoraphobia or severe anxiety have an associated depression.

Phobias
The anxiety may show itself in the form of a phobia—such as fear of going out of the house, fear of elevators, fear of cancer, fear of germs and so forth.

Guilt
You may have feelings of remorse and shame over real or imagined events. You may feel you shouldn't have done what you did and should have done what you didn't. You may feel guilty about not loving or functioning the way you used to.

Hopelessness
You may feel you are incurable, that there is nothing that can be done for you.

Helplessness
You may feel unusually dependent and unable to do much for yourself or to take care of yourself.

General Loss of Interest
You may take little pleasure in anything. You may be indifferent to family, friends, job, hobbies and other things previously important to you.

Irritability
You may be annoyed, impatient, jumpy, excessively angry or hostile about all sorts of trivial things. You may have the upsetting urge to harm those who are near and dear to you.

Social Withdrawal
You may avoid interacting with others and prefer to be alone more than usual.

Physical Changes
There may be almost any physical symptoms including constipation, nausea, chest pains, stomach cramps, rapid breathing, sweating, coldness, numbness or tingling of the hands or feet,

headache or feelings of pressure in the head, ears and neck. Often, the depressed person interprets such symptoms as deriving from some terrible disease that is destroying the body.

Suicidal Thoughts

This may range from wishing you were dead to actively planning suicide.

Delusions or Hallucinations

The most severe depressions may progress to what represents a partial break with reality. This is when the biochemistry is most disturbed and the person may believe thoughts that absolutely are not true (delusions) or see or hear things that are nonexistent (hallucinations).

HOW TO DIAGNOSE

Even with such a list of symptoms, depression can be hard to pinpoint. Women can go to the gynecologist and have a pelvic exam and PAP smear to check for cancer; you can have checkups for blood pressure or eye examinations for glaucoma. There is no single test, as yet, that will predictably diagnose depression.

A number of physical tests have been devised to shed some light on depression. A few psychological questionnaires are also quite accurate in determining the severity of depression. The test presented in this book is called the Carroll Rating Scale. It is an adaptation of the Hamilton Rating Scale for Depression, modified so that you can rate yourself rather than be rated by professionals. The Hamilton was devised in 1960 and is the test most often mentioned in psychiatric literature.

Naturally it is difficult to be 100 percent accurate without being interviewed by skilled professionals. A self-rating scale is good for general screening but should not by itself indicate an absolute diagnosis of depression because, naturally, there is a chance of denial, loss of insight, or exaggeration of symptoms. But this scale will give you an idea of where you stand.* If you think you are

*Psychiatrists have placed people with depressive symptoms into different diagnostic categories, depending upon the severity, duration and so on. Differen-

depressed and also test as depressed, you very likely are. If you think you are not depressed, but you test as depressed, obtain a professional opinion. If you score as not depressed but still think you might be, you'd be well-advised to seek further skilled evaluation. You might also re-administer the test periodically, especially to rate yourself as you progress with the self-help program in this book. (It might be helpful to write your answers on a separate piece of paper, so you can retake the test from a clean copy.)

CARROLL RATING SCALE

Complete *all* the following statements by circling YES or NO, based on how you have felt during the *past few days.*

1. I feel just as energetic as always	YES	NO
2. I am losing weight	YES	NO
3. I have dropped many of my interests and activities	YES	NO
4. Since my illness I have completely lost interest in sex	YES	NO
5. I am especially concerned about how my body is functioning	YES	NO
6. It must be obvious that I am disturbed and agitated	YES	NO
7. I am still able to carry on doing the work I am supposed to do	YES	NO
8. I can concentrate easily when reading the papers	YES	NO
9. Getting to sleep takes me more than half an hour	YES	NO
10. I am restless and fidgety	YES	NO
11. I wake up much earlier than I need to in the morning	YES	NO
12. Dying is the best solution for me	YES	NO
13. I have a lot of trouble with dizzy and faint feelings	YES	NO
14. I am being punished for something bad in my past	YES	NO

tiating the proper subtypes can be important, especially in those with manic-depressive illness. They are all described in the *Diagnostic and Statistical Manual for Mental Disorders,* third edition, and are condensed in the appendix of this book, if you prefer a more technical examination of diagnosis.

15. My sexual interest is the same as before I got sick	YES	NO
16. I am miserable or often feel like crying	YES	NO
17. I often wish I were dead	YES	NO
18. I am having trouble with indigestion	YES	NO
19. I wake up often in the middle of the night	YES	NO
20. I feel worthless and ashamed about myself	YES	NO
21. I am so slowed down that I need help with bathing and dressing	YES	NO
22. I take longer than usual to fall asleep at night	YES	NO
23. Much of the time I am very afraid but don't know the reason	YES	NO
24. Things which I regret about my life are bothering me	YES	NO
25. I get pleasure and satisfaction from what I do	YES	NO
26. All I need is a good rest to be perfectly well again	YES	NO
27. My sleep is restless and disturbed	YES	NO
28. My mind is as fast and alert as always	YES	NO
29. I feel that life is still worth living	YES	NO
30. My voice is dull and lifeless	YES	NO
31. I feel irritable or jittery	YES	NO
32. I feel in good spirits	YES	NO
33. My heart sometimes beats faster than usual	YES	NO
34. I think my case is hopeless	YES	NO
35. I wake up before my usual time in the morning	YES	NO
36. I still enjoy my meals as much as usual	YES	NO
37. I have to keep pacing around most of the time	YES	NO
38. I am terrified and near panic	YES	NO
39. My body is bad and rotten inside	YES	NO
40. I got sick because of the bad weather we have been having	YES	NO
41. My hands shake so much that people can easily notice	YES	NO
42. I still like to go out and meet people	YES	NO
43. I think I appear calm on the outside	YES	NO
44. I think I am as good a person as anybody else	YES	NO
45. My trouble is the result of some serious internal disease	YES	NO
46. I have been thinking about trying to kill myself	YES	NO
47. I get hardly anything done lately	YES	NO

48. There is only misery in the future for me	YES	NO
49. I worry a lot about my bodily symptoms	YES	NO
50. I have to force myself to eat even a little	YES	NO
51. I am exhausted much of the time	YES	NO
52. I can tell that I have lost a lot of weight	YES	NO

Compare your answers to those listed below and give yourself one point each time your answer is the same. Any score greater than ten reveals some degree of depression, and the severity of the depression increases with the score.

1. no	14. yes	27. yes	40. yes
2. yes	15. no	28. no	41. yes
3. yes	16. yes	29. no	42. no
4. yes	17. yes	30. yes	43. no
5. yes	18. yes	31. yes	44. no
6. yes	19. yes	32. no	45. yes
7. no	20. yes	33. yes	46. yes
8. no	21. yes	34. yes	47. yes
9. yes	22. yes	35. yes	48. yes
10. yes	23. yes	36. no	49. yes
11. yes	24. yes	37. yes	50. yes
12. yes	25. no	38. yes	51. yes
13. yes	26. yes	39. yes	52. yes

NOTE: If you have a medical disorder causing symptoms like fatigue, decreased sexual activity and other physical changes, then the diagnostic process is more complicated unless you also show a number of non-physical symptoms as well. If you are going through a particularly difficult life situation—the death of someone you're close to, the loss of employment—you may temporarily score higher on the test. However, if the symptoms continue for more than two weeks you should also consider depression.

WHAT DO I DO WITH WHAT I'VE LEARNED?

If you tested as severely depressed, you need professional help in addition to following the program in this book; please consult a psychiatrist.

Published with permission from Bernard J. Carroll, M.D., Ph.D., and previously published in *The British Journal of Psychiatry*.

If, from taking the test, you have discovered or had confirmed that you are depressed, it's a good idea to read the whole book before you start the treatment procedure. Some other factors may be contributing that must have attention before this program can work optimally.

Be hopeful. There is relief available for depression and you have already taken the first step: self-knowledge and proper identification of your problem can be the best news you've ever had! The nutrient program contained in this book may be exactly what is needed to put you on the road to health.

LOW MOODS WITHOUT DEPRESSION

Where do you fit and what do you do if you don't have the diagnosis of depression, yet you do have low moods? Have you ever known anyone who did not have occasional down days or cycles or low periods during the day? I haven't. We all have brief depressed feelings and such periodic gloom may run the gamut from slight to severe. What differentiates this from the illness of depression is the duration as well as the presence of the accompanying symptoms previously listed. Low moods are somewhat like masturbation, with 99 percent of us sometime or other experiencing this and the other 1 percent lying.

Even if you scored as totally normal on the Carroll Rating Scale, you'll likely have other times when you would not score so well. Low moods constitute those other times when you have some of the symptoms on the list, but they don't last for over two weeks at a time, or they involve fewer than four of the categories of symptoms listed earlier in the chapter. Any mood discomfort is not optimal health, and recurrent symptoms, even if intermittent, need recognition and attention.

Why suffer at all if you don't have to? It's worth trying available methods of relief and enhancing your life with a more consistent sense of well-being. If low moods are a part of your life, you may want to control them with intermittent nutrient use. The treatment described in this book is extremely effective for these temporary times of pessimism and dampened enthusiasm.

3 The Brain Amine Theory of Depression

Bacterial pneumonia and TB used to be major killers until we discovered they were caused by the presence of bacteria which could be eradicated by antibiotics. But not all illnesses have a single cause of this sort and therefore cannot be so successfully controlled or eliminated. The current major causes of death are diseases such as cancer, heart disease, stroke and Alzheimer's, which simply do not have any single basis of origin. They are multidetermined, with genetic, environmental, dietary, lifestyle and psychological causes all coming into play. Depression is one of these potentially multifactorial illnesses.

Among the causes of depression we do know about, research has shown that imbalances in certain brain chemicals play a critical role. In fact, *regardless of the overt triggering factors, the underlying chemical mechanism of depression is almost always a shift in the brain chemistry.* This understanding makes depression a treatable illness, though it is best treated in a way that addresses all the contributing factors involved in its development.

HISTORY OF DEPRESSION

Though this understanding of the chemistry of the problem is relatively recent, depression has been with us as long as recorded history. It has afflicted individuals of every rank in society, from King Saul and Alexander the Great to the humblest in their services. Through the ages this darkness of the mood has been variously viewed as caused by evil spirits, disobedience to God, moral failings, divine possession, black bile, anger and grief. Whatever the presumed causes, there were no answers and no predictable methods of cure. The depressed were misunderstood and stigmatized, treated with amulets, spells and bloodletting. The best, kindest treatment available consisted of suggestions to "feel better," entertainment with "amusing stories and diversion," and mild reprimanding of the sufferers' "groundless sorrow."

More recently, medical and psychiatric science have gone through numerous cycles in their attitudes toward depression. Ironically, in the nineteenth century depression was thought to be caused by imbalances in the body's chemistry and little attention was paid to the idea that psychological factors might be involved.

About the turn of the present century, Freud and Jung suggested that depression should be considered a psychological disease, caused by the activity of a demanding, exacting and punishing conscience. That attitude, for better or worse, dominated professional thought for much of this century and still exists in some circles.

DRUGS AGAINST DEPRESSION

The message? If you are depressed, be glad you live now rather than in the past. For only recently have we begun to unravel the provable, physiological causes of mood changes and thus to have predictable, physical treatment.

Such understanding began during the 1940's and 1950's when scientists who were researching a drug called reserpine for use as a tranquilizer and as a means to control high blood pressure noticed that it produced depression in some patients. Shortly thereafter, another group of scientists noted that some of the antihistamine drugs that are used in the treatment of allergies produced a lifting of depression in certain individuals. About the same time, an Australian doctor reported that lithium affected the mood of patients who took it.

Each of these discoveries implied that there is a strong relationship between our mood and our body's chemistry. Researchers began to watch more closely for any other hints that drugs could influence or change the moods of depressive patients or even create depression.

The point was this: if depression is purely psychological, as Jung and Freud suggested, then why are medications able to have such a marked effect on mood? The pendulum began to swing back: medical science again acknowledged the importance of chemical factors in the creation of depression. We now know that brain chemicals mediate virtually all feelings of love, hate, sadness, pleasure and anxiety in response to our experiences.

The present trend in medical science emphasizes the biochemical and genetic origins of depression. Psychological factors are now seen by many experts as catalysts that trigger a change in chemistry. Almost all psychiatrists now treat their patients both biochemically and psychologically. Research also makes it clear that in depressive illness, given the choice of treatment of only medication or only psychotherapy, medication alone far surpasses psychotherapy in effectiveness. However, I want to stress that both, together, work best.

There are now many different kinds of antidepressant drugs on the market and new ones with slightly different effects are discovered each year. One reason for this continuing search for new drugs is that not all antidepressants work equally well for all the people who suffer from depression. Indeed, this fact seems to support the theory that depression has many causes. Different types of depression respond to different kinds of medicine. Some antidepressants, such as Elavil, Ludiomil and Sinequan, act as sedatives for agitated, anxious and insomniac depressives. Others such as Aventyl, Parnate and Nardil work as stimulants for patients who are lethargic, immobilized and apathetic.

The very diversity of the disease makes it difficult to know ahead of time which medication will eliminate which depression. So far, physicians have simply used their best judgment in each case, drawing upon their own experience and the available medical literature to know what kind of depressed person usually responds well to which pill.

This trial and error approach puts us in something of a predicament, however, since most antidepressants have to be taken for two to six weeks before their full effects are experienced. You can imagine the additional suffering involved if the first or second drug chosen by the doctor proves not to be the best one. When these delays take place, the depressed person (who feels utterly hopeless and incurable in any case) may lose what little willingness he may have had to seek treatment in the first place, sometimes with terrible results.

My friend Joan was visiting from Florida. She was terribly worried about a dear friend, a gifted artist, who recently had withdrawn from his friends, stopped doing all the things he enjoyed, and starting drinking heavily. I suggested she tell him to seek professional help.

In a later visit, she again mentioned her friend. He had gone to a psychiatrist who had placed him on antidepressant medication. When he did not respond, a different medicine was tried, and then another—all without response. Then they tried shock treatment, which apparently also did not work. Because he was becoming progressively more desperate, Joan told him about the nutritional treatment. Though he was interested, because of his inertia he kept postponing a visit to Los Angeles to investigate.

A few months later Joan phoned me to say her friend had died of an overdose of drugs. To add to the tragedy, a ticket to Los Angeles for the following week was found on his desk.

A great deal of research is being devoted to discovering specific ways to predict what patient will respond best to what medicine. As yet, no one single type of cure works for all depressions, but all depressed people can be cured of any single episode of depression, or of chronic depression, by the appropriate treatment. Some sufferers may respond well to the first medication they try. Even more respond positively to the multinutrient health-promoting approach described in this book—an approach that covers many bases and is virtually free from negative side effects.

BRAIN AMINE THEORY

As it became more clear that depression was alleviated by the use of various medications, researchers began looking for the reasons why these responses took place. They began to measure all kinds of substances in the blood, the brain, the spinal fluid and the urine, to find out what chemical changes occurred during

depression, and what changes came about as a result of treatment. They discovered that depressed people often have alterations of several chemicals in their blood, spinal fluid and urine.
Such alterations are now called "chemical markers" for depression. In other research, abnormal sleep brain wave patterns have
been shown to accompany depression. Many of these chemical
and brain wave tests are still primarily performed at the research
level, although a few are available for clinical use.

NEUROTRANSMITTERS

While research into depression progressed, other neurological
and psychiatric scientists were discovering a group of substances
in the brain known as the neurotransmitters. So far, about forty
of them have been identified, and it is here that most professionals feel the greatest promise lies for understanding and treating
neuropsychiatric disorders.

Neurotransmitters are chemicals that are released at nerve
endings in the brain where one nerve cell is close to another.
They allow messages to pass from one cell to the next and are
essential for communication between cells. The releasing cell
that passes along an effect is called the presynaptic neuron and
the cell that receives the message is called the postsynaptic neuron. Their connection is called a synapse. After release, the
neurotransmitter attaches to a location on the receiving cell
called a receptor, that can link only with it and with no other
neurotransmitter. It's much like calling someone on the telephone. You need two phones (two cells) and a signal connection
between them, and each phone rings only on receiving the activation of its given number.

The function of the relayed message is dependent upon the
location of the nerve cell and the particular neurotransmitter it
releases. One neurotransmitter, for instance, helps to pass what
are called excitatory impulses through the nervous system, while
another transmits "inhibitory" impulses. This is a little like putting your foot on the accelerator or the brake pedal of your
car. Some neurotransmitters stimulate positive or "rewarding"
thoughts and behavior, while others produce negative or "punishing" responses.

The quantity of available neurotransmitters is important, but so also is the "sensitivity" of the receptor cells. An altered or impaired sensitivity is another marker of depression. Using the previous analogy, if you press your car brakes and such pressure is not received on the brake drum, your car will not stop.

When certain sites in the brain contain too much or too little of these chemicals, or when the receptors are not sensitive and connecting with the chemical, serious problems can result. Parkinson's disease, for example, is caused by an imbalance of the neurotransmitter dopamine in specific areas of the brain. It is a neurological disorder that usually comes on in older age and makes deliberate movements difficult. People with the illness walk with a slow shuffle, holding their arms stiffly at their sides with little free movement, and have mask-like faces devoid of spontaneous expression. They also usually have a tremor. Depression, forgetfulness and other "psychological" symptoms may go along with the disease. Happily, in the case of Parkinson's the discovery of which neurotransmitter was deficient led to the development of a treatment which replaces the missing substance, providing dramatic relief. Because of such successes, researchers are always looking for neurotransmitters in order to determine how they might relate to neuropsychiatric disorders.

Probably the most popularly known neurotransmitter is endorphin, which is associated with the relief of pain and can also produce a euphoria-like state. We have all read about the apparent increase of endorphin in the brains of those who jog regularly and for a sufficient length of time. The endorphins are considered to be the cause of the "high" that runners commonly experience.

Endorphin reacts or binds to certain "receptor sites" in the brain (as do all neurotransmitters). Interestingly, it reacts with the same receptor sites as do potent external medication pain killers such as Demerol, morphine and heroin. One reason people may feel little or no pain under severe trauma, like the loss of a limb, is because the body releases a flood of endorphin to block temporarily what would otherwise be excruciating pain.

According to one theory the heroin or morphine addict may have a brain deficiency of the naturally occurring endorphins, which could then lead him to crave outside endorphin-like substances. This provocative concept needs further exploration.

In addition to the general maintenance of all brain activity, the neurotransmitters regulate your mood and control your sleep, appetite, aggression, memory, alertness and many other functions. Their deficiency also creates depression, and there is now no question that many depressed people contain below average amounts of certain neurotransmitters in the mood centers of their brains. Their nerve signals are not relayed from one cell to the next at a fast enough rate to maintain a normal level of mood and behavior. Researchers have found that higher levels of neurotransmitters actually increased the amplitude of the message sent to the next cell. They have also learned that once depression is treated and cured, the neurotransmitters actually return to normal.

SEROTONIN AND NOREPINEPHRINE

Serotonin and norepinephrine are the most significant neurotransmitters that are depleted in the brains of those who are depressed. Norepinephrine is present in excess in the brains of those experiencing mania, which is, in many ways, the opposite or obverse of depression.

When researchers began to investigate how the different antidepressants work, they discovered that these medications tend to bring about the same end result—increases of serotonin and norepinephrine in the brain. This in turn produces a marked improvement in the mood and outlook of previously depressed people.

Since norepinephrine and serotonin belong to a chemical group called the amines, the theory of depression that emerged from all this very persuasive research became known as the *brain amine (or monoamine) theory of depression.* Ninety percent of these amines are located in an area deep in the brain known as the limbic system. This system controls emotions, pain perception, sleep, and involuntary functions such as digestion, elimination and so on.

Because the amines are so important, the normally functioning brain has a mechanism for conserving them. This process is called *reuptake.* After the reaction takes place, the nerve cell takes back about 85 percent of the amines it has released and conserves them for later use. The other 15 percent is broken down by an enzyme called MAO (monoamine oxidase) and usually leaves the body in the urine. Thus, in the normal brain only 15 percent of the amine concentration regularly needs to be newly manufactured in order to keep the nerve cell communication mechanism going.

What can happen to foul this astonishing chemical process?

1. There may not be enough amines in the first place because of inadequate "raw materials" or precursors, chiefly amino acids, and their necessary cofactors, enzymes, vitamins and minerals.
2. There may be a genetically determined excessive need for the substances required to form the brain amines.
3. The reuptake mechanism may not be functioning properly.
4. There may be too much MAO so there is excessive destruction of the amines. This tendency toward excess MAO may be inherited. Also, as we age we have increased MAO, a factor leading to higher risk for depression in the elderly.
5. The receptor cells may not be properly sensitive or receptive to a normal level of the amines.

The common purpose of all biochemical treatments for depression is to increase the amount of these neurotransmitters at the synapse. Some drugs, such as the tricyclics, block the reuptake mechanism, allowing more amine to accumulate in the synapse. Others, such as the MAO inhibitors, block the MAO enzyme and slow the breakdown. Other drugs increase the sensitivity of the receptor cells, and still newer medicines act by mechanisms we've yet to understand.

The precursor nutrients (amino acids, enzymes, vitamins and minerals) appear to be the safest, most effective way of increasing the brain amine levels. They simultaneously increase both norepinephrine and serotonin, while the more traditional antidepressant drugs generally increase only one or the other of these brain amines and may not work if both amines are depleted.

To put things bluntly, the research and results indicate we are almost to the point where ignoring such chemical factors in a person with major depression might constitute negligence, if not malpractice.

GENETIC CAUSES OF DEPRESSION

A 1981 report from Yale University begins with the words: "Inherited variations in the activity of enzymes involved in neurotransmitter metabolism are thought to affect individual differences in neurophysiology, behavior, and susceptibility to disease" (Pintar et al., J. Neuroscience). The tendency toward depression is one of those traits related to neurotransmitter metabolism that can definitely be inherited. This is one reason why family history may be important in determining diagnosis. Those depressions that begin before the age of thirty, and are severe or recurrent, are most likely to be strongly influenced genetically.

Though the exact mechanism by which depression is transferred from parent to child is not yet fully understood, we are already pretty certain that the trait can be transferred on many different genes. When only a few of these predisposing genes are inherited, they'll result in milder forms of depression; when many of the genes are inherited, severe depression can occur. This multiple gene action explains why mood disorders do not follow as set, or predictable a pattern as do some other inherited traits.

Also, we are ultimately products of the interaction between our genetic influences and our environment. What goes on in our lives can exaggerate or diminish our genetic tendencies. If our genes predispose us toward fat accumulation, sadly, we must eat less and exercise more than the lucky ones with lean producing genes. If we have inherited a tendency toward insufficient neurotransmitters, a little stress and a little alcohol may plunge us into despair, whereas our friend can drink every day, lead a fast-paced, stressful life and feel okay—for a while anyway.

If you are depressed, there is a 20 to 25 percent chance that what is called a "first degree relative"—your parents, children or siblings—is also depressed. If you are not depressed, the chances of a first degree relative of yours being depressed is only 7 percent.

When one parent is depressed, the lifetime risk for the children to be affected is 17 percent. When both parents are depressed, the risk to their children of developing depression at any time in their life is 55 to 75 percent. You can see that genetic counseling can be extremely important for depressed parents.

Some professionals attempt to explain these familial patterns by arguing that we merely copy or imitate the depressed moods of family members. Yet, studies have been done on depressed persons who have had little or no contact with their families. The findings? The percentage of hereditability is basically the same, even when the patients have never known any of their biological relatives. For instance, when identical, same-egg twins are raised in entirely different environments, there is a 67 percent chance of both being depressed, if one is depressed.

There is also evidence to suggest that genetic factors may operate in vulnerability to suicide: the suicide rate in the relatives of depressed patients is more than ten times that of control groups. A striking example of this kind of genetic loading was presented very early in my career. In medical school, the psychiatry professor who taught us about depression candidly told us the horrible story of losing both parents in his childhood when they committed suicide together in their carbon monoxide-filled garage. Thereafter he spent his life trying to understand depression. In the end, perhaps he understood the agony too well, for a few years after I completed medical school I heard he had chosen to take his own life with an overdose of sleeping pills. Later I learned that his son, too, was suffering from depression.

GENETIC ASSOCIATION WITH OTHER DISORDERS

Studies show a higher incidence of depression in families with alcoholism, drug abuse, eating disorders, anxiety disorder, agoraphobia and hyperactive children, leading us to believe that the genetic influences sometimes overlap in these conditions. Treatment for depression can often improve or eliminate these genetically associated conditions.

It's no surprise to find a connection between depression and eating disorders, because our appetite and mood control centers are in the same area of the brain and both are influenced by the same neurotransmitters.

As yet, orthodox psychiatry has not developed any treatment intervention that can work preventively to reduce such genetic risks. But those who are so disposed would be wise to be careful about diet, nutrient supplementation and stress reduction programs as means of decreasing or negating these tendencies.

We can't control our genetic inheritance. So what do we do with all this tremendously valuable information? We use it. Positively. Optimistically. And for all it's worth.

The Amino Acid Treatment Program

W_e have seen that people who are suffering from depression very often have less than normal amounts of the chemicals serotonin and norepinephrine in their brains. Adding certain amino acids and vitamins to their diet can relieve the depression by restoring the balance of these important substances. This process is known as *precursor loading* and is the basis for the treatment program.

Now let's go to work implementing an antidepressant therapy that:

1. Has far greater overall safety than conventional drug therapies;
2. Is preferable for long-term use;
3. Can be effective with intermittent usage;
4. Offers associated health benefits such as improved overall energy, improved mental and physical endurance and functioning, decreased infections and a myriad of other health benefits that can accrue from a basic balanced nutritional program;
5. Can prevent further depressive episodes;
6. Has flexibility, in that it can be adjusted to deal with a large variety of symptoms;
7. Has no associated withdrawal symptoms;
8. Has almost no toxicity and is virtually immune to dangerous misuse (in contrast, for example, to many standard antidepressant drugs);
9. Is composed of water soluble substances that don't accumulate in your brain or other tissues;

10. Is metabolized by enzymes designed by evolution for that purpose;
11. And, finally, relies on your brain's own remarkable ability to override and to shut off the process if the neurotransmitter concentrations become too high.

THE BASIC PROGRAM

We'll begin by setting out an ideal minimum program for achieving greater neurotransmitter production. This assumes that low mood or depression is the key concern and that there are few other problems and symptoms. If you have any serious medical illness, be sure to read Chapters 6 and 10 before beginning the program.

Once we've established the basics, we'll fine tune the program to adjust it to any of several special circumstances you may have, such as accompanying illnesses, severe insomnia, anxiety, fatigue, memory disturbance and so on. You will also later read what to do in the presence of other interfering conditions such as excess alcohol intake, sugar, premenstrual problems, stress, drug side effects, food allergies, physical illnesses, age, severe life problems or just hectic day-to-day living.

In my practice, where the results of the program have been excellent, I first look for and help my patients to eliminate as much as possible these other contributing conditions. The less interference with the basic program, the better.

THE PROGRAM EXPLAINED

Our basic supplements are the amino acids L-tyrosine and L-tryptophan, vitamin B complex, vitamin C and a multivitamin mineral. Generally, for more predictable and more rapid absorption, I recommend all supplements be taken in capsule or powder form rather than in hard tablets. (The "L" and "D" in these names refer to the chemical rotation of the molecule.)

L-Tyrosine
Take 500 to 3500 mg when you get up in the morning, and again in the mid-afternoon.

This should not be taken with any protein food (such as milk, cheese, eggs, etc.), because you will absorb less of this amino acid if other types of protein are being digested at the same time. I recommend you take it with some water, juice or fruit and that you don't eat anything else for at least thirty minutes.

Begin with 500 to 1000 mg twice daily for one week. (Children and the elderly should start with 500 mg *once* daily in the morning, and if an increased dosage is necessary, it should not exceed 1500 mg twice daily.) If you feel no improvement after one week, gradually increase your dosage, staying at each increased level for one week. In other words, if you started with one pill twice daily for the first week, you would raise it to two pills twice daily the second week as needed, and so on. Do not exceed the maximum daily dosages listed here. This warning is not because adverse effects have occurred at higher doses, but because little is known about the long-term effects of higher amounts.

With all supplements, including the amino acids, stop and stay with the amount that works for you and remain on this minimum effective dosage.

L-Tryptophan

Take 500 to 6000 mg at bedtime.

Tryptophan, too, should not be taken with any protein food, for the reason given above. There won't be any problem if you take it with water or some carbohydrates. Actually, simultaneous ingestion of tryptophan with carbohydrates can increase the absorption of tryptophan. Note that if you have severe sleep problems, you must try to avoid night-time sugar, fruits and fruit juices as they will stimulate you when you want to be calming down. The exception is grapefruit, which has a sedative effect due to its high magnesium content.

Vitamin B Complex

Take 50 to 100 mg with breakfast and again with the evening meal. (The 50 to 100 mg refers to the amounts of B_1, B_2 and B_6 in the product. The other ingredients will often be in amounts other than 50 to 100 mg.)

Deficiencies of almost any of the B vitamins can cause depression, so their importance cannot be overemphasized (see charts in Appendix to Chapter Seven). When low mood or depression is complicated by circumstances such as severe stress, illness and certain dietary habits which have nutritionally depleted you, very large supplements of B complex vitamins may be necessary. The recommended dosages in the basic program are conservative and completely safe.

B complex vitamins are often yeast-based. To avoid the occasional problem with yeast, or other allergy reactions, I prefer that the B complex be yeast-free and hypoallergenic.

When you buy a multi-B vitamin, it contains the whole range of B complex vitamins. Different manufacturers create products with slightly varying ratios of one ingredient to another. Don't worry if what you find is not exactly what is listed here as long as the amounts generally parallel these. When possible, obtain a product with the vitamins B_1, B_2 and B_6 in what are called the coenzyme forms. The approximate dose ranges that follow should be available in a single supplement:

B_1: Thiamine hydrochloride	50–100 mg
B_2: Riboflavin 5 Phosphate	50–100 mg
B_3: Niacinamide or niacin	30–100 mg
B_5: Calcium pantothenate	100–500 mg
B_6: Pyridoxal-5-phosphate	10–120 mg
B_6: Pyridoxine hydrochloride	50–100 mg
Choline	100–300 mg
PABA	30–100 mg
Biotin	100–400 mcg
Folic Acid	100–400 mcg
B_{12}	100–500 mcg

If your B complex vitamin does not contain vitamin B_6 in the pyridoxal-5-phosphate form, you will need to find this form of vitamin B_6 and add it to your program separately, 20 to 120 mg twice daily. Try to buy vitamin B_6 that is coated so that it will not be destroyed by stomach acid. (See appendix.) Vitamin B_6 is essential for the metabolism and usage of all proteins and amino acids.

Vitamin C:

Take 500 to 2000 mg in the morning and again with dinner. This can be taken with your first food in the morning and with your evening meal. If you tend to be an allergic person, use a corn-free vitamin C compound.

Multivitamin Mineral Capsule

Take half the daily dosage in the morning and half in the evening.

For the purpose of implementing the basic program, here's what to look for in a multivitamin mineral. Find the product that comes closest to these specifications and take half the daily dose with breakfast, half with dinner.

	DAILY DOSAGE
Vitamin A (preferably in the form of beta carotene)	10,000–25,000 IU (International units)
Vitamin C	100–1000 mg
Vitamin B_1	25–100 mg
Vitamin B_2	25–100 mg
Vitamin B_3	25–500 mg
Vitamin B_5	25–500 mg
Vitamin B_6	25–500 mg
Vitamin B_{12}	100–1000 mcg
PABA	25–500 mg
Biotin	100–800 mcg
Folic acid	100–800 mcg
Vitamin E	100–400 IU
Vitamin D	100–400 IU
Calcium	250–1000 mg
Magnesium	125–500 mg
Potassium	50–200 mg
Manganese	10–30 mg
Zinc	15–50 mg
Selenium	50–200 mcg
Chromium	50–200 mcg

A wide range is listed for each substance because vitamin manufacturers use slightly different combinations of dosages, and it might be difficult to find a specific fixed formula for this kind of multisupplement. Some preparations may contain other ingredients besides those listed here. These should generally pose no problem.

You may have noticed the exclusion of copper from this list,

Dosage Schedule for Basic Program

	Morning upon Arising, without Food	With Breakfast or First Food	Midafternoon without Food	With Dinner	Bedtime without Food
L-Tyrosine capsules	500–3500 mg		500–3500 mg		
L-Tryptophan capsules					500–6000 mg
Vitamin B complex		50–100 mg		50–100 mg	
Vitamin C		500–2000 mg		500–2000 mg	
Multivitamin mineral		Half the total daily dosage		Half the total daily dosage	

Use a quarter to half of the above dosages for children (preferably free of or with less than 30 IU of vitamin E); also give a multi-amino acid supplement as mentioned on page 59.
Use a quarter to half of the tyrosine and tryptophan dosages plus full vitamin dosages for the elderly.
Begin with a minimum tyrosine and tryptophan dosage for all.
See page 44 for multivitamin and vitamin B complex specifications.
DO NOT EXCEED RECOMMENDED DOSES.

even though it is required for neurotransmitter formation. Copper deficiency is rare; more often we find a copper excess—which can create depression as one of its symptoms. If your multivitamin does contain copper, it should be no more than 500 micrograms (0.5 mg).

Iron has also been omitted. If you are pregnant, menstruating, a vegetarian, poorly nourished, are over seventy years of age, or have any evidence of iron deficiency, use a multivitamin mineral which contains amino acid chelated iron in the amount of 50 to 200 mg. Unless you fall into one of these categories, use iron-free supplements.

Please note that the amount listed on the side of the vitamin bottle is usually for anywhere from one to six capsules daily to provide the specified dosage. In other words, to get what you need you may have to take one to three capsules in the morning with your first food and the same amount with your evening food.

You will notice I have said "capsules," not tablets. You can also use powder or liquid forms, if available. Tablets can sometimes pass right through you, and not be digested at all. This was reported to me often enough for me to realize the best laid plans can go awry. Now I suggest the use of capsules whenever possible, unless you have a sensitive stomach and want very slow release to avoid the possibility of irritation.

A CRITICAL NOTE

Before beginning this treatment, be sure to see Chapter 6 in order to adjust the program to your own special circumstances. These may include associated medical or psychiatric diagnoses or a preponderance of particular types of symptoms.

It is also important to follow the complete program outlined in this book, not just the supplement program in this chapter. In my office, I always attempt to evaluate the possible contributing situations because that enhances the chance for complete effectiveness.

A COMMON ADJUSTMENT TO THE BASIC PROGRAM

If after four to six weeks there are insufficient results, one of the first things I do is to add L-phenylalanine to the program. If a person initially has physical pain as a part of her depression, I add D,L-phenylalanine right from the beginning.

L-phenylalanine or D,L-phenylalanine

Use 1000 to 3000 mg in the midafternoon with food to replace the afternoon tyrosine dosage. Continue taking the tyrosine in the morning.

Actually, more research has been done on the use of phenylalanine than on the use of tyrosine for treating depression, but since my patients have generally had better results and better tolerance with tyrosine, I prefer to use it.

As Dr. Arnold Fox described in *DLPA to End Chronic Pain and Depression*, the D form of phenylalanine helps relieve pain by slowing the breakdown of pain-relieving endorphins in the brain.

L-phenylalanine can convert to tyrosine, but it also has other important metabolic pathways, one of which is to form a substance called 2-PEA (2-phenylethylamine). PEA is believed to be a neurotransmitter which is closely related to norepinephrine. The amphetamines, the stimulant Ritalin, and the antidepressant Tofranil all cause an increase of 2-PEA in the brain, and this is one mechanism through which they exert their excitant effects.

Some depressed people have insufficient 2-PEA and when this is so, phenylalanine may be necessary. Since PEA is more of a direct stimulant than norepinephrine, phenylalanine usage can give those people who don't apparently need the extra PEA a "wired" feeling. This is one reason why it is not usually my first choice, but only needs to be added in approximately 10 percent of cases.

WHERE CAN I GET THE SUPPLEMENTS?

You may purchase the supplements at health food stores, at pharmacies or by mail. I prescribe very specific products because

I feel relatively certain of their quality and potency. On a number of occasions people who have been doing very well using a certain product have then run out and replaced it with an inferior product and relapsed. When we figure out what has happened and again use the original brand, they again improve.

When possible, buy encapsulated hypoallergenic supplements, which have no corn, yeast, sugar, dyes, preservatives or other additives.

The brands I like, which are available in most health food stores, are Country Life, Twinlab, Integrated Health, Alacer and Nutricology. Tyson and Associates products are available through pharmacies. All of these manufacturers produce high quality nutritional supplements. I am sure there are others as well. Please refer to the back of the book for more detailed information.

THE FORMS OF THE AMINO ACIDS

The chemical form of the amino acid is extremely important. For precursor loading to work properly, the amino acids must be taken in fairly large doses to make sure the digestive system manages to absorb enough of them. Further, they must be taken in what is called the singular "free form." This means they do not have to go through complicated digestive processes that may or may not occur, but are in the form that is ready for immediate assimilation and use by the body. This clearly bypasses the problem of poor digestion interfering with their usefulness. These free form amino acids are so pure and effective they are the official food supplement for astronauts, for U.S.S.R. parachute jumpers, for some professional athletes and for others who must have optimal performance. Extra protein, protein powders or protein supplements are not the same and will not give good results. If you use them for other purposes, they must be taken at a different time than the singular free form amino acids or they will interfere with the program.

There are many different kinds of amino acids on the market. Basically, four different grades are available:

The Feed Grade

The first is called the feed grade, because it is used in animal-feed supplements. Ironically, these are the amino acid tablets that are often for sale in health food stores.

The problem here is that when the amino acids are heated and compressed into tablets during manufacturing, they may lose some of their potency. Hard tablets sometimes go right through your body without breaking up or being digested, and it's not clear how much of the amino acids you are assimilating. Although they are the least expensive, I don't recommend feed grade supplements.

The Cosmetic Grade

This second grade of amino acid is used in shampoos, hair conditioners, face creams and so on.

The Pharmaceutical Grade

The pharmaceutical grade is a pure, potent amino acid, used by drug companies that manufacture amino acid-related products used in most high quality supplements.

The IV Grade

This grade of amino acid is pure enough to be used intravenously. It is more concentrated and, not surprisingly, is the most expensive. It is not readily available and is not used in oral supplements.

My Own Recommendation

My patients use the pharmaceutical grade with good, consistent results. Take it in powder or capsule form. Again, remember to look for what are called "free form amino acids."

WHO CAN BENEFIT?

Years of practice have convinced me that *everyone* who improves his diet and takes appropriate supplements will benefit. Therefore, anyone who reads this book and selects those elements which relate to him will be helped—whether or not he is actually depressed.

But if you have low mood or depression, this treatment has a good chance of working if you take the supplements regularly and as directed. It will work even better and more lastingly if you are willing and able to change your thought and life patterns in the ways we will discuss later. Such an approach requires that you take more responsibility and do more for yourself, but the payoff can be worth it.

For the unlucky ones prone to illness, getting well and staying well may require a consistent long-term application of will and behavior—with an occasional digression, of course.

Those with only intermittent low moods or with mild to moderate depression can also use this complete treatment safely and productively, following the precautions mentioned in Chapter 6.

NOTE: *If you are severely depressed, not functioning, anxious and agitated, or have serious suicidal intent, you should see a psychiatrist in conjunction with following this program.*

OTHER USES

If you are in a situation where you need intense mental concentration, focus and output, short-term use of tyrosine or phenylalanine together with the B complex vitamins is excellent for this purpose. Such circumstances might include studying for and taking exams, presenting a case in court, or completing an important project.

When experimental animals are given drugs which decrease the amount of norepinephrine in the brain, the animals' capacity for learning is blocked. Then, when the animals are given an injection of norepinephrine, the ability to learn returns. This has many unexplored implications for the use of norepinephrine precursors for improving learning.

When you use amino acids for this purpose, *only use them intermittently.* If you are not depressed, your amino acids are likely already in balance. You do not want to unbalance them by sustained supplementation. Generally I recommend against any such repeated or prolonged supplementation in the nondepressed individual. However there are balanced amino acid formulas which are safe for long-term use in these instances.

HOW TO BEGIN?

How you launch the program really depends upon how motivated you are, how easy it is for you to follow a consistent program and how eager you are to feel better.

If you are the "gung ho" type and want to plunge in totally, you can buy everything at once and get started. Generally, though, it is best to begin slowly, adding one new supplement daily until you are on the full program. This allows your body to adjust gradually to the substances and also lets you know which, if any of them, doesn't agree with you (this rarely happens).

HOW SOON CAN I EXPECT RESULTS?

You may respond dramatically and immediately to this treatment, or it may involve several months of gradual improvement. If your problem is merely low moods, you may have a rapid and consistently lasting improvement as early as within one day of starting the treatment program. Most of my patients have a partial or complete response within one to three weeks of the initiation of total treatment. Researchers using single substances such as tyrosine or phenylalanine (not a complete program as in this book), have usually seen a response in those with depressive illness by three weeks of treatment.

Often, others will notice improvement in your condition before you yourself become aware of it. This is especially true if you have been severely depressed. Almost consistently, depressed hospitalized patients are seen by others to be getting better before they themselves notice the change. It takes a while to sink in, since you are so accustomed to feeling bad. A good way to measure and compare your progress is to take the self-rating test in Chapter 2 once a month for several months after starting this program.

I had personally been on the nutritional program for three or four months before I realized one day I had been having a general sense of well-being for some time. Then I made an agreement with myself never ever again to even consider the option of suicide, as I had done on many previous occasions. No matter what came my way I would search for positive ways to cope rather than waste my energy in these destructive escape fantasies.

Having made such a decision, it has been easy to stick with it. At times, I find myself truly happy on all levels. I could never feel that way before. Even at best, something inside or outside was always interfering. I am no longer dependent on the outer world for the maintenance of my mood. Instead, I depend on my thoughts, attitudes and biochemistry, my inner world. It's amazing, when this happens, how well outside life falls into place.

When you begin to feel better it may come in starts and stops. If all your days have been bad, you'll begin having some partially good days. At the beginning you will swing back and forth in your moods. Gradually the shift will be toward more of the partially good days. Eventually you'll have *totally good days,* after which your mood will become stable and *up* most of the time. The transition usually takes place in this gradual fashion. Those who have been depressed for years will need to feel good for a period of time before they trust and feel safely rescued from low moods.

You'll find yourself elated that you're feeling better, and then when a low day recurs, you may become frightened and discouraged, believing the mood monster has returned. Avoid this discouragement: the mood angel will come again to lift your spirits and she will visit more and more frequently. Do not give up or abandon the program. It is totally natural for your course to fluctuate until you have returned to a state of consistent well-being. This pattern is the one most often experienced in those recovering from a "depressive illness."

One patient with seventeen years of chronic depression under her psychological belt refused to believe she was really free of her depression until she had passed four consecutive months with no evidence of low mood. When she began the program, she said she was "skeptical" but desperate and didn't want to go back on medication. In the first-month follow-up visit she felt much less depressed but felt "it is too soon to trust it." The second month, she continued to feel well and was surprised, still not daring to get her hopes up too much. The third month was the same.

Finally, on the fourth-month visit, she said, "You've convinced me, I'm a believer. I haven't felt this good for this long in fifteen years." She is a mental health professional and has sent me many patients since then.

How Long Should I Continue This Treatment?

When a depressed person is given the usual antidepressant drugs, the treatment generally continues for six months after her symptoms have disappeared. Subsequently, the dosage is gradually reduced. But some people must continue using traditional antidepressant medications for years.

I use a similar approach with nutrients. I advise people who have severe depression to stay on the program longer than others. If you have occasional low moods or one of the moderate forms of depression, you might start tapering the dosage after three or four months, until you find the minimum amount you can take that still leaves you feeling good. If you have suffered from severe or chronic depression, continue the treatment for six to eight months after you feel well. Then gradually taper off. Some people have to stay on a minimum dosage indefinitely, which should and can be accepted freely, without guilt or concern.

This has been the case with several of my patients. Janet, who is a nurse, has been taking the supplements and feeling well for several years, after sixteen previous years of depression. Each time she drops her nutrients below a specific dosage she has a relapse, but as long as she takes the minimum nutrients necessary for her, she maintains her sense of well-being. Certainly, for those who need such long-term chemical regulation, these substances, which are natural to the body, are preferable to drugs, foreign compounds which stress the system.

It shouldn't be necessary for most of you to stay on this program for the rest of your lives even if you have a significant genetic predisposition to depression. After you have responded favorably and may even have tapered off the supplements completely, you can always return to them if your depression or low moods come back. You can also keep a supply of the nutrients on hand for use on those occasional low days when you wake up feeling a little under par.

You will do particularly well if you also use the supplementary suggestions later in this book for creating overall health and well-being.

HOW DOES THIS TREATMENT COMPARE WITH USUAL ANTIDEPRESSANT MEDICATION?

It must be emphasized that if you are severely depressed, you may need traditional medication to begin with. Furthermore, if you are already on medication do not abruptly stop it. Follow the guidelines on page 73. It is unwise to discontinue most of these medicines abruptly, for you can develop withdrawal symptoms such as nightmares, insomnia, anxiety, agitation, irritability and gastric distress. You can also precipitate a relapse of depression.

What are the advantages of a nutritional program versus the more traditional chemical therapies?

First, when both tyrosine and tryptophan are used, both the neurotransmitters norepinephrine and serotonin are increased. Antidepressant prescription medicines also increase the neurotransmitters, but most of them only increase one or the other, not both. Valuable time can be lost giving a drug that, for example, increases serotonin, when low norepinephrine is the problem. One way to determine which neurotransmitter is low or has missing precursors is to conduct an amino acid chromatography test.

Second, many people who have only mild or moderate depression, or only intermittent low moods will not want to take a medication with many possible side effects. After all, if you only feel low five or ten days out of every month, or if your moods fluctuate during the day, why take a daily prescription medication?

Third, some chronically depressed people have a relapse every time they try to decrease or stop their medication. Hence, they remain medicated for years. The likelihood of such relapses is high in those who suffer from the actual "illness" of depression. Some studies report a relapse rate of 12 percent in the first month after stopping treatment, 25 percent within three months, and 50 to 90 percent within two years. For these persons, the value of a

good, safe nutritional program which they can continue indefinitely is quite obvious as an alternative to chronic long-term
medication usage with its attendant side effects.

Fourth, this combination of amino acids and vitamins is usually
effective within the first two weeks of use, compared to the four
to six weeks usually required for most antidepressant medication
to take effect.

Last, there is a considerable difference in side effects between
the two methods.

It bears repeating that some severely depressed people who
are already using medication must, initially, continue to follow
that line of treatment even while beginning this one. If your doctor wants you to continue your medication and do nothing else
for the time being, then follow your doctor's advice and later,
when you are improved, implement this program as a guard
against relapses. If the severity or associated symptoms of your
depression warrant strong sedative medication to quell extreme
agitation, or associated psychotic thinking, you need to be willing
to take the medication and not be put off by the possibility of side
effects.

POSSIBLE SIDE EFFECTS OF TRADITIONAL ANTIDEPRESSANTS

In medical practice, the risk of side effects from medication is
always weighed against the risk of the effects of the illness itself.
Since the mortality associated with the diagnosis of *major* depression is 15 percent, physicians and patients alike have been
willing to tolerate side effect risks. Fortunately, many of the side
effects are benign and transient. A list of possible side effects
from prescription antidepressants follows.

1. Orthostatic hypotension (This is most common and is described as a delayed adjustment of the blood pressure to
   changes in body position, especially abrupt changes. It can
   cause dizziness sometimes associated with falls, especially
   in the elderly. Also, other blood pressure changes may occur,
   such as elevated blood pressure.)
2. Sedation and fatigue
3. Sleeping too much

4. Constipation
5. Dry mouth
6. Blurred vision
7. Impaired orgasm or delayed or painful ejaculation
8. A switch to mania
9. Temporary thinking defects, especially related to memory and concentration
10. Palpitations and rapid or irregular heart beat
11. Sensitivity to the sun
12. Itching and skin rashes
13. Weight gain
14. And, *very rarely:* urinary retention, a paralytic response of the small bowel, glaucoma or global depression of blood cells

All these risks increase in the treatment of the elderly and additionally complicate the treatment of children. Also, these medications must be administered with caution to those with epilepsy, Parkinson's disease, heart rhythm problems, glaucoma, high blood pressure, liver insufficiency and certain urinary disorders. The newer classes of antidepressants are slightly less risky, but still present a number of possible problems.

Generally, quantities of antidepressants greater than 1250 mg at once can be fatal. This is about six to eight times the therapeutic dose, and ironically a number of depressed persons commit suicide with their antidepressant medication before the medication has had time to exert a positive effect.

Because of such side effects most doctors, including myself, have had to discontinue or change antidepressant medicines on a number of occasions. Yet, by contrast, *in all the years I have been treating depression with amino acids, I have never had to discontinue the treatment because of side effects.* I have, at most, had to modify the tyrosine and phenylalanine usage in cases of preexisting high blood pressure.

POSSIBLE SIDE EFFECTS OF THE NUTRIENT PROGRAM

Side Effects of L-Tryptophan

1. Slight morning drowsiness
2. Stomach queasiness or mild nausea

3. Erratic dreams
4. Slight headaches
5. Transient agitation
6. Blood pressure changes in a few who have a preexisting high, unstable blood pressure and who are over sixty years old

Since we are discussing a relatively new treatment, let's go over these possibilities in more detail, so as to be on the safe side. Bear in mind, though, that my patients have not experienced effects other than drowsiness. Other researchers, however, have reported them as possibilities.

In Great Britain tryptophan has been used over a period of many months to treat depression. Daily doses of 6000 to 9000 mg have been taken with almost no side effects reported and, even more important, no withdrawal symptoms on abrupt discontinuance.

Tryptophan is rapidly metabolized and cleared from the body so there is no toxic buildup over time. Thus, side effects are extremely rare, other than a slight, short-lived morning drowsiness in some patients who have taken it late the night before. This drowsiness is trivial compared to the heavy sedation experienced with some of the traditional antidepressant medications. No patient under my care has had to stop tryptophan because of side effects. There have been reports that larger than usual doses on an empty stomach can sometimes produce mild queasiness or nausea. Rarely, very sensitive people experience an increase in dreamlike sensations as they are falling asleep, or have erratic dreams while sleeping. Other physicians who prescribe L-tryptophan have reported that a few of their patients experience slight headaches or transient agitation. Some studies, on the other hand, report that tryptophan suppresses migraine headaches.

Because some physicians have reported problems, we advise that nobody who has taken MAO inhibitor drugs should use tryptophan within ten days.

Researchers report that tryptophan taken alone without B complex vitamins can produce dizziness, light-headedness and blurred vision in a few cases. My patients have not experienced this, but neither have they taken the tryptophan without the B complex vitamins. It's important to take the B complex vitamins

both because they eliminate this possibility and also because
they improve the tryptophan metabolism.

There are conflicting studies and reports on how tryptophan
affects blood pressure. Animal studies indicate it has a slight
blood pressure lowering effect, yet a few humans, especially
those over sixty who already have high blood pressure, occasionally experience a transient increase in heart rate and blood pressure with the use of extra tryptophan. This effect has not been
noted in those with normal blood pressure. Those few who do
have this reaction are a small subgroup who apparently metabolize tryptophan unusually or may already have excess serotonin
in their brains for some other reason. Again, I have not noted this
problem in my practice, but it is a possibility.

If you have high blood pressure, you can ask your doctor to
measure your blood and urine for free-circulating serotonin levels. If they are low to average, you are likely to be safe in taking
the tryptophan. Begin at the lowest dose and gradually increase
as needed. If the serotonin is high, refrain from taking the tryptophan, but follow the rest of the program. It may work quite well
for you.

Side Effects of L-tyrosine

I personally have not come across any side effect problems
with L-tyrosine, though there is a report of one case of a manic,
over-stimulated episode being attributed to the substance. If you
are manic-depressive, there is always the *risk* of inducing a
manic state whether you take traditional antidepressant medications or the antidepressant nutrients. In any event, for patients
diagnosed as manic-depressive nothing, including this program,
should be undertaken without a doctor's strict supervision.

Tyrosine has been given safely, but cautiously, to those with
heart disease and to those taking what is known as "beta
blocker" medicine, circumstances which make classical antidepressants risky.

Though there is some worry about its potential for increasing
already high blood pressure, a double blind study suggested the
opposite. Because it increased norepinephrine in certain areas of
the central nervous system, tyrosine actually produced a decrease in blood norepinephrine concentrations in the rest of the

body. The researchers concluded that tyrosine could possibly be of benefit in treating certain cases of high blood pressure.

Side Effects of L-phenylalanine

L-phenylalanine is considered to have a slight potential for creating changes in blood pressure in a few people already suffering from severely high, erratically fluctuating blood pressure. Two such patients of mine who were monitoring their blood pressure levels several times daily noted a ten point increase in their blood pressure one to two hours after taking this amino acid. This is not a dangerous increase and the levels returned to normal an hour or two later. Other researchers have not observed this effect, and Dr. Arnold Fox reports the safe use of the form called D,L-phenylalanine on hundreds of his patients. All the same, this possibility does exist and if you have such blood pressure problems, use phenylalanine and tyrosine cautiously, starting with a minimum dose and gradually increasing while, at the same time, monitoring your blood pressure.

With excess dosage, headaches, insomnia and irritability have also been reported occasionally.

IS THERE ANYTHING ELSE TO BEAR IN MIND?

Theoretically, taking certain amino acids separately could create an overall imbalance of amino acids in your body. So far, neither the medical literature on the subject, nor the clinical experience of physicians using this type of treatment has shown any signs of this kind of problem occurring at these suggested doses. If you were taking a dosage of more than 20 g (20,000 mg) daily, it might create an imbalance and consequent problems of some type, but we are using much smaller amounts.

Depression is an illness characterized by less than the usual amounts of amino acid end products in the brain. Therefore, those who are depressed generally need more of certain specific amino acids than the rest of us do. In other words, taking amino acid supplements when you are depressed is likely to balance an already unbalanced system, rather than the reverse. This hypothesis has been borne out by blood amino acid studies before and after treatment.

Add a multi-amino acid preparation (that includes seventeen to nineteen of the amino acids) if you continue taking the amino acids for more than seven to eight months, or when the single amino acids are used by those under fourteen years of age. Take them with breakfast and with dinner. If you have three or more alcoholic drinks or eat a lot of sugar daily, use a mixed amino preparation that contains an extra amount of glutamine, which helps to reduce alcohol and sugar cravings. Do not use a protein powder in these instances, use a pure form amino acid preparation.

How Much Does All This Cost?

The cost will vary depending on whether you respond to a minimal program, or have to take the top dosages, or have to add in substances mentioned in later chapters. The price also varies depending on where you purchase your products.

Considering the substances and dosage ranges in this chapter, the monthly cost should range from fifty to a hundred dollars. For those on antidepressant drugs, the average monthly cost is usually thirty to sixty dollars, depending upon whether a trade name product or a generic form is used. Thus, for slightly more cost, you can often achieve the same or better results and gain overall general improved health.

One Last Question

If this treatment is as simple, safe and successful as you say it is, why aren't more doctors using it?

In general, most doctors only feel comfortable using treatment methods with which they are totally familiar, or which have long been accepted as standard approaches. It's not surprising: nobody would be very happy if doctors were always trying new treatments on their patients with very little knowledge of the treatment or of its results.

What all this adds up to is expressed in the phrase, "What doctors are not up on, they are down on." That can be a pity, when a successful new field like using nutrition for actual treatment of various ills is just developing. It is unfortunate, in my opinion, that doctors who haven't had the chance to familiarize themselves with this new and comprehensive way of viewing disease discourage their patients from trying it. Nutritional medicine is really a subspecialty in itself. Information in nutritional science doubles every three to four years, so that keeping up with the immense flood of new research in the field demands considerable interest and time commitment. Nutritional medicine is not the same thing at all as what a "nutritionist" does, but is the application of general medical knowledge to the understanding of the interaction among nutrients, biochemistry, physiology, anatomy and genetic patterning.

In a 1985 report, *Nutrition Education in U.S. Medical Schools,** a committee found that some medical schools only require a total of three hours training in nutrition! The best of the schools surveyed only require 56 hours, which would be about one hour weekly for one year. This is almost negligible compared to the time spent on other subjects. They also found among the schools that teach the least amount of nutrition are some that have the best reputations for superior academic strength!

Doctors are already swamped by the amount of work they have to do just to keep up with their own practice and the developments in their own field of specialization. Learning an entirely new field is an immense undertaking. That is why your physician is unlikely to know that much about nutrition, unless he or she has gone out of the way to become knowledgeable in the field.

After all, the first serious medical text† devoted entirely to the treatment of depression with amino acids and vitamins was published only in 1983. And, although there has been a recent rash of articles in the medical journals, most physicians are only now beginning to learn that this kind of treatment exists.

If you or your doctor are interested in taking a look at some of the research supporting this approach, you can check the appropriate sources in the bibliography.

If you are looking for a physician in your area who believes in

Nutrition Education in U.S. Medical Schools, a report from the National Academy of Sciences Press, 2101 Constitution Avenue, N.W., Washington, D.C.
†*Management of Depression with Monoamine Precursors,* 1983, edited by H.M. van Praag and J. Mendlewicz, S. Kargen Pub., Inc., N.Y.

and is familiar with nutritional treatment, you can check the appendix for a list of organizations with referral lists.

Many people who come to my office already have their own internist, rheumatologist or cardiologist, and so on. They confide to me that they are afraid to let their doctors know they are using nutritional treatment for fear the physician will object, ridicule them, or give them negative suggestions. Some patients even play a little game: they simply don't reveal they are using this kind of treatment until the doctors themselves comment on how well they are looking and doing.

Some of my patients never tell their doctors. One woman, who improved dramatically as a result of this kind of treatment, is very amused when she goes to her doctor for a checkup every now and then. He's made it clear he is not in favor of the idea of using nutritional supplements. But when he sees her, he always tells her, "I don't know what it is that you're doing, but whatever it is, keep doing it."

Still, more and more physicians are becoming interested in this rapidly expanding field and more and more are experiencing the satisfaction and benefits concomitant to nutrient therapy. Certainly, we might conclude that Thomas Edison saw the light when he said, "The doctor of the future will give no medicine, but will interest his patients in the care of the human frame, in diet, and in the cause and prevention of disease."

5   Amino Acids, Brain Amines and Precursor Loading

Individual amino acids are the very basis of the successful use of the treatment program we have just outlined. It therefore may be helpful to know something of what they are and how they work.

There are twenty-two major identified amino acids that make up body protein. Many other minor amino acids that participate in body functions are less understood and new amino acids are still being discovered. Each one has its unique functions and potentials, yet all are necessary. Many scientists believe amino acids are the most elementary and essential of all food substances, even though all nutrients are interdependent. In fact, without amino acids we would have no structural bodies. While carbohydrates and fats give us energy with which to drive our body machines, twenty of the amino acids are the actual physical body builders that create "us" in the first place. They are imperative to the formation and maintenance of our skin, bones, muscles, blood, organs, hair and nails. They also help form our body's enzymes, hormones, antibodies and brain neurotransmitters.

Since amino acids are the very basis of the successful nutritional treatment of depression, and since one of the most important aspects of obtaining a good diet is the balancing of amino acids, we'll take a closer look at the ways these food substances function.

AMINO ACIDS AND PROTEINS

Each protein food is made up of a unique combination of amino acids, in a specific order. The body's need for protein is really a need for amino acids.

Of the basic twenty-two, there are ten essential and twelve nonessential amino acids. The label "nonessential" does not mean not important. All of the amino acids are vitally necessary and have their various and unique functions in your body. The essential ones can only be obtained from your diet, whereas the nonessential amino acids can also come directly from your diet or be created in your body by conversion from the essential dietary amino acids. In order for this conversion to take place, there has to be an adequate level of an essential amino acid left over after it has performed its primary functions in your body. Even then, the conversion can only take place when other nutrient and enzyme substances are present to facilitate the process.

Nature's irrepressible law of balance is persistently evident in our nutritional needs and is especially highlighted when it comes to amino acids and proteins. The essential amino acids must be consumed in proportions that closely approximate the pattern required by our bodies. The lowest level of an individual amino acid in a meal is called the limiting amount, and the meal is nutritionally useful only to that extent. For example, a lunch containing 100 percent of your body's phenylalanine requirement, but only 20 percent of your tryptophan requirement, results in only 20 percent of the protein in that meal being used by your body for the vital functions of replenishing and building tissue. The rest of the protein you've eaten can be used only for fuel, thereby creating more of the unwanted waste products of urea and uric acid.

Some foods have the full range of essential amino acids in relatively balanced amounts. These are fish, fowl, red meats, eggs, milk, cheese, sesame seeds and pumpkin seeds. Other foods such as nuts, beans, rice, vegetables and grains have low levels of certain amino acids and adequate levels of others. To be effective in building tissue, the full range of essential amino acids must be eaten at the same time, not part at one time of day and the rest at another time or on another day. Therefore, when some amino acids are low or completely missing in a food, that food must be combined with a complementary protein food which makes up for the deficiency in order to provide amino acid balance. Such combining is well described in the popular book *Diet For a Small Planet,* by Frances Moore Lappé.

The RDA (Recommended Dietary Allowance) for amino acids has little practical value, as Doctors Roger Williams, Jeffrey Bland and others have demonstrated in their research on biochemical individuality. Each person is unique in his needs for all nutrients. These variations can be marked, so there are considerable differences between individuals in their amino acid requirements. You may need four times as many amino acids as your husband, for instance. Perhaps some cases of depression are only secondary to an individual having an unusually high need for certain amino acids. Or stress may create a situation in which nonessential amino acids cannot be adequately produced to meet our brains' needs. Also, a nonessential nutrient can become essential when our body processes fail to work optimally in their conversion processes.

The basic amino acids are listed on page 66.

Often in my practice I do an analysis of my patients' diets. Among other things, this reveals how many grams of protein they are eating daily and what the amino acid breakdown of the protein is. Even when the total protein intake is in the normal range of 45 to 80 daily depending on size, age, and physical activity, some of the component amino acids are often low because, although they are eating *enough* protein, it is not good quality. Even excessive intake, such as 100 to 150 of protein daily, can still result in amino acid deficiency. This pattern, together with high

1. Fish	7. Peanuts	13. Garbanzo beans
2. Poultry	8. Brazil nuts	14. Lima beans
3. Red meats	9. Almonds	15. Brown rice
4. Cottage cheese	10. Cashews	16. Eggs
5. Sesame seeds	11. Lentils	17. Milk
6. Pumpkin seeds	12. Soybeans	18. Cheese

*Information abstracted from *Nutrition Almanac,* Nutrition Search, Inc., John Kirschman, Director. New York: McGraw-Hill, 1973.

ESSENTIAL AMINO ACIDS	SUGGESTED OPTIMUM DAILY INTAKE
Phenylalanine	4100–6600 mg
Tryptophan	1000–2000 mg
Arginine*	Not available
Histidine*	Not established
Leucine	7300–12,200 mg
Isoleucine	5200–8600 mg
Lysine	7000–12,000 mg
Methionine	2400–3700 mg
Threonine	3600–6100 mg
Valine	5300–9300 mg

NONESSENTIAL AMINO ACIDS

Proline	Asparaganine
Taurine	Aspartic acid
Tyrosine	Ornithine
Glutamine	Serine
Glutamic acid	Alanine
Cysteine	
Glycine	

*These two are essential and important in youth and old age but not during the inbetween ages.

fat intake, is often found in those who eat large amounts of dairy products.

The usability of protein from various foods is as follows in decreasing order of availability:

METABOLIZING AMINO ACIDS

Interestingly, some studies show only 60 percent of apparently healthy people have normal levels of *all* the amino acids in their blood.

As you have seen, one reason for such deficiencies is that we eat protein in forms that don't include a full range of the amino acids. Additionally, food protein contains amino acids in what is called a "bound" form, where chains of several amino acids are linked together. When you eat protein your digestion, assimilation and metabolic processes must operate to release or separate the amino acids from the chain or bound form into what is called the "free form" state. If this separation process does not take place, the protein is useless to you.

Here are the basic requirements for the healthy metabolism of amino acids:

1. You regularly eat enough, but not too much, amino acid balanced protein or properly combine those proteins which are not complete to achieve an overall balance.
2. You have no problems digesting this protein and breaking the chains down into their component amino acids.
3. All the other necessary ingredients and nutrients which interact with each amino acid are also available in your body:
   a) A large number of digestive enzymes, many of which are formed by amino acids. Poor usage of amino acids creates digestive enzyme deficiencies, which in turn lead to even less efficient digestion of protein.
   b) Vitamins and minerals. Amino acid deficiencies are prominont in poroono with vitamin deficiencies because certain vitamins and minerals, especially B_6, B_3 and B_{12}, are necessary for the metabolism of protein.
4. There are no genetically determined variations in your usage, metabolism or need for amino acids.
5. All the other body functions that involve amino acids are operating normally.
6. You do not have severe stress interfering with these basic metabolic processes.

PRECURSORS AND PRECURSOR LOADING

Certain neurotransmitters are among the most critical chemicals formed by amino acids. Since a deficiency of certain neurotransmitters can cause depression, how can we increase their quantities in our brains?

Key neurotransmitters like norepinephrine, serotonin, dopamine, acetylcholine and histamine are known to be precursor dependent. Because of this they can be increased by the process called "precursor loading"—increase the amounts of the precursors in your diet to increase the amount of the end products in your brain. Each meal you eat alters and modifies the amount and nature of these particular neurotransmitters in your brain. "Precursor loading" means eating more of the nutrients that the body converts into the neurotransmitter.

As we've seen, simply eating more food protein does not guarantee such a process. Further, the different amino acids actually compete with each other for absorption, so that even when they are all present together in the digestive system some are more readily absorbed than others.

For precursor loading to be effective the amino acids must be taken separately in the form of singular free form amino acids— and taken in large enough quantities to ensure that enough of the final products do reach the brain to form the neurotransmitters.

In a person experiencing a normal mood, we can assume that dietary protein, as well as certain vitamins and minerals, are present in sufficient quantity, that the metabolism is normal, and the brain is functioning properly in regard to mood regulation. This person does not need singular free form amino acid precursor loading to feel well. But when a person has low moods, he probably has nutritional deficiencies or poor metabolism, or both. Such an individual needs precursor loading to achieve normal neurotransmitter levels.

Since the neurotransmitters serotonin and norepinephrine are the brain amines most important to the cause and relief of depression, increasing their precursors in your diet is the direct route to increasing the levels of these essential chemicals in your brain. This, in turn, will improve the biochemical functioning of your brain to specifically counteract any tendency toward depression that you may have.

The precursor to serotonin is the amino acid L-tryptophan. The precursors to norepinephrine are the amino acids L-tyrosine and L-phenylalanine. If the precursors are chronically deficient, the neurotransmitters they form will also be low.

A current study by Aatron Medical Laboratories indicates *none of the depressed persons examined have had completely normal blood amino acid levels.* So far, the five hundred patients analyzed show a pattern of low tyrosine, phenylalanine and tryptophan. Fifty percent of them have low glutamine, which is another important brain fuel and stimulant.

L-TRYPTOPHAN AND SEROTONIN

As we have seen, L-tryptophan is one of the essential amino acids and the required intake for optimum health in the "normal" person is 1000 to 2000 mg daily. The person with depression may be getting less than this amount, or may actually need more because of various metabolic problems. Paradoxically, merely eating extra protein to try to get more tryptophan will actually give you less, because of the competition from other amino acids. (On the other hand, a high carbohydrate and low protein meal will stimulate insulin production, which helps drive more tryptophan into your brain.)

Tryptophan is carried into your brain, where it is converted to serotonin and then released to carry messages as a neurotransmitter. These messages influence your mood, sleep, appetite, sex drive and pain perception, and the secretion of certain hormones. They also aid in the inhibitory control of a variety of complex behaviors. Increasing brain serotonin levels decreases the perception of pain and stimulates the sex centers in the male and female brain. Evidence now supports the role of a serotonin deficiency in depression, alcoholism, eating disorders, chronic pain, short attention span in childhood, seizure disorders, violent behavior and Alzheimer's disease.

Serotonin's role in normal sleep has been getting a lot of attention recently. When a normal body biorhythm is operating, serotonin naturally increases at night to promote the onset of sleep. Low serotonin levels are therefore related to certain cases of insomnia.

Extensive research has shown that there are reduced levels of serotonin in the brains of some depressed people. There is also a link between low serotonin levels and suicidal or aggressive impulses. Autopsies on many suicides reveal a low brain serotonin content. A recent study also found a 44 percent increase in the number of serotonin receptors in a part of the brain of suicide victims. It is speculated that there is a need for more sensitive and a greater number of receptors when serotonin availability declines. It's as if the brain is hungry for this particular brain food and develops many extra receptors to try to gobble it up.

The chemical reaction and necessary ingredients for the formation of serotonin from tryptophan are listed in the appendix.

L-PHENYLALANINE, L-TYROSINE AND NOREPINEPHRINE

L-phenylalanine is another essential amino acid that the body cannot manufacture from the other amino acids. L-tyrosine is nonessential and can be obtained from the conversion of L-phenylalanine.

The optimum dietary intake of phenylalanine is 4100 to 6600 mg daily for the person with normal metabolism and conversion processes. Your body will derive part of the tyrosine it needs from this phenylalanine and part directly from your diet. Eating more protein helps increase the levels of these amino acids in your brain. The best food sources are meats, eggs and dairy products. However, food sources alone will not provide the pure forms and quantities necessary for correcting low moods and depression.

Two neurotransmitters, norepinephrine and dopamine, can be derived from tyrosine and phenylalanine. (Low dopamine is also implicated in some depressions, but the focus of this book remains with serotonin and norepinephrine.)

Norepinephrine is involved in mood and appetite regulation, and influences those centers of the brain having to do with reward and punishment behavior, specifically helping one to feel purpose, pleasure and gratification with a consequent elevated, positive mood. Norepinephrine is also important in promoting drive, ambition, alert mental functioning and memory.

The synthesis pathway of norepinephrine from precursors is detailed in the appendix.

ENZYMES AND COENZYMES

Enzymes and coenzymes are substances whose presence makes chemical reactions possible. Vitamins B_6, C, biotin and folic acid, as well as the minerals magnesium, zinc, copper, iron and manganese, are coenzymes necessary for creating the chemical changes we are discussing. They are essential to the success of the process. Pancreatic enzymes are also necessary.

A deficiency in any of these can indirectly lead to lowered mood because any chain of metabolic events in the body is only as good as its weakest link. A reaction depending upon seven nutrients cannot occur properly if only six are there in sufficient amount. This again underlines the importance of nutritional balance. *No single vitamin, mineral or amino acid functions entirely on its own.*

CONCLUSION

Tryptophan, L-tyrosine and L-phenylalanine are amino acids that act as precursors to brain amines. If for any reason the body does not have sufficient quantities of these substances, low moods and depression are the likely result. And, of course, the prevention and treatment of these conditions is dependent on these "big three" of the amino acids.

6 Program Adjustments for Special Circumstances

The approach in this book has been devised for use in the relatively uncomplicated cases of low mood and depression that most people experience. If you are reading this book and considering its program, the chances are that you will respond to this nutritional treatment. The more complex and severe your illness, however, and the more problematic the accompanying circumstances, the more likely you'll need professional help in tailoring the program. If you follow all the advice and still are not relieved, you'll need to consult further because other significant health conditions may be influencing you, or your depression may be one of those few that do not respond to this form of treatment.

If someone close to you seems to be severely depressed, this person may have a difficult time following any program, especially if he is self-destructive or lacking in self-esteem or the ability to take care of himself. Initially, he may need the support of a family member or doctor to administer the treatment, but it cannot be forced. You have to want to follow this plan and be willing to change harmful life patterns for it to work.

Also, if you are seriously suicidal, you need to be in the hospital for your own protection, support and treatment until this time passes, as it will. Once you are past the acute stage, the nutritional treatment, in consultation with the presiding doctor, becomes more essential than ever.

This leads us to the question of how psychiatric treatment meshes with the nutritional program. In my opinion, though psychiatry is a branch of medicine, it became separated from the medical mainstream during the first fifty years of our century. It is now returning to the medical field with the discovery of the mind-body-stress-biochemical interactions.

Psychiatrists, like other doctors, usually do the best they can, but they are not omnipotent. They are trained in medicine and in the special understanding of the psychological processes from both a psychodynamic and a physiological point of view. They can work in partnership with you toward the relief of symptoms which are experienced as "psychological"—though the causes can range from divorce to a brain tumor.

Many psychiatrists will not be familiar with this form of treatment. If that is the case, you may encourage your doctor to learn more about it or to refer you to a consultant who does understand the relationship between nutrition and depression.

ALREADY TAKING ANTIDEPRESSANT MEDICATIONS

If your physician has prescribed medicine for your depression, you should not change your dosage without working closely with her. But we recommend that, under supervision, you gradually increase the amino acids as you carefully and slowly decrease your medication. Do not stop your medication abruptly or you will likely have withdrawal symptoms and could relapse if the nutrients haven't had time to work. For the *severely* depressed, the usual length of time it takes to get off the medication and on to the nutrient program and to maintain a stable improvement ranges from two to six months.

If you are taking medication for depression, you can easily *add* the full doses of vitamins and minerals. If your medicine is any kind other than what is known as an MAO inhibitor, you can also add the amino acids. Some research has indicated that adding tryptophan increases the beneficial effects of traditional antidepressants. Start with the lowest dose and build up gradually as needed.

Because of side effects and food restrictions, MAO inhibitors are not widely used in this country. The research is contradictory about using them with amino acids. Do not use these substances together unless your doctor specifically advises you to.

It makes sense that the more severe and long-lived your depression, the more difficult it is to treat, just as is so with any illness. This is often the rule with traditional therapies and may also be the case with nutrient treatment, but some people who have been ill a long time improve rapidly with this new approach.

PROGRAM MODIFICATIONS FOR OTHER PSYCHIATRIC DIAGNOSES

Associated Diagnosis of Schizophrenia

The depressed person with schizophrenia needs an altered nutritional treatment program and should be under a doctor's care. All the vitamins and minerals are useful, but much larger doses of certain B vitamins are needed. Also, a doctor should be monitoring the tyrosine and tryptophan doses. Sometimes schizophrenic symptoms improve with tryptophan, sometimes they worsen.

There is a great deal of literature available on the orthomolecular treatment of schizophrenia. For a list of available books, articles and pamphlets, contact The Schizophrenia Association of Greater Washington, Inc., Wheaton Plaza Office Building North, Suite 404, Wheaton, Maryland 20902, phone (301) 949-8282, or The Huxley Institute, 900 N. Federal Highway, Boca Raton, Florida 33432, phone (800) 847-3802, in Florida (305) 393-6167.

Associated Diagnosis of Manic-depressive Illness (Now Called Bipolar Disorder)

If you are manic-depressive, the amino acids can potentially lift you out of your depression if you follow the program in Chapter 4. They can also potentially push you over into mania—as can any traditional antidepressant medication. Even though this can happen, the treatment of the depressive phase of manic-depressives is still essential and most of the time does not precipitate mania. Be aware of the possibility and proceed with antimania treatment, should it be necessary. See the appendix to Chapter 2 to learn the clear signs of moving into a "high" state. Some nutrients can help treat mania, such as:

LECITHIN Double-blind, placebo-controlled research has now shown that the nutrient lecithin, which contains choline and inositol, has anti-manic effects. In one study lecithin, in a 90 percent pure form, brought about rapid improvement in four manic patients—three of whom immediately worsened when the lecithin was discontinued. The phosphatidyl choline form is most effective, and the strongest commercially available form has a 55 percent concentration. Take one to four capsules three times daily during a high phase.

TRYPTOPHAN Tryptophan has been useful in controlling some cases of mania, but it has made others worse. Amounts up to 12,000 mg daily in four divided doses have been safely used for this purpose. Tryptophan is worth a trial in all manic disorders.

PROGRAM MODIFICATIONS FOR CERTAIN MEDICAL CONDITIONS

If you are under a doctor's care for depression, heart disease, hypertension or other serious illness, discuss the program with your doctor and refer to Chapter Ten. Remember, though, that most doctors don't know about or fully understand nutrients, so you might want to consult with one who does, or ask your doctor to read this book.

The following medical conditions require changes in the treatment as specified.

High Blood Pressure
As we have seen on page 57 through 58, you should consult with your physician before trying the nutritional program if you have high blood pressure.

Pregnancy
During pregnancy it is wise to be careful of drugs and excessive nutrient dosages. A number of pregnant women have received this treatment, have experienced no problems and have delivered normal babies. If you are depressed, you can safely take a multivitamin mineral, usually with iron. Take the B complex vitamins, up to 50 mg twice daily, and vitamin C, up to 500 mg twice daily. If you are still depressed after two to four weeks, take the lowest amino acid dosages—only up to 1000 mg daily of tyrosine and tryptophan. Remember, all these substances are present nat-

urally in food, but pregnancy limits have not been determined, so take them only with the approval of your doctor.

Severe Liver Disease

Since the diseased liver is unable to remove the ammonia formed in the body by the breakdown of protein, any person with severe liver disease must have a protein-restricted diet. Such a person is also unable to take traditional medications because his liver is unable to metabolize them properly. If you are in this situation, do not take the amino acids, but follow the vitamin and mineral program and the other suggestions in the book.

Severe Kidney Disease

Those with serious kidney malfunction may be placed on protein-restricted diets because their kidneys cannot rid the body of ammonia, a by-product of protein metabolism. There is some literature available on the successful treatment of such people with the "free form" amino acids, but, since this point remains unclarified, avoid the amino acids and any extra magnesium if you have a severe kidney disorder.

Overactive Thyroid

The individual with hyperthyroidism (an overactive thyroid) already has an excess of, and poor breakdown of tyrosine. Such a person should avoid extra tyrosine and phenylalanine, but can follow the rest of the program.

Parkinson's Disease

People with this disorder being treated with the drug L-dopa should not supplement their diet with vitamin B_6, as it can cancel the effect of this medicine. However, L-dopa lowers tryptophan levels, so those who take this medicine may develop depression. This has been successfully treated with 1000 mg of tryptophan daily, as reported in several research reports.

Depression is common with Parkinson's because this illness is caused by decreased amounts of the neurotransmitter dopamine throughout many areas of the brain. Therefore, the precursor tyrosine is sometimes very useful.

Phenylketonuria

Because they lack an enzyme essential for the metabolism of phenylalanine, people with this extremely rare genetic condition should not take any phenylalanine and should be on a restricted diet devoid of this amino acid. Phenylketonuria is quite evident in infancy or early childhood—that is, if you have it, you know it by now.

Malignant Melanoma

One last potential theoretical problem is for those suffering from this rare type of skin cancer. One by-product of the breakdown of tyrosine and phenylalanine is melanin, and you would not want to risk increased melanin production with this condition. I should emphasize that this is theoretical and there are no reported cases in fact, but some researchers are attempting to treat melanomas with diets limited in tyrosine and phenylalanine, with as yet unclear results.

PROGRAM MODIFICATIONS FOR ASSOCIATED SYMPTOMS

You may wish to modify the program when various clusters of symptoms predominate. Such modifications are as follows.

Insomnia, Anxiety, Agitation and Irritability

TRYPTOPHAN If you have a tendency toward agitation, insomnia and anxiety, you may have decreased brain serotonin levels and need more tryptophan. If you sleep excessively when you are depressed, try omitting this amino acid entirely. Tryptophan has also been found to be useful in those with poor control of their aggressive and hostile impulses.

There are now many double-blind studies showing the sleep-inducing effects of tryptophan. Unlike regular prescription sleeping pills, tryptophan does not alter the sleep brain wave patterns and there is no risk of developing a dependency or tolerance and having withdrawal symptoms on abrupt termination. In research, the sleep-inducing dosage of tryptophan has ranged from 1000 to 6000 mg, with 3000 to 4000 mg being optimal.

Most of you have heard of alpha brain waves, the brain electrical activity that occurs when you are in a relaxed awake state—somewhat meditative. EEG's done on subjects taking L-tryptophan showed that any brain wave changes induced were of a desirable type, in contrast to undesirable brain wave changes caused by barbiturates and other hypnotics.

If you are insomniac without agitation or anxiety, take the regular tryptophan dose one hour before bedtime. If there is accompanying anxiety and agitation, low doses of tryptophan throughout the day may be useful, ranging from 250 to 500 mg, three times daily. Bear in mind that, as with most substances, there can be what is called a "paradoxical" or opposite reaction. Thus, about 1 percent of people become more agitated with tryptophan.

LECITHIN Phosphatidyl choline (triple strength lecithin) is also calming. Take it at 55 percent concentration, 2 to 3 capsules, 2 to 3 times a day.

GABA Gamma amino butyric acid (GABA) is a calming neurotransmitter that is sometimes used in a pure form and at other times is combined with inositol and vitamin B_3, all of which are relaxing to the nervous system. Take twice a day for a total of 1000 to 2000 mg of GABA, 200 to 500 mg of B_3, and 1000 to 5000 mg of inositol.

MAGNESIUM In Chapter 7 we will discuss how magnesium deficiency can be associated with agitated states. If you are agitated, try adding magnesium, preferably in the orotate form. Begin with 100 mg, two to three times daily, and increase to 500 mg, two to three times daily, if a higher dose is needed.

If your anxiety, insomnia and agitation are beyond what can be handled nutritionally, you may at first need a traditional, strongly sedative antidepressant drug. You can start the nutrient program at the same time, or you may wait until you respond to the medication and then make a gradual transition to this program.

Apathy, Fatigue and Slowed Behavior

Sometimes depressive people experience slowed movement and speech, general apathy, lower levels of anxiety and little insomnia—in fact, they may sleep too much. Such people are more likely to have low brain norepinephrine and should take more tyrosine or phenylalanine and less tryptophan.

This type of depression is also likely to be associated with vitamin B complex deficiency, so if you have these symptoms you may try doubling or tripling your vitamin B complex dosage. Folic acid is important here. Make sure you are getting a total of about 1000 to 1500 mcg of folic acid when you add up the total amounts in the multivitamin and vitamin B complex. Folic acid is usually listed in micrograms and 1000 mcg equals 1 mg. Additionally, take 1000 to 2000 mcg of sublingual vitamin B_{12}.

Predominant Memory and Concentration Problems

All of the B complex vitamins are important in improving memory, as are tyrosine and phenylalanine. The basic program will be sufficient in most cases of memory impairment. If you don't experience a significant restoration of your memory as your mood improves, you may wish to add in extra memory-enforcing substances. Some companies make combination products for memory. You may wish to try a combination product before adding the following single agents:

CHOLINE The choline mentioned in the section on manic-depressives is important in improving memory, especially in the elderly. It is part of the B vitamin family and is a precursor for the formation of the neurotransmitter acetylcholine, which influences mood, memory, learning, long-term planning and primitive emotions and drives, and also helps control muscle tone and activity.

We are not sure whether acetylcholine deficiency relates to Alzheimer's disease, though that is now being investigated.

Researchers administered a continuous infusion of an acetylcholine-producing drug into the brains of Alzheimer's victims. Several improved during treatment and then relapsed when the drug was replaced by placebo salt water infusions. Also, there is promising research using high doses of the nutrient choline for this condition. So far, the results are mixed, with some improving and others realizing no benefit. In one study, a single oral dose of 3 g improved memory and serial learning ability in the subjects. In another study, a dose of 10 g produced similar results.

Avoid the choline chloride preparations—they will make you smell like a dead fish. One of my seventy-seven-year-old patients had read about the use of choline for memory stimulation and had started taking it on her own. One day she came in for an appointment and my office and the waiting room were suffused with a terrible stench. When I asked her if she was taking choline, she said she was, in the chloride form. The problem disappeared when she promptly switched to phosphatidyl choline.

Alcohol and excess estrogen can cause a choline deficiency. Too much or too little choline can contribute to depression, so balance is very important here. Doses over 3000 mg can deepen a depression, so discontinue it if you have such a response. No RDA has been established for choline, but our usual daily intake is 250 to 1000 mg. The treatment doses have ranged from 1000 to 10,000 mg daily and no toxicity has been reported.

L-GLUTAMINE This amino acid is a unique brain fuel important for optimum mental functioning and is useful in some cases of depression. It is what is called an "excitatory" neurotransmitter. It also helps to protect against the effects of alcohol, helps decrease the desire for alcohol, and in some cases decreases the desire for sugar. The dosage is generally 1000 to 3000 mg daily, all to be taken before four in the afternoon. It can be taken at the same time as your tyrosine.

DMAE DMAE-H3 (dimethylamino-ethanol) is a concentrated solution of the nutrient PABA (para-amino benzoic acid). In liquid form, take ten drops in the morning. This and sublingual vitamin B_{12} (2000 mcg in the morning) can be added if three to four months of the other nutrients have not sufficiently enhanced your memory.

OTHER USES

If you are in a situation where you need only occasional intense mental concentration, focus and output, short-term use of tyrosine or phenylalanine together with vitamin B complex is excellent for this purpose. Such circumstances might be studying for and taking exams, presenting a case in court, or completing an important project.

When experimental animals are given drugs which decrease the amount of norepinephrine in the brain, the animals' capacity for learning is blocked. Then, when the animals are given injections of norepinephrine, the ability to learn returns. This has many unexplored implications for the use of norepinephrine precursors for improved learning.

Part II

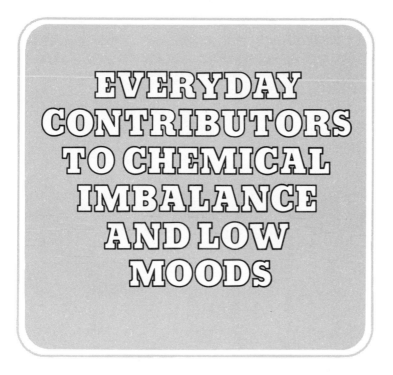

EVERYDAY CONTRIBUTORS TO CHEMICAL IMBALANCE AND LOW MOODS

I will apply dietetic measures for the benefit of
the sick according to my ability and judgment;
I will keep them from harm and injustice.

—from *The Hippocratic Oath,*
translation by Ludwig Edelstein
Ares Publishers, New York, 1979

Whether healthy or depressed, active or sedentary, whether we're eighteen, thirty-eight or sixty-eight, all of us are affected by the same principles of health maintenance. Some of the hearty ones can get by with poor nutrition and unhealthy habits for many years before the cumulative negative results begin to manifest. This makes it easier for us to deny the connection between our lifestyles and our health. Yet, in the final analysis, we cannot avoid the simple fact that what goes into our bodies absolutely affects our overall health, quality and quantity of life, and *mood.*

Everyone has stories about exceptions, like uncle Jack who drank three whiskies a day and lived relatively well and happily until age ninety-four. My own grandfather drank one to two bottles of wine daily for all the years I knew him and then died suddenly and peacefully at home when he was eighty-three, without obvious suffering or illness. My grandmother likes to boast he had no gray hair and all of his original teeth, with no cavities. She fed him well—and regularly—and I say good genes contributed, because his smoking but non-drinking sister recently died at one hundred three and another sister died at ninety-six. His cirrhotic liver did make a difference, and likely cut short his own genetic plan.

Usually it's no single factor that does us in, but the combination that gives such a negative potential. A heavy drinker who eats marvelously healthfully or takes vitamins will withstand the wear far better than the boozer who skips many meals and subsists primarily on the "beverage."

Since there are so many variables influencing us, and since

some of them can interfere with or undermine this nutrient treatment, it is important that you read on in order to understand the program within the context of overall good physical and mental habits. Certain conditions in your life may need to change to ensure the long-lasting excellent benefits others have achieved.

As you read about all the variables capable of influencing your mood, you may need to evaluate specific health conditions further. Perhaps you will suspect allergies, thyroid problems, chronic yeast infection or blood sugar problems. Though laboratory tests are not necessary to undertake this treatment, you may refer to the appendix for a list of tests I've used in evaluating many patients who come to me.

We will now consider some factors leading to the unbalanced brain chemistry that, in turn, causes mood changes or even actual depression.

7 Nutrient Deficiencies

The branch of psychiatry that deals with the psychological effects of common nutritional deficiencies is called orthomolecular psychiatry. The avant garde group of psychiatrists who use this approach evaluate and treat many mental symptoms and illnesses from a nutritional point of view.

Even Freud, if he were alive today, would likely recognize and commend these methods. In his later years, when vitamins and minerals were first being identified and studied in earnest, he wrote, "The future may teach us to exercise a direct influence, by means of particular chemical substances, upon the amounts of energy and their distribution in the mind. . . . I am firmly convinced that one day all these disturbances we are trying to understand will be treated by means of hormones or similar substances."

ORTHOMOLECULAR THERAPY

Nobel Laureate Dr. Linus Pauling coined the term "orthomolecular." He defines it as "the treatment of mental disease by the provision of the optimum molecular environment of the mind, especially optimum concentrations of substances normally found in the human body."

The rationale behind the orthomolecular approach is the following: there is ample evidence, as described in Part I, that some psychologically disturbed people have unusual or abnormal metabolism of one or more vitamins, minerals, amino acids or essential fatty acids. These people often have nutrient needs above the average and far above the "minimal" standards set in the RDA. Some researchers have described these states of increased need as a vitamin dependency syndrome.

Even the general so-called healthy population has demonstrated individual biochemical diversity and a consequent wide range of daily nutrient needs. You may flourish on 5 mg of vitamin B_6 daily, while your neighbor may need 500 mg to achieve the same results. The average American diet is deficient in several nutrients by RDA standards and even more so by optimum health standards. Many life habits or conditions either interfere with absorption or utilization or use up excessive amounts of certain nutrients.

There is sufficient clinical evidence that inadequate vitamin levels initially cause a depression of the vitamin enzyme activities. These enzyme activities facilitate most of the chemical reactions in our bodies. When they are malfunctioning, the first symptoms produced are those of subtle psychological and physical impairment rather than the full symptom complex of a frank deficiency syndrome.

RDA VERSUS OPTIMAL LEVELS

In using nutritional treatment, I make a clear distinction for my patients between the RDA and optimal nutrient levels. The RDA is the *minimum* amount necessary to avoid a deficiency illness, but is not the recommended amount for good health.

Plain common sense tells us that what we need to keep from being ill is different from what we need for the best of health. The amount of food needed to keep us from starvation is quite different from that required for our ideal weight, in the same way that the amount of water and fertilizer which keeps a rose bush alive is hardly enough to produce a plant resplendent with aromatic, opulent bloom.

But the rose can receive too much water and fertilizer. Quantities and balance are extremely important. There are optimum dosages beyond which beneficial effects diminish, and even harmful effects can occur. It is wise not to exceed these dosages.

Food Alone Is Rarely Enough

Even by conservative RDA standards, the average American diet is commonly deficient in vitamins B_1, B_2, B_6, folic acid, C, E and iron. Naturally, other deficiencies also occur. Only the rare "balanced diet" of the best natural, unrefined, unprocessed, wholesome foods has a possible chance of meeting all of our nutritional needs. And how many of us daily eat the following traditional idea of a balanced diet?

1. Four portions of whole grain products
2. Four portions of fresh fruits and vegetables (with at least one of each being uncooked)
3. Two portions of meat products (or fish, poultry, eggs, beans, peas or nuts)
4. Two to three portions of milk or milk products

I know I would be fat if I ate this much every day, and such a diet excludes vegetarians, those who must restrict cholesterol, those on caloric-restricted diets, those with allergies and many others.

Computer analyses of hundreds of patients' food intake has revealed no diet with fewer than three to four nutrient deficiencies by RDA standards and even more deficiencies by optimum measurements. I personally have tried eating a variety of healthy, seemingly balanced diets only to find that my diet remains stubbornly deficient after all. Further, *I have never seen a single patient whose diet tested adequately in all the B vitamins at RDA levels.* Worse, they rarely test at the optimum level in even *one* of the several B vitamins.

These dietary analyses have also revealed the following trends:

1. Low complex carbohydrates
2. High refined carbohydrates
3. High protein (but unbalanced amino acid intake)
4. High fat
5. Low fiber
6. Low vitamin B complex
7. Low vitamin C and bioflavonoids
8. Variable amounts of minerals, but generally low magnesium

Any one of these trends is undesirable. Put several of them together, as is usually the case, and we're just a short step from creating the biochemical imbalance that can cause mood changes and other health problems. Many of us are more careful about giving our animals the proper diet than we are about what we feed ourselves. It is truly a tribute to the adaptive capacity of the human organism that we do as well as we do, although several large population studies have revealed that 80 percent of us suffer from some sort of "dis-ease."

There is a tremendous amount of scientific data to support these observations and it has frustrated me at times to see best-selling books by novices in the field saying the opposite, that what you eat is sufficient for your needs. There really should be no controversy. In lieu of faddish reading, please refer to the appendix for a list of excellent books on nutrition written by experts with years of training and experience in biochemistry, clinical practice and research.

Rarely does food alone supply an "adequate," let alone "optimal" amount of all the different essential nutrients. Also, there are many "elective" circumstances that necessitate greater than usual amounts of certain nutrients, circumstances that interfere with absorption and metabolism, procedures for food growth and processing that deplete the nutrients in your food, and so on. For instance, if you are a smoker each cigarette causes your body to utilize 25 mg of vitamin C—at one and a half packs daily that would be 750 mg of vitamin C just to break even, without having any left over for the multitude of bodily functions related to vitamin C. When you consider that the average diet I see contains from 100 to 300 mg of vitamin C, you get some idea of the potential for deficiency.

HABITS AND CONDITIONS

Any of the following can create a similar increased need for one or more nutrients and hence can lead to deficiencies.

1. Stress (who is excluded from this?)
2. Excess caffeine (more than one cup of coffee a day—see page 116) or alcohol (more than two drinks daily)

3. Excess sugar or other refined carbohydrates such as white flour, pastas, etc.
4. Tobacco use
5. Street drug use (such as cocaine, heroin, amphetamines, marijuana)
6. Regular use of aspirin, sleeping pills or tranquilizers
7. Use of birth control pills
8. Use of certain prescription medications (See page 121)
9. Dieting for weight loss, exclusion diets for food allergies or special diets for various illnesses
10. Vegetarianism
11. High fiber or phytate diets
12. Exposure to pesticides via water, air or food, and other pollution
13. Work with chemicals (painting, gardening, photo developing, etc.)
14. Drinking chlorinated or fluoridated water
15. Pregnancy or nursing
16. Puberty
17. Old age
18. Physical illness, especially: cancer, anorexia nervosa, burns, post-surgery or post-trauma, diabetes, chronic kidney or liver disease, any kind of gastrointestinal disorder, infections and inflammations, psoriasis, AIDS or ARC, and intestinal parasites

WHICH NUTRIENTS CAN INFLUENCE YOUR MOOD?

It is probably safe to say that all of the essential nutrients needed by our bodies are also needed by our brain cells. An inadequate supply of any will cause some aberration in brain function, however subtle. Still, as we saw earlier, certain substances are more related to mood control than others. Especially important are:

• The amino acids tyrosine or phenylalanine, and tryptophan
• The B vitamins—in particular, B_6, folic acid and biotin
• Vitamin C

• The minerals (as enzymes)—magnesium, zinc, iron, copper, and manganese
• Pancreatic enzymes

In addition to the above brain amine forming nutrients, vitamins B_1, B_2, B_3, B_5 and B_{12} also influence your mood by different mechanisms.

Each nutrient has multiple bodily effects, but our focus is on the role of these particular nutrients in orchestrating your moods, on how to determine if you have specific deficiencies, and how to go about correcting them. The charts beginning on page 197 in the Appendix summarize this information.

VITAMINS AND MOOD

The B Vitamins
The first clinical effects of insufficient vitamin B complex are mood changes, insomnia, changed appetite, sugar craving, impaired drug metabolism and a decrease in immune function.

The B vitamins are "synergistic" with each other, which means that each one works best in the presence of an adequate amount of all the others. Therefore, a distinct deficiency of any of the B vitamins can partially impair the effectiveness of the rest. Also, an excess or toxicity of any B vitamin is more likely to occur if it is taken singly, without the addition of the entire vitamin B complex group. Different manufacturers use varying ratios of B's in the vitamin B complex supplements. What is important is that the vitamins all be present in sufficient workable quantities, rather than in absolutely equal amounts.

As a group, the B vitamins play an important role both in alleviating depression and in relieving the anxiety and restlessness which often accompanies it, perhaps partly because of the effect of the B vitamins on lactic acid. Exercise and certain metabolic processes cause the formation of lactic acid when there is inadequate vitamin B complex or oxygen. It is this accumulation of lactic acid in your muscles that makes them sore if you strenuously exercise without gradually building up to it. Excess lactic acid can also produce anxiety.

Vitamin B₆ (Pyridoxine)

Vitamin B_6 has major importance in regulating your moods, and is the most implicated of all the vitamins in the cause and treatment of depression. Depressed persons show evidence of insufficient vitamin B_6 as commonly as they show decreased tyrosine, phenylalanine or tryptophan.

Without adequate vitamin B_6, the amino acids are not much use to you. Vitamin B_6 literally controls all the amino acid metabolism and transformations in your body. It also regulates amino acid absorption from your gastrointestinal tract and directly participates in carbohydrate and fat metabolism as well as in the formation of red blood cells and antibodies. It is also required for the proper functioning of over sixty enzyme systems in our bodies.

As previously mentioned, the American diet tends toward high protein and high fat. This creates a greater requirement for vitamin B_6. But the average daily diet only contains about 2 mg of this vitamin. This supply is further depleted by stress, alcohol, tobacco, birth control pills, pregnancy, antibiotics and many other medications.

It is important to take the active coenzyme forms of the B vitamins for these vitamins to function adequately. Many supplements contain the inactive pyridoxine, or pyridoxine hydrochloride, form of B_6, which your liver must convert to a usable form. If, for whatever reason, this conversion does not take place, B_6 cannot be used by your body.

In 1983 there was an uproar in the press about so-called toxic problems with vitamin B_6. These were reported in a few self-medicated individuals who took 1000 to 6000 mg daily over a period of two to forty months, without adding in other B vitamins or a multivitamin mineral. This amount of B_6 taken alone over that period of time would create a severe imbalance and interfere with the other B vitamins. The reversible neurological side effects experienced with these megadoses were theorized to be the result of vitamin B_6 toxicity, yet toxicity was never proven, and more likely contributors were the multi-B vitamin deficiencies and magnesium depletion, which would occur on such a lopsided program. Some researchers also feel the symptoms were related to taking the B_6 in the inactive pyridoxine form rather than in the usable coenzyme form mentioned above.

The message is simple: only take vitamin B_6 when you are also taking vitamin B complex and keep the dosages somewhat proportionate. If you stay within the limits recommended in this book, you should have no problems. Remember the rule is one of *balance.*

Vitamin B_1 (Thiamine)

This vitamin is essential for nerve stimulation, and for metabolism of carbohydrates to give brain energy as well as body energy. It is also needed for the synthesis of the neurotransmitter acetylcholine.

Vitamin B_1 is commonly deficient because stress, alcohol, sugar, refined carbohydrates, and particularly caffeine, deplete our bodies of this nutrient. For instance, research on rats showed that daily consumption of tea for twenty-five weeks produced a 60 percent decrease in total brain B_1.

You can suspect a deficiency of vitamin B_1 if, in addition to low mood, you have at least five of the following: chronic fatigue, irritability, memory loss, personality changes (including aggression), insomnia, anxiety, restlessness, night terrors, appetite loss, sensitivity to noise, numbness and tingling in your hands and feet, and circulation problems—and no other explanation for your symptoms has been found.

If you have five or more of these symptoms, consider doubling the vitamin B complex dosage on page 45, and add an extra 200 to 500 mg of daily vitamin B_1 for the first three months of the program. Carefully follow the whole program as outlined.

Vitamin B_2 (Riboflavin)

Vitamin B_2 is important in all the cell energy systems in your body, especially in assisting in the metabolism of proteins, carbohydrates and fats. Together with vitamin B_1, it promotes the effectiveness of thyroid hormone and insulin, both of which can influence your mood. It is also related to the stress response.

Although vitamin B_2 itself has not generally been associated with emotional states, researchers find that diets restricted only in riboflavin produce adverse personality changes, including aggressive personality alterations, as the first symptom of dietary inadequacy.

Riboflavin indirectly participates in amino acid metabolism because it is necessary for your liver's activation of vitamin B_6 into the form your body can utilize. Taking a large amount of the pyridoxine form of B_6 without having sufficient B_2 for this conversion will do you little good and is another example of the need for balance among the B vitamins.

Vitamin B_3 (Niacin)

Niacin deficiency has been associated with depression and anxiety. One link may be that niacin can be formed from tryptophan. If there is a dietary deficiency of niacin or an unusual need for it, tryptophan may be used to make niacin, leaving less of it available to form serotonin, one of the neurotransmitters implicated in depression.

Niacin works with vitamin B_1 to help with the oxidation of sugar and to promote proper brain metabolism. It helps to maintain our energy by degrading carbohydrates, fats and proteins and participates in the manufacture of certain hormones and proteins. It helps with irritability and other mental disturbances, binding to the same "receptor sites" in the brain as do the tranquilizers Librium and Valium, and producing a similar calming response.

With mood disorders I generally do not prescribe any more vitamin B_3 than is present in the vitamin B complex and multivitamin mineral capsules, unless an individual is severely agitated, anxious or has an associated form of schizophrenia. In some cases high dose niacin in the niacinamide form can actually create a side effect of depression, so it is important to avoid daily doses of niacinamide over 500 mg unless there is a clear indication for it. Vitamin B_3 in very high doses is one of the basic orthomolecular therapeutic agents successfully used in treating schizophrenia, together with other nutrients, especially vitamin C and the other B vitamins. There are many publications available on this treatment that can be obtained through sources in the appendix.

Supplemental vitamin B_3 comes in both a niacin and a niacinamide form. The niacin form can cause nonharmful temporary skin flushing, itching and nausea in some individuals. These side effects can be decreased by using a time-release pill. It can also slightly raise blood sugar and aggravate ulcers, so if you have diabetes or ulcers, refrain from large doses of niacin. The niacinamide form does not cause flushing or stomach irritation or other side effects at this dosage of 500 mg.

Vitamin B₅ (Pantothenic Acid)

Vitamin B_5 is a precursor essential for the formation of certain hormones and for certain biochemical reactions. Vitamin B_5 also promotes amino acid uptake and antibody synthesis. It is active in the formation of the neurotransmitter acetylcholine, which can be involved in some depressions. A deficiency can cause depression, fatigue and allergies. This vitamin is particularly prone to depletion with chronic stress.

Vitamin B₁₂ (Cyanocobalamin or Hydroxycobalamin)

This vitamin is important for the health and maintenance of your nerve cells and of the nerve tracts in your spinal column. The mental changes caused by a deficiency of vitamin B_{12} can range from difficulty in concentrating or remembering, mental fatigue and low moods, to a severe stuporous depression, intense agitation, hallucinations and manic or paranoid behavior. There can also be neurological problems and anemia.

You can only absorb about 1 percent of the vitamin B_{12} in your diet or in supplements. Fortunately, under optimal conditions you only need 1 to 3 mcg daily and you would have to take only 100 to 300 mcg to get this, allowing for the poor rate of absorption.

Because of the poor stomach absorption, I usually do not give vitamin B_{12} orally except for what is present in the vitamin B complex combination. Instead, I give it in a "sublingual" form available in most health food stores. You dissolve the tablet under your tongue upon arising in the morning. Since the substance goes into your blood stream through the blood vessels under your tongue, you absorb more than you would by the gastrointestinal route.

If you are over fifty-five, vegetarian or alcoholic, have extreme fatigue, poor memory, low thyroid or weight loss, I recommend you take 1000 to 2000 mcg of the sublingual form every morning.

Though it is extremely rare, an untreated vitamin B_{12} deficiency can ultimately be fatal.

Folic Acid

Folic acid is needed to form brain norepinephrine and serotonin. It also helps maintain the secretions of steroids from your adrenal glands and so is particularly useful in times of stress. It has a major function in DNA and RNA synthesis and helps form antibodies as well.

Perhaps one reason that folic acid is one of the most commonly deficient vitamins is that alcohol interferes with its metabolism. If you drink regularly, you probably need extra folic acid. The elderly also commonly lack folic acid. In one study of elderly people unable to care for themselves, 67 percent had a folic acid deficiency. Besides the elderly and those using alcohol, those on anticonvulsant drugs, birth control pills and certain other medicines are at high risk for deficiency.

Folic acid deficiency can create depression, memory problems, fatigue and anemia. Since a similar anemia is also caused by vitamin B_{12} depletion it's important, to avoid further complications, to use them both as supplements. Vitamin B_{12} and folic acid are present in vitamin B complex preparations. Those in the high risk groups for deficiency should double their vitamin B complex dosage.

A person in depression with easy fatigability may respond well to folic acid therapy, because folic acid is energizing. However, excess amounts of more than 5 mg daily can create the side effect of a hyperexcited, overactive, irritable, insomniac, euphoric state and may aggravate seizure problems.

Folic acid helps increase estrogen levels, so it can be useful for those with menopausal symptoms, but since female hormone administration may be associated with breast and uterine cancer, those with cancer should avoid large doses of folic acid. In these conditions 600 to 800 mcg daily would be the top supplemental limit.

If you are on anticancer chemotherapy, ask your doctor if the chemotherapy drug is an agent which blocks folic acid metabolism. If it is, do not exceed a total dose of 600 to 800 mcg. Your multivitamin mineral and your vitamin B complex added together will supply this amount.

Biotin

Biotin is one of the coenzymes helping to form brain serotonin. It is essential for normal metabolism of fat and protein. Known biotin deficiencies are not common, but a group of human volunteers placed on a biotin-deficient diet developed depression, weakness, hallucinations and panic. Generally, skin and hair problems also develop with biotin deficiency.

Raw egg whites contain a substance which destroys biotin, so someone eating a great many whole raw eggs could encounter a deficiency. Also, those on high doses of antibiotics can develop a biotin deficiency.

Vitamin C

Vitamin C is needed to form both norepinephrine and serotonin. It also helps to protect against the oxidation or breakdown of norepinephrine.

Vitamin C has a profound stimulating effect on the adrenal glands, so that, during times of stress, our bodies require more vitamin C.

Few diets have enough of this vitamin for its basic uses in the first place, without considering that extra amounts are needed when we are exposed to dietary and inhalant chemicals, alcohol, smoking, drugs, stress, mercury, lead, cadmium and a myriad of other toxins. This is because vitamin C acts as a detoxifier to actually help remove these unwanted substances from our bodies. With low vitamin C, the toxins are free to accumulate gradually, finally contributing to many disease states.

Magnesium

Magnesium, another of the coenzymes needed to form the brain amines, is active in the metabolism of amino acids and carbohydrates, and aids in your body's utilization of vitamins C and E. Magnesium also helps convert the B vitamins into a form your body can use; thus a magnesium deficiency could indirectly lead to a vitamin B complex deficiency. Very large amounts of vitamin B complex, or vitamin B_6 without sufficient magnesium, tend to deplete available magnesium as well as limit the usability of the B complex vitamins. Put simply, the more vitamin B complex you take, the more magnesium you need.

Magnesium deficiency can create depression, restlessness,

irritability, an increased sense of hearing accompanied by a pro-
nounced startle response, agitation, anxiety, insomnia, disorient-
ation, confusion and even hallucinations. Researchers have
found significantly lower levels of magnesium in the blood and
cerebrospinal fluid of depressed patients, and the lowest levels
in suicidal patients. (It's interesting that lithium, the well-known
antimanic and antidepressant drug, helps increase the magnesium level in the blood; we can wonder if this contributes to its
effectiveness.)

Deficiency is common because the typical American diet only
provides one half to one third of the 400 mg RDA. Alcoholics have
particularly depleted magnesium, and its lack is one of the causes
of delerium tremens, or DT's. Extra magnesium is also required
when its absorption and retention are decreased by other factors
such as physical and mental stress, a moderate intake of sugar,
alcohol and caffeine, and a high intake of protein, fat, calcium,
salt, refined carbohydrates and phosphates. The blood concentration of magnesium varies in relation to that of calcium, and this
ratio in turn affects nerve transmission and muscle contraction.
Excess calcium such as you would get with a high intake of dairy
products would tend to decrease your magnesium levels. For this
reason, given the American lifestyle, the RDA would be more
accurately increased to 500 to 800 mg daily.

People living in soft water areas such as the southeastern U.S.
tend to have much lower magnesium levels than those in "hard"
water areas such as the southwest. It would be interesting to
know if there is a greater percentage of depression in the soft
water areas, because these regions do have a high rate of kidney
stone disease, also related to the insufficient magnesium. Magnesium deficiency also plays a significant role in the development
of heart disease and irregularities, and high blood pressure, and
many cases are successfully treated by appropriate supplementation.

The preferred forms are magnesium orotate or aspartate, because they are readily absorbed. Sufficient vitamin B_6 and thyroid
hormone also promote magnesium absorption. Supplemental
magnesium should not be given to those who are in kidney failure, or suffering from the rare Addison's disease or myasthenia
gravis.

Zinc

Zinc is necessary for brain amine formation. It is also involved in multiple physiological functions, and deficiency can be associated with many physical and some psychiatric disorders.

The average American diet contains about 10 mg daily, while the RDA is 15 mg. Zinc is reported to be deficient in the soils of thirty-two of our states. In addition, a high-fiber diet impairs the absorption of zinc if taken at the same time, so do not take minerals with bran or a fiber supplement. Estrogen pills and high copper levels in the body will contribute to zinc deficiency. On the other hand, excess zinc over 100 mg daily on a long-term basis can cause your body to lose copper and iron and to actually develop an iron or copper deficiency anemia.

Vitamins E and B_6 are synergistic with zinc, so it may not be possible to correct a zinc deficiency without also insuring adequate amounts of vitamins E and B_6.

Iron

Iron is a coenzyme needed to form the brain amines. It is also needed for proper metabolism of the B vitamins. An iron-related depression would likely be associated with poor attention span, listlessness and fatigue. There may also be irritability, headaches, feelings of numbness and tingling, and a burning sensation on the tongue.

Iron deficiency is the most common chronic disease in the world. Government surveys show that American women, children and teenagers have been in a dietary decline since 1950 in terms of meeting the RDA for iron (whereas the average American man has enough, if not too much, iron).

Most women have had iron deficiency anemia at some time in their lives. This condition is especially common during pregnancy. At least twenty million people in the U.S. are deficient in iron, including young women, children, those who are socioeconomically oppressed and the elderly infirm.

Vitamin C will enhance iron absorption, while caffeine, antacids, high-fiber cereals and tetracycline will inhibit absorption. It's easy to get a blood test measuring the iron level and total iron storage (ferritin) in the blood. This can be a guide for whether supplementation is indicated. It is possible to store and accumulate too much iron, which can be toxic. Because of this potential,

I recommend iron-free vitamins for men and post menopausal women. Children and menstruating or pregnant women often need some additional iron. If you do take iron, avoid the ferrous sulfate form, as it is less tolerable to the digestive system. Also use an amino acid chelated iron product, 50 to 100 mg, three times daily, or buy a multivitamin mineral which contains iron.

Manganese

Manganese is needed for brain amine formation, so a deficiency can be associated with depression. Manganese also activates a number of enzyme systems necessary for the utilization of vitamins C and B complex. It is essential for proper pituitary functioning and therefore indirectly helps regulate hormones. Those with insufficient manganese levels also tend toward allergies and mood-changing low blood sugar problems.

Dietary manganese deficiencies are not uncommon because our soils are depleted of this mineral, which affects our vegetables and fruits. Because large amounts of calcium and iron inhibit manganese absorption, people who eat a lot of dairy foods, or who supplement too much calcium or iron, need to take a multivitamin mineral containing manganese. Excess phosphorus, such as is found in soft drinks and junk food diets, can also inhibit manganese absorption.

ARE NUTRIENT TOXICITIES POSSIBLE?

"Balanced" supplements are essential. If you are going to supplement at all, this approach will decrease the likelihood of problems with doses of single substances. Sometimes a person reads about the merits of a particular nutrient, starts taking it, and goes overboard on the dosage thinking "these same positive effects can be increased in the proportion that I increase the dose." Wrong! *Optimum dosages should be followed and not exceeded unless prescribed by a nutritionally aware doctor as treatment for specific medical conditions or symptoms.*

Toxic reactions are possible with some nutrients at extremely high doses. It is very important not to overdo vitamins A and D, because they are stored in the body.

In general, though, vitamins are essential to your health and are

Depression-Related Vitamins and Minerals

daily dosage and toxicity levels for adults

	RDA	Optimum	Treatment	Side Effects	Toxicity
Vitamin B$_1$ (Thiamine) (mg)	1.5	10–25	10–500	Over 1000	8000–24,000
Vitamin B$_2$ (Riboflavin) (mg)	1.8	10–15	10–500	Over 1000	No Known Toxicity
Vitamin B$_3$ (Niacin) (mg)	15–20	50–150	100–3000	Over 3000	70,000–280,000
Vitamin B$_5$ (Pantothenic acid) (mg)	5–10	50–200	10–1000	Over 10,000	No Known Toxicity
Vitamin B$_6$ (Pyridoxine) (mg)	2.0	10–25	10–500	Over 2000	Over 210,000
Vitamin B$_{12}$ (mcg)	3.0	20–100	10–2000	None Known	No Known Toxicity
Folic Acid (mcg)	400	400–1000	400–10,000	Over 3000	No Known Toxicity
Biotin (mcg)	100–200	300–600	300–1200	Over 50,000	No Known Toxicity
Vitamin C (mg)	45	250–4000	100–10,000	Over 10,000	50,000–100,000
Magnesium (mg)	300	400–800	400–1200	None Known	Over 15,000
Copper (mg)	2–3	2–5	2–5	Over 7	Over 250
Iron (mg)	18	10–25	10–300	Over 50	Over 100
Manganese (mg)	2.5–5	3–20	10–100	Over 200	Over 1000
Zinc (mg)	15	15–30	25–200	Over 200	Over 1000

relatively harmless. In some instances you have to take amounts thousands of times the RDA before toxicity can occur. By comparison, many standard prescription drugs have no such leeway; sometimes just doubling the dose can prove poisonous, or even fatal.

If you are uncertain about safety, the accompanying chart will tell you the minimum RDA and the optimum amounts for improving and maximizing health, the treatment dosages used by orthomolecular physicians to treat various conditions, the dosages which can create symptom side effects, and the amounts which can be toxic if indeed a substance has a toxic potential.

The dose ranges of the treatment program recommended in this book are far below any of the side effect amounts and on the low side of the treatment dosages.

Remember, balance is vital. You do not need to take more unless there is an indication of the necessity. "If some is good, then more is better" does not apply.

Certain individuals may be allergic to some vitamins because they are manufactured with starches, fillers, dyes, yeasts, corn, sugars and so on. This reaction is different from a reaction to excessive dosage. If you know you have allergies, use special hypoallergenic products. Only rarely are individuals allergic to the actual vitamin itself.

If you have any serious medical illness, then when supplementing any more than the lowest level of the treatment doses listed in this table consult a nutritionally-oriented physician of any specialty whose subspecialty is "orthomolecular or nutritionally-oriented medicine."

8 Other Food–Mood Connections

Our nutrient program has had satisfying and consistent results, but it will not work as well if your other health habits are physically or psychologically damaging. In addition, though nutritional status is important, there are other factors that can influence your mood and engender depressed feelings, including excess sugar, hypoglycemic reactions to sugar and refined carbohydrates, vegetarianism and food sensitivities or allergies.

SUGAR IS NOT SO SWEET

I don't talk about sugar from any lifelong position of abstinence. I used to live on Hostess Pies, Snickers, Mars Bars, Reese's Peanut Butter Cups, chocolate bridge mix, See's Candies, Swensen's peanut butter chocolate ice cream, and Coca-Cola. I often used to bake five dozen chocolate chip cookies, eat half the batter while they were cooking, and then finish off the cookies in a few days—with a "little" sharing, of course. And while "dieting," I slinked down to the vending machines in the medical school dormitory basement to get my nightly fix. No wonder I was depressed.

Because of such excesses I am now limited in what I can eat, and probably forever. Even small amounts of sugar can spell trouble for people who are allergic, diabetic, hypoglycemic or yeast-infection prone, but excess sugar can create a real health danger to anyone. Many people are hooked on sugar and, unknowingly, profoundly influenced by it.

Now, what constitutes "excess"? The average American consumes 126.8 pounds yearly, over a third of a pound daily! This consumption is up 11 pounds per year from what it was a decade ago. Sugar constitutes 25 percent of our daily calories, and sweet drinks make up 25 percent of that sugar intake.

Most of us are not aware that our intake is this high, as we are surrounded by hidden as well as overt sugars. If you read labels, you'll notice how omnipresent sugar is (and it isn't even included on all labels). Remember that there are many other names for sugar—corn syrup, corn solids, fructose, sucrose, glucose, dextrose, etc. Try buying a cereal without sugar and you'll likely only be left with a choice of shredded wheat and grape nuts; try buying sugar-free canned or frozen vegetables and you'll be severely limited in your choice; even many already sweet fruit juices are sweetened; note all the loaves of bread with added sugar; the canned beans; the sauces and ketchups—sugar, sugar everywhere. What helps sell sugar and what is particularly alarming is that the taste, as well as the effects, have proven addictive. Even laboratory animals will choose sugared food and water over their non-sweetened counterparts when given the option.

The case seems clear, the evidence overwhelming; sugar is one of the most powerful common foods capable of affecting our minds and our moods. A twelve-year-old girl was brought to me complaining of severe depression and "attacks" of anger during which she provoked and verbally assaulted her parents, and verbally and physically abused her sister. As time passed, it became clear that this behavior occurred whenever she ate sugar. As long as she refrained from sugar there were no such mood swings or angry attacks. Now she is eighteen years old and has been doing well on a nutrient program. However, she has called me with occasional relapses through our six years of knowing each other. My first question is always about sugar and each relapse turns out to have been precipitated by her returning to her sugar habit. She usually needs a few booster sessions to bolster her discipline and then does well again until the next slip.

Sugar, white flour, alcohol and other refined carbohydrates are nutritionally useless. They provide "empty" calories that can only convert to energy when certain vitamins are present. Those vitamins must be obtained from other more nutritious foods or supplements. If you indulge too many of these empty calories and not enough nutritious foods to help with their metabolism, you will create a depletion of certain vitamins. The empty calories can thus push you into a negative nutritional state.

Here is a dramatic example of an empty-calorie junk food diet and its consequences. A thirty-year-old woman came to me complaining of daily headaches and stomach pain, saying, "My mind is constantly racing. I can't fall asleep because I'm thinking about horrible things that are going to happen. I keep seeing my son in a coffin. My moods are always changing; my poor son having to deal with me, he'd be better off without me." This woman suffered from chronic anxiety interspersed with panic attacks, confusion, restlessness, difficulty concentrating, memory lapses, suicidal thoughts, dizziness, palpitations and tightness in her chest, muscle weakness, pain and cramps, and chronic fatigue.

Here is a three-day sample of her diet at the time:

MONDAY	TUESDAY	WEDNESDAY
1 apple	1 cup of coffee	1 cup of coffee
2 chocolate chip cookies	2 donuts	2 slices of American cheese
3 slices of American cheese	1 hamburger patty	1 chicken pie
1 hamburger on a plain bun	1 Like soda	1 Pepsi Free
French fries	1 slice of American cheese	potato chips
1 Pepsi Free	1 candy bar	2 bean and cheese burritos
1 Like soda	1 Pepsi Free	1 Pepsi Free
1 bowl Rice Krispies with sugar	some "Red Hot" candy	1 Like soda
2 more Pepsi Free's	1 McDonald's McRib with french fries	1 candy bar
1 slice of American cheese	1 Tab	
	1 hot dog and bun	

This type of eating pattern had continued for a long time. Where is her daily protein, her vegetables and fruit? Her diet only consistently contained one of the five basic food groups, grains. No wonder she felt so terrible, and yet was too discouraged to make any lasting changes. She might try to eat healthfully for a few days, then when she didn't notice an immediate, significant improvement, she lapsed into her old habits. It would take a good six months or a year in this woman's case to make up for or undo ten years of deprivation.

Her diet is hardly unusual. I am often appalled by the lists of food intake which people bring to me. Sometimes I wonder how they can live and move at all. And there is no greater offender than sugar in these harmful diets.

Put simply, sugar is a drug which, besides being addictive, is actually toxic to our systems in large amounts. Vitamins B_1, B_2 and B_6 are needed to detoxify and metabolize it. Our bodies particularly need vitamin B_1 to metabolize sugar. The more sugar we eat, the less vitamin B_1 we have, and fatigue, depression and other problems follow. The damage and symptoms are directly proportionate to our indulgence and to whether or not we use supplements or get enough B_1 and B complex vitamins some other way. Sugar also leads to depression by increasing the magnesium and calcium excretion in our urine and by decreasing the overall magnesium absorption from our food.

Excess sugar may also contribute to amino acid deficiencies, because research in animals indicates that sugar and amino acids compete for absorption in the intestines. Specifically, the influx of the amino acids tryptophan and phenylalanine are inhibited by sugars. Therefore it may be unwise to eat sugar and protein at the same time. High sugar intake also undermines your immune system: it has been shown to decrease the white blood cell count and to lower resistance to colds, flu and other infections.

HYPOGLYCEMIA

Hypoglycemia is a condition of abnormal sugar metabolism resulting in low blood sugar, which many experts believe may be brought about in certain susceptible individuals by the ingestion of too much sugar or too many refined carbohydrates.

Is hypoglycemia a hype? Some doctors think so, but I don't. What makes it so controversial? One reason is that, as with most illnesses with multiple yet vague symptoms, doctors tend to get uneasy. The temptation is to pass the symptoms off as obsession, hypochondriasis, a bad marriage. . . . If hypoglycemia had a list of clear-cut, well-defined physical manifestations, it would be more readily accepted and agreed upon as a specific malady in need of treatment. On the other hand, hypoglycemia may have been over-diagnosed, too often passed off as the cause of all sorts of vague symptoms by a public made aware of hypoglycemia.

But we are now discovering that certain mental symptoms and diseases are indeed associated with altered or disturbed glucose (sugar) utilization in the brain. There are computerized brain X ray tests called positron emission tomographic (PET) brain scans which measure glucose utilization in the brain. Depressed patients show an overall reduction in glucose metabolism that is most marked across the front and on the left side of their brains. Since the B vitamins are necessary for sugar utilization and metabolism, could it be that B vitamin deficiencies are actually contributing to this faulty glucose metabolism?

PET brain scans of schizophrenics, depressives and other diagnostic groups have helped to substantiate the effect that low blood sugar or rapidly changing sugar levels have on brain function and thus on emotional states, moods and perceptions. The proper concentration of sugar (glucose) in the proper areas of the brain at the right time is an essential component of good mental and physical health, but eating more sugar to create sugar in your brain is not the answer and in the long-term can actually create less.

Here's why: sugar rapidly absorbs into your system and your body reacts or overreacts to this with an outpouring of insulin from your pancreas. This causes the level of blood sugar to go down. Fine tuning of the sugar level with just the right amount of insulin can be difficult: if the blood sugar drops too low, the body pours out substances called growth hormone, glucagon, cortisol and adrenaline to push it back up; this can then cause a further release of insulin, and the sequence bounces back and forth until a balance is established.

Your liver, pituitary body, pancreas and adrenal gland are all involved in this process of your body's efforts to achieve blood sugar balance. Problems can develop when they are overworked and taxed by a regularly incoming sugar load or by sporadic excessive sugar. High insulin output can also create major changes in brain chemistry as well as brain swelling.

Sufficient quantities of the proper nutrients can promote proper glandular function and hormone production and otherwise aid in the metabolism of the sugar. Eliminating caffeine also helps to level out your blood sugar.

If you have early morning, or before lunch, or late afternoon fatigue which is relieved by a seeming "pickup" of sugar and you find yourself reaching for candy bars, sodas, or other quick sugar fixes at those times, suspect a problem. *More than 50 percent of patients who go to a doctor complain of fatigue as one of their symptoms. The most common cause is eating sugar.*

The following is a list of symptoms induced by rapidly fluctuating or low blood sugar, that is, by hypoglycemia. Please note that many of these symptoms also occur with depression. Those symptoms marked with an asterisk more clearly indicate blood sugar problems and help to differentiate the two.

Symptoms of Blood Sugar Instability

   1. Depression
   2. Nervousness
   3. Irritability, anger, rage attacks
   4. Exhaustion
*5. Faintness, dizziness
*6. Tremor, cold sweats
*7. Weak spells, especially between meals
   8. Headache, especially in the morning
   9. Digestive disturbances
10. Forgetfulness
11. Insomnia
12. Nighttime awakening, inability to return to sleep
13. Constant worrying
14. Unprovoked anxieties
15. Mental confusion
*16. Internal trembling
17. Palpitation of the heart
*18. Rapid pulse

19. Muscle pains
20. Numbness
21. Social withdrawal
22. Antisocial behavior
23. Indecisiveness
24. Crying spells
25. Lack of sex drive
26. Allergies
*27. Uncoordination
*28. Leg cramps
29. Lack of concentration
*30. Blurred vision
*31. Twitching, or jerking of muscles
*32. Gasping for breath
*33. Itching of skin
*34. Feeling like you can't get enough air
*35. Staggering
36. Sighing and yawning
37. Impotence
*38. Unconsciousness
39. Night terrors
40. Nightmares
41. Phobias, fears
42. Suicidal ideas
43. Nervous breakdown
*44. Convulsions
*45. Craving for sweets
*46. Blackouts
*47. Light clammy perspiration
*48. Fluctuating mood and personality throughout the day
*49. Feeling better right after eating and feeling worse two to six hours after eating or upon arising in the morning

If you regularly eat sugar, drink alcohol, have a family history of sugar-associated illnesses, and have at least ten of these symptoms (especially if many are with the asterisk), read *Fighting Depression,* by Harvey Ross, M.D., and proceed with appropriate hypoglycemia testing, in addition to—not in place of—following the program in this book. Refer to the appendix for further information on hypoglycemia.

VEGETARIANISM

Strict vegetarianism is not without risks. It takes a conscientious person with a fair amount of nutritional sophistication to follow this life style successfully. Those who omit dairy products and eggs are especially vulnerable to long-term difficulties. Vegetarians are particularly prone to develop iron, vitamin B_{12} and amino acid deficiencies. All of these can be associated with low energy and low moods.

Fish, fowl, meats and cottage cheese are the primary single foods supplying balanced amino acids. Most vegetarian foods do not supply such a balance on their own. They must be intelligently combined to provide the nutritional equal to what you would get from a meat and dairy diet. Popular books such as *Diet For a Small Planet,* by Frances Moore Lappé, can help you to ensure a properly balanced amino acid intake.

If you are strictly vegetarian be sure to take supplemental iron and vitamin B_{12} as mentioned on page 40, in addition to the basic nutrient program. It would also be wise to get a complete blood count, blood vitamin B_{12} level, and blood amino acid analysis every few years.

ALLERGIES OR SENSITIVITIES

Over the past several years, there has been a lot of controversy about food allergies or sensitivities, how to detect them and whether, in fact, they exist. To me, this is somewhat like refusing to accept the fact that the sun rises daily, whether or not you see it that day. Anyone who has suffered from sensitivities to food will have trouble understanding the medical establishment's disagreement on this issue.

Such allergies not only exist but are increasing. The combination of stress, nutrient deficiencies and exposure to chemicals in food, water and air, as well as recreational drug use and abuse, can alter the immune system and cause overreaction to many substances, including food.

The most common foods producing reactions are wheat, corn, coffee, sugar, yeast, eggs, soy, beef, pork and milk. Some who have symptoms from alcoholic beverages are reacting to the yeast, corn, grains, hops, grapes and so forth in these drinks.

Acute food allergies may be obvious, but chronic allergies are not so well defined. We are often "addicted" to the foods to which we are reacting negatively. As part of the allergic response, a person may be initially stimulated and may feel better for a while after eating a particular food. The negative symptoms arrive later and, since we don't associate them with the food, we get hooked on this initial stimulatory effect and eat more and more, creating a plethora of confusing symptoms.

The "target organ" is the specific part of the body affected or attacked by the allergy. With emotional symptoms, the target organ is the brain. Why should it be exempt? Why should allergic effects be limited to the skin, with itching and hives, or to the upper respiratory system, with sneezing, hay fever and asthma, or to the gastrointestinal system, with colic, diarrhea and cramps?

Food and chemical allergies can change your emotions and cause low moods and sustained depression. They can create psychological symptoms such as the following:

Depression	Poor work habits	Hyperactivity
Withdrawal	Slurred speech	Restlessness
Listlessness	Stuttering	Confusion
Crying jags	Disorientation	Tension
Mental dullness	Mental lethargy	Silliness
Anxiety	Difficulty concentrating	Stuporousness
Panic attacks	Memory loss	False beliefs
Irritability	Indifference	Delusions
Aggressive behavior	Poor comprehension	Hallucinations
Anger	Excessive daydreaming	Suicidal feelings
Learning disabilities	Negativity	

Moderate and variable allergies can produce fluctuating, unpredictable moods. Often they are bearable because the fluctuating course does give times of relief. Sometimes they are not bearable.

A certain subgroup of allergic people are what are called "universal reactors." They have become allergic to so many substances in the air and the food supply that their life is severe.

They may suffer so wide a range of physical and psychological symptoms that they find relief only in isolation units in hospitals or in natural settings far from most of the offending agents.

HOW CAN YOU TELL IF YOU ARE REACTING NEGATIVELY TO FOOD?

Unfortunately, allergy detection can be bewildering and complex, because people's reactions are inconsistent. Whether or not you react at any given time may depend upon how much stress you're experiencing, your total biochemical and nutritional state, and how many other simultaneous inhalant, chemical and food allergies you are exposed to. This is described as the "total allergic load." Eating three foods you are sensitive to may not create a problem, but adding the fourth overwhelms your system and you get symptoms. Or, if you are already reacting to mold and pollen, and then you add the wrong food, you feel worse.

Researchers are constantly working to discover new and better ways to measure adverse reactions to foods and inhalants. Strictly speaking, an allergy involves an immune globulin E (IGE) reaction, an immediate reaction directly linked to the food intake as, for example, blisters following the eating of shellfish or coughing right after eating wheat.

Other adverse reactions to food, mediated by immune globulins G, A and M, are called "sensitivities" and create delayed reactions, with the symptoms occurring anywhere from an hour to three days later. Irritability and muscle tension the day after eating a lot of wheat is an example. If the offending food is eaten daily, producing a gradual buildup and overlap of symptoms, it is particularly difficult to pinpoint the offending agent. Yet the bottom line is the same—unpleasant reactions to certain foods. You can track down your problem by trying a food-mood diary. Keep a list of what you eat, at what times, and of what moods follow and when. If you do this for a while, you may notice the emergence of certain patterns.

Fasting: *under a physician's supervision,* try a program of fasting and drinking only water for a few days. If you feel much better, part of your symptoms are probably reactions to food. Do not fast if you are hypoglycemic or diabetic.

You might try to stop eating all the foods you regularly use and eat other less common foods. Do not repeat any food more often than every fourth day. If you feel better on this program, food reactions were contributing to your symptoms.

Your doctor may wish to try one of a wide range of tests for allergies and sensitivities. Allergy detection tests are rapidly changing. Ask your doctor for the most up-to-date determination available in your area. Some of these tests are listed in the Appendix.

There are traditional allergists, and there is a new medical specialty called clinical ecology. These doctors are devoted to the research and treatment of multiple allergies related to our changing chemical environment and usually employ a different approach from what is considered traditional.

If you have any family history of allergies or can detect any fluctuating mood changes which seem to connect to food intake, look to food as part of your problem. If your mood states shift a lot, or if you feel better when you don't eat or feel best when fasting, you should be checked for allergies. If you have a depression which hasn't been responsive to usual treatments, suspect allergies.

Allergy sufferers respond well to a balanced hypoallergenic nutrient-supplement program. They have responded well to tyrosine, partially because it helps to fortify the immune system and perhaps partially because one breakdown product of tyrosine is epinephrine, which has traditionally been used to treat many allergy victims.

If food reactions are influencing your moods, the amino acid program will work best if coupled with a three month abstinence from the offending foods and a gradual reassimilation of the foods into your diet. See the bibliography for books that will be helpful.

9 Life Habits and Exposures

Many of us regularly use substances that can add to chemical disequilibrium and therefore adversely affect our moods. These include caffeine, alcohol, cocaine, tobacco and some prescription medicines. They are prevalent in our culture, are part of our daily activities, and can undermine the effectiveness of the amino acid program described in this book.

CAFFEINE

Caffeine is the most widely used drug in the world, and is popular because it is mentally stimulating.

It is found in coffee, tea, soft drinks and some over-the-counter pain pills, and in the energy producer "Guarana," which is sold in health food stores. Very recently, colas replaced coffee as the number one source of caffeine intake in our country. This is especially worrisome because children, who consume so much of these beverages, are very susceptible to the adverse effects of caffeine.

Caffeine is a potent, addicting drug. Abrupt discontinuance may cause headaches and other withdrawal symptoms. Caffeine use affects your brain, nerves, heart, circulation, digestion, the release of adrenaline from your adrenal glands, and the degree of tension in your muscles.

It can adversely affect certain medical conditions and should be entirely avoided in the following circumstances: high blood pressure or heart irregularities; insomnia and anxiety; ulcers, gastritis, or other stomach problems, because it stimulates gastric acid secretion; pregnancy, because it has been associated with birth defects and abnormal pregnancies; hypoglycemia; fibrocystic breast disease; and pancreatic cancer.

Small doses of 65 to 130 mg enhance physical and mental performance and induce alertness, wakefulness, talkativeness and water elimination. Larger doses, over 150 to 250 mg, can produce toxic effects including insomnia, anxiety, panic attacks, restlessness, irritability, delirium, ringing in the ears, flashes of light, gastrointestinal disturbances, tense or trembling muscles, fast or irregular heart beat, low-grade fever, headaches, fatigue, dizziness, weakness, and mood fluctuations with depression.

Depending on your weight and associated health conditions, your daily intake should not exceed 150 to 200 mg. You can use the caffeine-free alternatives when you have reached your self-assigned quota.

AVERAGE CAFFEINE CONTENT OF BEVERAGES

	CAFFEINE/OZ	8 OZ CUP	12 OZ
Brewed coffee	15–30 mg	120–240 mg	
Instant coffee	13–20 mg	104–160 mg	
Tea	2–10 mg	16–80 mg	
Over the counter stimulants:			
Mountain Dew			50 mg
Tab			41 mg
Diet Shasta Cola			38 mg
Shasta Cola			38 mg
Sunkist Orange			38 mg
Dr. Pepper			37 mg
Pepsi-Cola			35 mg
RC Cola			34 mg
Coca-Cola			32 mg
Diet Pepsi			32 mg
Pepsi Light			31 mg
King Cola			29 mg

*Abstracted from Woodrow Monte and Samy Ashoof, "Caffeine Content of Selected Soft Drinks," *Journal of Applied Nutrition,* Vol. 37, No. 1, 1985.

CAFFEINE AND THE BRAIN AMINES

Psychiatrists are seeing the toxic effects of caffeine enough to have included a diagnosis of caffeine intoxication, or "caffeinism," in the diagnostic manual (DSM-III).

Caffeine stimulates the release of norepinephrine and other brain amines. This release takes place in the brain and body, and is the reason a small amount of caffeine may give a lift. Chronic use of larger amounts will result in depletion of the amines unless there are plenty of precursors for replacement. Under the conditions of depletion, a caffeine user will progress to feeling nervous and fatigued.

Caffeine also importantly affects mood by interfering with vitamin B_1 absorption and metabolism. Thus, chronic high intake could ultimately result in a vitamin B_1 deficiency.

One study also presented evidence that 300 mg of caffeine caused a 50 percent increase in the loss of magnesium (which is related to depression) and a 100 percent increase in the loss of calcium and sodium in the urine. Dietary magnesium and calcium intakes are often low anyway, so caffeine adds an additional mineral-exhausting stress to your system.

Aside from the problems of caffeine, coffee and tea significantly inhibit iron absorption when taken with a meal or up to one hour following a meal. Tea blocked iron intake by 87 percent in studies of the absorption of radioactive iron. Since low iron can contribute to depression, this is another mood altering hazard of these popular drinks.

I always ask my patients about their use of caffeine and the importance of doing this was underscored when a woman visiting the United States from her native Japan came to see me. Her complaints were depression, withdrawal, insomnia, fatigue, weakness, muscle tension, irritability and racing thoughts. When we talked, I learned she owned and operated a gourmet coffee shop and drank about fifteen cups of brewed coffee daily. The primary treatment I prescribed was that she discontinue the coffee and add B vitamins; all her symptoms cleared in several weeks.

FROM BOOZE TO BLUES

Alcohol affects our moods as well as our general well-being. Alcoholism is also our nation's number-one health problem and third largest killer. We have about twelve million alcoholics and many more million heavy drinkers, meaning they consume more than fourteen drinks a week.

Most studies indicate that more men than women are alcoholic, whereas twice as many females as males are depressed. Many of the male alcoholics appear to have a depression that is masked by the alcohol problem. Because it is hard for many men to admit depression, they may turn to substance abuse or antisocial behavior to escape their psychological pain.

Even though inner conflict and stress can precipitate heavy drinking, we now feel fairly certain that alcoholics fall prey to their illness because they metabolize alcohol differently from nonalcoholics. This is either secondary to a genetic predisposition or to the disruptive biochemical effects of heavy drinking.

ALCOHOL AND NUTRITION

If we look at the destructive effects of regular drinking from a purely nutritional point of view, we see that, like sugar, alcohol gives you "empty" calories, with no vitamins, minerals or amino acids. It induces malabsorption of many nutrients and creates a greater need for them. Alcoholics have deficiencies of all the B complex vitamins, of amino acids and of some minerals. In fact, even small amounts of alcohol taken regularly will create vitamin B complex problems because alcohol decreases the absorption of vitamins B_1, B_2 and folic acid. Vitamins B_6 and C are destroyed by acetaldehyde, a breakdown product of alcohol produced by the liver. Alcohol also increases urinary excretion of zinc, magnesium, calcium, and vitamin B_{12}, and thus leads to depletion of those substances as well.

As we have seen, almost all these substances can be related to mood, and many of them help form the brain amines. Recent studies of brain amine metabolism have shown alcohol reduces the synthesis of neurotransmitters from tyrosine. And, it should be noted, a significant number of alcoholics have an associated depression.

If you are not alcoholic but do have daily drinks, you need supplementation to offset the drain on your body's nutritional status. Occasional social drinking should not pose this kind of nutritional threat and does not require the same replacement efforts.

The nutritional approach to treating depression works well in drinkers because it is totally safe to mix nutrients with alcohol and because the alcoholic needs the nutrients anyway. On the other hand, the mixture of traditional antidepressant drugs with alcohol can be very dangerous, making orthodox treatment risky. Even when counseled to avoid alcohol, there is no guarantee a person will do so, and a number of suicides have eventuated from the combination of alcohol with antidepressant medication or tranquilizers.

Many drinkers, especially those involved in AA (Alcoholics Anonymous) programs, are advised by their support groups to avoid psychiatric medication of any kind. This can create problems for those who need biochemical help to eliminate depression. The nutrient program poses no such dilemma.

After treatment with specific diets and nutrients, many alcoholics naturally lose the craving and compulsion to drink. Therefore, the self-discipline required is in taking the supplements, more than in avoiding the alcohol.

COCAINE

We've all heard about the widespread use of cocaine among professionals and athletes, and in the white collar sector.

We also know that a new cocaine trend is cause for much greater alarm. The villain is "crack," a cheap, smokable, readily available form of cocaine that is highly addictive and is considered to be far more dangerous than the usual powdered, snorted variety used by the older crowd.

A 1985 University of Michigan survey indicated that 17 percent of high school students had used cocaine. What will happen to this number now, when cheaper, more addictive forms of cocaine spread across our land? And what will happen to the moods and psychology of our teenagers, who are already on biochemically induced emotional rollercoasters from sugar, alcohol, tobacco, caffeine and other drugs?

The following set of symptoms is common among cocaine users: blurred vision, panic attacks, hyperactivity, severe headaches, weight loss, nasal problems, paranoia, convulsions, *depression* and precipitation of manic states.

Because of its high or euphoric effect, many people use the drug to counteract drops in mood and energy or, ironically, to treat their own depression. In fact chronic cocaine usage creates depression. Cocaine causes our brain cells to release the stored neurotransmitters norepinephrine and dopamine into the space between nerve cells (synapse) where they chemically interact with the next cell to produce stimulatory effects. Cocaine not only causes increased release of these neurotransmitters but also decreases the reuptake of norepinephrine, dopamine and serotonin back into their storage cells. Cocaine also temporarily inhibits the enzyme that breaks down the neurotransmitters. The net effect is to keep this system of nervous pathways excited and "on" in an unnatural way. But when the neurotransmitters are finally metabolized, not only is there an end to the high, there is also a deficiency until the body produces more, or until another cocaine dose stimulates release of the gradually depleting "stores" of neurotransmitters. When cocaine use is repeated a sufficient number of times without adequate nutrient replacement of the neurotransmitter precursors, a final depressed, depleted, exhausted state can occur.

Several studies have reported successful treatment of cocaine addiction using the amino acids L-tyrosine, L-tryptophan, L-glutamine, and L-phenylalanine, plus vitamins and minerals. These nutrients replace the depleted neurotransmitters and relieve the underlying mood disorder that may often lead to the addiction in the first place.

TOBACCO

Smoking depletes your body of vitamins A, B_1, B_5, B_6, C and E, and of the amino acid cysteine. Smokers tend to have vitamin C levels about half that of nonsmokers; they also have lower vitamin B_6 levels. These deficiencies are importantly connected with depression. Tobacco may contribute to mood fluctuations from an allergic standpoint as well.

For these reasons, among other important medical considerations, it's important to stop smoking. However, those who do smoke particularly need to replace their depleted vitamins and amino acids with a supplemental nutrient program.

Drugs That May Cause Depression

The following substances may cause depression. (The generic name is listed first and the trade names are in parentheses.)

Antibiotics (When you take antibiotics, be sure to take vitamin B complex daily also.)
Cycloserine (Seromycin)
Gram negative antibiotics
Sulfonamides (Bactrim, Azo Gantanol, Cotrim, Septra, Sulfatrim, Sulfa Methoxazole)
Neomycin
Tetracyclines
Metronidazole (Flagyl)

Antimalarials
Sulfadoxine
Pyrimethamine (Daraprim, Fansidar)

Arthritis or Pain Medicines
Phenylbutazone (Azolid, Butazolidin)
Indomethacin (Indocin)
Piroxicam (Feldene)
Sulfasalazine (Azulfidine)
Aspirin (including Bufferin, Anacin, Ascriptin)
Phenacetin (A.P.C. with Codeine, Propoxyphene Compound, Soma Compound)

Birth Control Pills and Other Hormones
Estrogens
Progesterone
Steroids (may also cause euphoria or even mania)

Chemotherapy
Vinblastine sulfate (Velban)

Methotrexate
Procarbazine hydrochloride (Matulane)

Diet Pills
Amphetamines (Obetrol, Dexedrine, Desoxyn)
Benzphetamine (Didrex)
Diethylpropion hydrochloride (Tenuate, Tepanil)
Phenmetrazine hydrochloride (Preludin)
Mazindol (Sanorex, Mazanor)
Fenfluramine hydrochloride (Pondimin)
Phendimetrazine tartrate (Plegine, Melfiat, Bontril)
Phentermine (Ionamin, Fastin, Adipex-P)

Diuretics
Furosemide
Triamterene (Dyazide, Dyrenium)

Heart Medicines
Digitalis (Digoxin, Lanoxin, Cedilanid, Crystodigin)
Procainamide (Pronestyl, Procan SR)

High Blood Pressure Medicines
Hydralazine (Apresazide Apresoline)
Methyldopa (Aldomet, Aldoclor, Aldoril)
Clonidine hydrochloride (Catapres, Combipres)
Guanethidine (Ismelin, Esimil)
Propanolol hydrochloride (Inderal, Inderide)
Bethanidine
Reserpine (Chloroserpine, Regroton, Diupres, Diutensen-R,
    H-H-R Tabs, Hydropres, Serpasil, Unipres, Ser-Ap-Es,
    Naquival, Metatensin, Hydromox, Hydro-Fluserpine)

Medication for Parkinson's Disease
Amantadine hydrochloride (Symmetrel)
Levodopa (Larodopa, Sinemet) (may also cause mania)

Drugs for Psychosis
Phenothiazines, (Compazine, Phenergan, Sparine, Stelazine,
    Temaril, Thorazine)
Haloperidol (Haldol)
Thioxanthene (Navane)

Seizure Medicines
Succinimide derivatives (Celontin, Zarontin, Milontin)
Carbamazepine (Tegretol)
Mephenytoin (Mesantoin)

Tranquilizers and Sleeping Medicines
Librium, Valium, barbiturates, other sleeping pills

Miscellaneous
Disulfiram (Antabuse)
Physostigmine (Antilirium)
Tagamet (ulcer treatment; creates various nutritional deficiencies if taken for a long time)
Choline (a nutrient supplement good for memory, but large doses can cause or exaggerate low moods. Consequently, it is helpful to give this to a manic person to help lower the mood to normal)
Lecithin (this is a nutrient combination of choline and inositol)
Penicillamine
Cholestyramine

Do not stop any of these medications without consulting your doctor.

Specific Physical Illnesses and Low Moods

Very often people who feel depressed when they are ill believe their feelings are only a psychological reaction to their sickness. However, medically ill people who become depressed and remain that way beyond the initial discomfort, fear and frustration of the first three to four weeks of their illness may also have brain amine changes that are adding to their mood disturbance. People who are depressed need to be screened for physical illness and those who are physically ill need to be evaluated for depression.

The stress and disturbance caused by disease can rapidly deplete your body of nutrients at the time you need them most. A number of studies have measured nutrients in post-surgical and severely ill patients and have found significant deficiencies. Also, any illness that decreases the amount of oxygen circulating through your body can increase the likelihood of depression. Research has shown that the enzymes which initially break down tyrosine and tryptophan (tyrosine and tryptophan hydroxylase) are regulated by oxygen. Thus, low oxygen can inhibit brain amine synthesis.

While virtually any illness can coincide with depression, some illnesses are far more likely to create mood problems than others. Though all sick people are dealing with the psychological stress of illness, only some have the distinct constellation of neuro-chemical imbalances which adversely affect mood.

The physical conditions that most often predispose a person to mood disorders are low thyroid, premenstrual syndrome, chronic candidiasis (fungal infections), viral infections, high blood pressure, stroke, other cardiovascular diseases and Parkinson's disease. Because of the chemical imbalances involved, patients with some of these illnesses have benefited a great deal from the nutritional program in conjunction with the medical attention their condition may require.

THE THYROID CONNECTION

The neurotransmitters directly influence hormone levels. For this reason, people who are depressed often have associated hormone changes. Likewise, a primary hormone disorder or glandular malfunction can lead to depression.

There is a delicately balanced system of hormonal regulation originating from your hypothalamus, an area deep in the bottom center of your brain. It regulates your pituitary, the part of your brain that controls the glands and their hormone production. Your hypothalamus responds to the chemical environment of your body and prompts your pituitary to stimulate your glands to secrete. Your glands, in turn, must have the necessary ingredients for hormone formation; these include essential fatty acids, amino acids, vitamins and minerals. Once formed, these hormones then feed messages back to your hypothalamus and other brain parts, directly affecting your neurotransmitter mechanisms.

We know that neurotransmitter depletion is the biochemical cause of depression, and one of the areas of the brain most depleted is the hypothalamus. Therefore, besides affecting mood, deficient neurotransmitters can create hormonal and metabolic imbalances and also disrupt normal biological rhythms.

The most consistent, best documented hormonal changes associated with depression are related to the thyroid, adrenal and ovarian hormones. In my practice, I find low thyroid function in a number of those who are depressed.

A forty-eight-year-old woman who came to my office said, "I've had depression all my life." She had been hospitalized on numerous occasions over the previous nineteen years, had had many doctors and years of psychotherapy, so she knew the psychological jargon and the psychological answers. She had tried to kill herself repeatedly, once by wrist cutting and nine times by drug overdose. She said, "I feel I can't even succeed at killing myself, so I don't try anymore. But I think, wouldn't it be nice if I would just die?"

At the time of our first meeting she was taking the antidepressant medication Elavil, the major tranquilizer Navane, Cogentin to counteract the side effects of the Navane, Catapres for her high blood pressure, and the diuretic hydrochlorothiazide for her high blood pressure. She also had a history of heavy drinking. Beyond these physiological pollutants, she had been an abused child and had led a chaotic life. Family history revealed she had a schizophrenic sister who was also a drug addict, a schizophrenic brother and two alcoholic brothers.

On an initial health questionnaire she indicated the following huge list of symptoms: headaches, faintness, imbalance, sleepiness soon after eating, insomnia, sneezing, watery itchy eyes, blurred vision, hearing loss, chronic cough, gagging, canker sores, frequent yawning, sensitivity to light and sound, tight feeling in her chest, sudden changes in blood pressure, severe constipation, bloating, belching, feeling of fullness long after finishing a meal, abdominal pains and cramps, skin rashes, itching, sweating, chronic fatigue, weakness, muscle cramps, swelling of hands, feet and ankles, binge eating, severe depression, mental lethargy, confusion and suicidal thoughts.

Initial laboratory tests showed low thyroid, low magnesium, low potassium, extremely high cholesterol and triglycerides, slightly elevated blood sugar and high uric acid (gout).

We began treatment with thyroid, a multivitamin mineral, vitamin B complex, vitamin C, bioflavonoids, an extra calcium-magnesium-zinc preparation, another 400 mg of magnesium orotate, 3200 mg a day of tyrosine and 3000 mg a day of tryptophan. She was instructed to eliminate sugar, red meat, milk, eggs, and cheese from her diet in order to treat the gout and high blood sugar.

Within two months this patient was able to stop her medications for blood pressure because her pressure had normalized. Within three months she was able to stop all other medications she was taking at our first visit and to remain on only our treatment program. Her depression was completely cleared and she was feeling much better in every way. It is now two years later, and she continues to have a totally normal mood and normal blood pressure. She is, in every respect, a "changed woman."

The literature indicates that 15 to 20 percent of depressed people are also hypothyroid. This is no surprise because the thyroid hormone regulates metabolism in all of your body cells, including your brain cells. Very slight shifts toward a lowered thyroid state can affect our very responsive brain cells, which seem to be more reactive to subtle thyroid lack than are other body cells.

Depression is the major mental manifestation of those with hypothyroidism. In fact, 40 percent of those diagnosed as hypothyroid also suffer depression. They may also experience other mental changes such as poor memory and concentration, and overall slowing of mental processes. At times, paranoia and even psychosis can result. Other possible symptoms are:

Chronic fatigue, especially in the morning
   Muscle weakness and lethargy
   Excess sleepiness
   Menstrual changes or problems
   Weight gain with swelling and puffiness
   A deepened or hoarse voice
   Constipation and other digestive symptoms
   Cold intolerance
   Decreased sweating
   Hair or eyebrow loss
   Dry, coarse rough skin
   An average morning underarm temperature below 97.2 degrees

As if we need more to complicate the diagnosis, thyroid dysfunction may not readily be discovered by doing the usual thyroid blood tests measuring so-called T3, T4 and TSH. Studies have shown that approximately 20 percent of depressed patients have antithyroid antibodies in their blood. This condition is called autoimmune thyroiditis and some now believe it is the most frequent thyroid disorder in our population. It is like an allergic inflammation of the thyroid gland. It occurs eight to ten times more often in women than in men, primarily between the ages of thirty to fifty years, although it can appear at any age. Most of these same patients have normal T3 and T4 and TSH blood levels.

Another blood test that may reveal thyroid problems is called the TRH test. You can request it if you suspect you have thyroid problems that the usual tests have not revealed.

Tyrosine and iodine are required for the formation of thyroxine, the thyroid hormone. When tyrosine becomes depleted, our bodies may first use tyrosine for thyroid formation before it is used for norepinephrine formation. This seems to be the case because low thyroid is less common than depression.

I have not seen research evidence on the use of tyrosine to treat these instances of subtle low thyroid, but some investigators have reported lower tyrosine blood levels in hypothyroid patients. In my practice, I have successfully used tyrosine in several patients with borderline low thyroid, and the thyroid levels have increased to the midnormal range. This approach certainly makes sense when used in conjunction with 75 to 200 mcg of iodine daily. If, however, the levels of thyroid are clearly below normal, then thyroid hormone should be added as well.

Many different circumstances can predispose a person to low thyroid. First of all, there is a strong genetic component to thyroid disease. Additionally, chronic stress and pain can inhibit the release of thyroid hormone, so people experiencing these would do well to ensure sufficient tyrosine and iodine in their bodies. Other conditions which contribute to decreased thyroid formation are aging, and excess vitamin A, iodine, fluoride, chloride and bromide. Those who have excess thyroid in their bodies already have too much tyrosine in their systems and should not take extra amounts.

If you suspect thyroid disorder in yourself, see your doctor for complete evaluation and also read the excellent book called *Hypothyroidism, The Unsuspected Illness,* by Broda Barnes, M.D.

PMS—PREMENSTRUAL SYNDROME

We know now that PMS is a condition of biochemical disequilibrium which can be related to increased activity of monoamine oxidase (the enzyme that breaks down the neurotransmitters), nutritional deficiencies, antibodies to ovarian tissue, chronic fungal infections, estrogen and progesterone imbalances, thyroid disorders and other possible contributing factors.

Now that PMS is finally receiving the validating attention it deserves, we are able to discover more about its impact on America. Studies indicate that between 30 and 50 percent of women from twenty to fifty years of age are affected, and most studies are toward the 50 percent figure. This can have staggering consequences in many areas besides the approximate one hundred billion dollar yearly loss to the work force because of PMS-related absenteeism.

By definition, the sufferers from PMS must have at least one symptom-free week per month, and a somewhat consistent pattern of increased symptoms anywhere from three weeks to one day before the onset of menstruation, which then abate with menstrual flow. The severity of the symptoms can and does vary from month to month.

Depression and anxiety are common aspects of PMS, and some researchers believe there is a relationship between PMS and mood disorders. Studies do suggest that premenstrual malaise predicts an increased vulnerability to depressive illness.

PMS has been treated with tranquilizers, antidepressants, diuretics, progesterone, oral contraceptive pills and amphetamines. None of these have had the clear-cut positive results we would hope for.

Guy Abraham, M.D., has been a major contributor to the understanding of what he calls PMTS (Premenstrual Tension Syndrome), especially as it relates to nutritional factors. He and others in the field believe that malnutrition and stress are common factors underlying PMS. In general those with PMS should avoid sugar, caffeine, chocolate, nicotine, alcohol, salt, fatty and fried foods, and excess dairy products. Women with PMS need to eat plenty of fresh fruits and vegetables, lean meats, beans and whole grains.

Estrogens are central nervous system stimulants, while progesterones are central nervous system depressants. The balance of these two hormones has a profound effect on moods and this balance can be nutritionally influenced. The nutritional treatment in this book should significantly help with most cases of PMS. When this basic program does not completely eliminate PMS, the magnesium supplement can be doubled or tripled, the vitamin B complex doubled or tripled, and the vitamin B_6 doubled or tripled. When breast tenderness is a problem, additional vitamin E up to a total of 1600 IU daily may be useful. Extra vitamin E should only be used in those women who have no problems with hypertension. It is contraindicated otherwise. In those cases where nutrients are not completely effective, there should be an evaluation for the presence of yeast overgrowth.

FUNGUS INFECTIONS

In my practice, the infection I have found to be most commonly associated with depression and other psychiatric symptoms is the condition of yeast, or fungal overgrowth. The favorite places for this growth are the mucous surfaces of the body. The infection is called monilia when in the vagina, thrush when in the mouth, and candidiasis when it is more widespread, such as in the gastrointestinal or genitourinary tracts.

Coyotes and rabbits may coexist in a certain balance in the neighboring hills. But if someone comes along and kills the coyotes, we'll have a rabbit population explosion. Likewise, this yeast lives in all of us and usually coexists in proper balance with its other normal neighboring microorganisms. Under certain conditions this internal environmental balance is disturbed and there is a yeast population explosion.

Antibiotics can create this imbalance because while they are killing unwanted harmful organisms, they can also kill the friendly bacteria that help to keep the yeast in balance. This especially occurs with repeated antibiotic use. These normal bacteria can be reintroduced by eating yogurt or taking lactobacillus acidophilus capsules, especially if this is begun at the onset of antibiotic usage.

Certain other conditions help sustain the yeast either by feeding it or by providing an optimum growth environment. This particularly occurs after the overgrowth process has already begun. Excess sugar in the blood and other alterations in the internal environment related to hormones, such as cortisone or birth control pills, can promote proliferation of yeast cells. After they are established, the yeast organisms are often very resistant to attempts to control their population. Once an individual has developed this tendency, the yeast seems to be ready and waiting for the slightest opportunity to multiply. It may only take the help of a few days of eating sugar or breads high in yeast, drinking yeast-filled alcohol, or returning to antibiotics to cause a flare-up. Once the fungal infection has taken hold, it creates chemical imbalances, including amino acid imbalances that predispose to depression.

Though this nutrient program will contribute to the general well-being of people with persistent and serious yeast infections, they need additional antiyeast nutrients or medications and must follow a specific antiyeast diet.

Yeast overgrowth has become such a major problem that I discover it relatively often in those who come to me for treatment. If they score high on the candida questionnaire, I then order a blood test for what are called anticandida antibodies, for confirmation. When this test is abnormal, we proceed with appropriate treatment.

VIRAL INFECTIONS

I have seen and known a number of patients who had a totally normal mood when physically well but could progress to a severe depression with any viral episode. The exact mechanism by which this occurs is unknown, but it clearly tips the scale in those with already delicately balanced systems. Be alert to any mood swings accompanying viruses and treat them with this program. Depression is known to accompany or follow viruses such as mononucleosis, hepatitis or influenza.

HIGH BLOOD PRESSURE AND HEART DISEASE

Hypertension is the second most common illness after depression, and often the two coexist. This isn't surprising, since many drugs used to treat this condition cause depression. There is also increasing evidence that low vitamin B_6 and low magnesium contribute to high blood pressure as they do to depression.

A complicating situation is that some traditional antidepressants should only be used with caution in those with hypertension or on antihypertensive medication. There are even precautions to be followed when giving amino acids to severe hypertensives. (See page 57.)

Those who have suffered heart attacks or who have other forms of heart disease often suffer from depression. In studies on patients with heart attacks, 60 percent are depressed during their hospitalization, 20 to 30 percent are still depressed one year later, and 15 to 20 percent never return to work. Again, one reason for such statistics may be that many of the common heart medicines can actually create depression as a side effect. But there are also nutritional and biochemical mechanisms involved in this process that can be ameliorated by the food supplement program.

STROKE

People who have suffered from strokes experience mood disorder more commonly than other patients with equally disabling medical illnesses. Depression in these patients cannot be fully explained by the severity of their impairment. Rather, it seems to be the result of physiological changes in the brain in response to the localized injury of the stroke. The incidence of depression is highest when the damage is to the anterior left portion of the brain. Also, the closer the damage is to the left front, the more severe will be the depression. In contrast, when the stroke is in the *right* frontal area, the patient may become indifferent and, conversely, even tend toward jocularity.

Some investigators have surmised that the injured brain cells may switch from producing neurotransmitters to synthesizing protein for regeneration of the damaged cells. This would suggest that depletion of the amines following injury to certain brain areas could contribute to causing some post-stroke mood disorders and additionally supports the entire biochemical theory of depression.

Because of the statistics and because many people with strokes can't talk or otherwise express themselves well, it might be especially prudent and highly beneficial to proceed with the safe, antidepressant amino acid treatment that is the subject of this book.

PARKINSON'S DISEASE

Parkinson's disease is often related to depression, which is especially interesting because it is a disorder caused by neurotransmitter deficiencies of certain areas of the brain that relate primarily to movement.

Depressed people with Parkinson's disease can benefit from the nutritional program in this book, but if they are taking L-dopa they must not supplement extra vitamin B_6. L-dopa lowers tryptophan levels, so when depression is present these people should supplement tryptophan as well as tyrosine.

ORGANIC AILMENTS AND DEPRESSION

Because of the frequent simultaneous occurrence of depression and certain physical illnesses, we cannot be certain that an intrinsic biochemical vulnerability to depression does not in some way predispose people to certain organic ailments and vice versa.

It does become apparent that costs, severity and duration of illness, and mortality can be reduced by appropriate evaluation and treatment for depression. Otherwise, normal healing processes may be compromised, the immune system may be altered and an already ill person may become more vulnerable to infection as well as many other complications.

A side effect of the nutritional treatment of depression is overall improved general health as well as improved moods. Such a promotion of healing and wellness is far more desirable than the emotional, social and monetary costs of being ill.

Stress and Traumatic Life Events

M any studies clearly indicate that traumatic life events can trigger biochemical depressions—as well as numerous other physical disorders. In fact, stress precedes most episodes of illness and is associated with the onset of 70 to 80 percent of depressions.

Since severe stress can create both physical and emotional problems, we cannot assume an illness evolving from psychological stress is necessarily purely psychological. Each of us has our genetically inborn body system vulnerability—the part of the dam which cracks first. The same degree of stress may give Joe an ulcer, and make Mary wheeze from asthma; it may overwhelm your best friend with feelings of inadequacy and leave you feeling challenged and alive.

LOSS AND DEATH

Life events scales have been devised which list all the stressful events in our lives and rate them according to severity and the likelihood of precipitating illness. The most weighty and potentially damaging stress of all is when someone we love dies, especially if we are quite dependent on them, such as in a long-term marriage or a child's loss of a parent.

Other potentially incapacitating stresses are divorce, illness, and various losses such as failure of a business, loss of money, a demotion in position or importance, and consequent losses of self-esteem. When the person suffering the loss does not have enough support from her family and friends, the damage is multiplied.

We all have problems with loss and need to work to prepare ourselves not to overreact to it. We have numerous other options besides breakdown, but we need to understand them before we can use them.

Because of its finality, the most devastating loss we can sustain is the death of someone we love. This loss is also the most complex to work through because we can no longer interact with the real person but must interact with our memories of her, with what we have been able to incorporate into our psyche.

Approximately eight million Americans will experience the death of an immediate family member this year and 10 to 20 percent of their grief reactions will progress to depression. Loss is the bottom line for all the psychological explanations of depression. There is nothing about which we feel more helpless and immobilized, and no change we may more innately want to resist. Nothing challenges our adaptive and coping capabilities more than loss by death. By its very nature of engendering our sense of helplessness, it sets us up for extreme stress reactions.

Attachment and bonding are powerful forces, and the pain of severing any emotional bond can be hard to bear, but the brutality of the experience is directly related to our philosophy about life, about continuing on and about losses. Those who believe in reincarnation or who have strong spiritual beliefs in the continuity of life after death do seem to deal with loss better than those without such belief systems. Those prone to extreme dependency, bitterness and a sense of victimization, or to spiritual doubt and disbelief are vulnerable to exaggerated, prolonged loss reactions.

Yet no matter how you may prepare yourself, when loss comes through the death of a loved one it can be temporarily overwhelming. The key word is "temporary." It must be temporary to avoid a total erosion of your life and health. You must reach out for support and help. You must not withdraw and isolate yourself. If you have no close friends or family to turn to, you must find support organizations, telephone hot lines, church groups, whatever and whoever will lend you an understanding, supportive, caring ear, along with positive suggestions for how you may get through this period without too much damage. (You will also find some reading suggestions in the bibliography.)

Remember that any temporary destructive escapes will only make you feel worse in the end. Alcohol, drugs and other self-abusive behavior will directly deplete your brain's chemical resources for fighting stress or depressed feelings. Force yourself to eat well, and make sure to use the supplements recommended in this book.

We always have choices—we can eat or starve, we can sleep or wake, we can wallow or win, we can emotionally lie down and give up or we can keep searching until a new life line is cast our way.

MOURNING OR DEPRESSION?

Pure grief is temporary. Initially intense and seemingly overwhelming, it remits as time goes by. The bereaved may be consumed with sadness and tears, disbelief, thoughts of the lost one, and so on. This can be constant to begin with, but as regular life continues, the grieving feelings will begin to come and go. Your basic mood improves between bouts of acute feelings of grief. In time, these intense feelings of loss come less and less frequently as a new life is developed. This normal grieving process can take anywhere from six months to two years.

"Uncomplicated bereavement" is the psychiatric label given to this normal grief response, even though, temporarily, it can look like a full depressive syndrome with poor appetite, weight loss and insomnia.

Grieving is abnormal when it gets worse with time or is prolonged and protracted. The grief periods exceed the relief periods. Feelings of worthlessness, prolonged or marked impairment in functioning and slowed activity indicate that depression has set in.

The psychological process of grieving is important to experience. That is why we have funerals, wakes, shivas. These procedures are for the survivors, not for the departed. It is healthy to immerse oneself in the feelings of loss in order to express and gradually release them. Unexpressed, unacknowledged grief cannot be released.

Because they have avoided clear acknowledgment of their loss, many of my patients progress to later depression. They have not attended the funeral, they have never visited the gravesite (if there is one), they have refused to "release" the lost one. This holding on keeps them emotionally bound and leads to depression.

One person in particular comes to mind. Janet was young, intelligent, beautiful, happily married, with everything going her way. She was also depressed.

As an only child in white South Africa, Janet had developed an intensely loving and dependent bond with her mother. Her mother had died six years earlier. Janet did not attend the funeral and on some level continued to hold on to her mother. She desperately wanted a child but had had two miscarriages. As the problem became more evident, I asked her to confront the situation by writing a "goodbye letter" to her mother. She was to say everything she would want to say if her mother were sitting right before her for the last time. At the end, she was to say goodbye and to let go. She first responded with horror, cried and said she couldn't do it.

Finally, after a few weeks, at my urging she spent several painful days writing the goodbye letter. At last she truly mourned and it had a remarkable effect on her. The depression lifted. She soon became pregnant and was able to carry the baby to term. She had finished therapy by then, and it was wonderful later to receive a photo and announcement of the birth of her beautiful baby girl.

Saying goodbye does not mean erasing the person from your mind. It involves holding onto your loving, good thoughts about him, and giving up your own feeling of loss and of being torn apart.

The grief reaction is one of the most stressful psychological events we endure. There is some suggestion that even in a "normal" grief reaction biochemical changes occur in the brain. We know, for example, that grieving infant monkeys who were separated from their mothers recovered from their grief when treated with an antidepressant drug.

UNIQUE RESPONSE TO TRAUMA

We all have traumas in our lives, and each of us has different ways of responding emotionally to these unfortunate events. We are stressed in varying degrees by all painful experiences, but some of us react more intensely than others.

One of the most positive persons I have ever known responded to the death of a loved one by sitting and watching television for two solid days and nights—after which she miraculously bounced back to being her usual cheerful self.

Another, very negative person decided she loved a man from her past with whom she had had no contact for years and who had subsequently married. She built up a fantasy about their undying love and proceeded to pursue him. When he did not respond similarly, she slid into a deep depression and entertained ideas of suicide.

We don't yet completely understand the myriad factors which determine the intensity and type of response each individual may have to stress, but flexibility and adaptability are significant parameters in determining our ability to cope with the vicissitudes of life.

Researchers believe we are born with certain patterns of reaction, some of which make life harder and others which make life easier. Studies on newborn babies have clearly indicated extreme variations of reaction to the same stressful stimuli, such as unpleasant noise. This is not a learned response, but something inherent. Perhaps these reactions to unpleasant noise (that is, to stress) are mediated at a purely biochemical level. If this is so, the intensity of the reaction might then be determined by the intensity of the electrochemical discharge which is created by stressful stimuli, and by the subsequent imbalance created by these biochemical changes brought on by the stress reaction. Perhaps the ultimate degree of reactivity and subsequent chemical disruption is genetically determined.

In an interesting study, a group of rats was subjected to the stress of immobilization for thirty minutes. During and following the stress, their amino acids were measured. Some of the amino acids were decreased and others were increased by the stress, and the patterns of response were consistent from animal to animal. But the magnitude of the responses varied considerably, with some rats having much greater chemical changes than others, suggesting the possibility of individual biochemical patterns of reaction to stress.

Optimum nutrition, healthy habits of living, and cultivated "right thinking" dramatically help to protect us from the potentially damaging effects of stress by decreasing the magnitude of our biochemical stress reactions within the framework of our own body systems.

WHAT IS A BIOCHEMICAL STRESS REACTION?

Emotion per se is the experience of physiological and psychological arousal. You not only experience fear in your thoughts—you sweat, your heart pounds, your stomach turns and your muscles tense. Fear, hate, love, loneliness—virtually any emotional state can and does cause biochemical changes in your body. The critical factor is whether the emotion is positive or negative.

Technically, a stress response is a physiological event during which your bodily chemistry and reactions change in response to your environment. So really any emotion constitutes some kind of stress. But the intensity of any stress or emotional reaction is created by how we personally and uniquely perceive what happens to and around us as well as by our individual biochemistry.

Two young American women, along with two Indonesian boatmen, were lost on a small boat in the South Seas for twenty-one days. When they were rescued, the women only needed a good meal and a full night's sleep to recover, while the men were treated for shock and dehydration. What made the difference? The men had been convinced they were going to die, and lived in a state of panic for most of the time at sea. The women were certain of their eventual rescue. Fear changed the men's chemistry and, in essence, poisoned their systems with stress chemicals.

Even though it has been researched intensively, the biochemical stress reaction is too complex yet to be fully understood. We do know there is no "single" stress hormone, but that, in stressful situations, our body temporarily produces more of certain chemicals. Three of the most important are epinephrine, norepinephrine and cortisol.

Epinephrine (adrenaline), the "fight or flight" hormone, accounts for the feeling you get following a near accident in your car, sounds of trespassers in your backyard at night, and so on. It is secreted by your adrenal glands. Your body requires a certain optimum release of adrenaline for best functioning; either too much or too little will interfere with your mental and physical performance. Any arousal by either pleasant or unpleasant stimulation will increase your adrenaline levels as compared to a neutral non-arousing condition.

Norepinephrine is one of the powerful mood determining neurotransmitters we've already discussed. It also functions as a hormone in some body reactions. When it acts as a neurotransmitter, it is secreted by certain brain cells in the area where it exerts its action, and when it functions as a hormone, it is secreted by the adrenal glands.

When you experience chronic stress, your body is constantly creating and utilizing extra amounts of norepinephrine. And when there are not enough precursors available for this continuous replacement, depletion with subsequent low moods or depression can follow.

Besides affecting norepinephrine levels, stress has been found to deplete your brain levels of tryptophan directly, by changing how tryptophan binds to a substance called albumin, which carries tryptophan into your brain.

Cortisol (cortisone) is a multifunctioning hormone also secreted by your adrenal glands. Among other things, it increases the excitation of your brain and causes the release of other body hormones. The chronic excess cortisol produced by sustained stress will increase the amount of tryptophan used by your body. This makes less available for the creation of serotonin in your brain and can indirectly lead to the biochemical disturbance of mood disorders.

NOREPINEPHRINE VERSUS EPINEPHRINE

Under normal, nonstress conditions norepinephrine production is four to five times greater than epinephrine (adrenaline) production. In other words, they exist in an approximate four to one ratio.

Your body's ability to produce norepinephrine increases with physical fitness. Physically fit people also release less norepinephrine per workload, but can attain overall much higher levels during increased exercise than can those who are sedentary. This supports the obvious: a fit person responds better physiologically to stress than an unfit person does.

Some research indicates that physical work or exercise causes a 200 percent increase in norepinephrine and a 50 percent increase in adrenaline. This is one reason physical activity can elevate your mood. Conversely, psychological stress causes only a 50 percent increase in norepinephrine but a 100 percent increase in adrenaline. Thus psychological stress reverses the usual normal ratio from four to one to one to two and upsets the normal balance of these substances.

Perhaps norepinephrine is more important to daily bodily processes than is epinephrine, because it exists in greater supply under normal nonstress conditions and because it is conserved by our bodies—unlike adrenaline, which is entirely metabolized and excreted in the urine.

Research has shown that the better you secrete norepinephrine and adrenaline in response to acute threat or challenge, the greater is your well-being and performance efficiency—up to a point. If you are regularly stressed and secreting these chemicals on an ongoing basis, you will have more sickness and earlier death. Also, animal studies have shown increases of norepinephrine release following acute stress and an ensuing depletion of stores after chronic stress. It is as if intermittent stress is okay, even desirable—but continuous stress can spell disaster. If you are going through a period of consistent stress in your life, but are not depressed, using the basic vitamins and minerals mentioned in Chapter 5 and a balanced amino acid preparation can help protect you from some of the physical and psychological consequences of that stress.

CONTROL VERSUS HELPLESSNESS

Even if you are exposed to chronic adverse events, you will have less adrenaline response to them when you feel "in control."

The damaging chronic adrenaline responses occur when you are feeling helpless and not in control.

If I'm moving to a different house because I love it and have chosen to live there, it's very different from moving to a different house because my husband has left me, the bank has foreclosed on the mortgage and I am unable to think of any other resources. But even in this situation it's important for me to exercise my choices and to get help in creatively recognizing all my positive alternatives, if I'm unable to think of them on my own—in other words, to take some control of the situation.

Compared to those who never get depressed, the person prone to depression is more inclined to emotional passivity and to not taking control, even when not depressed. This behavior can be extremely hazardous to your health. In recent research it was found that those who felt helpless showed little or none of the normal expected changes in brain norepinephrine and adrenaline when they were challenged with a difficult situation. They were probably already chemically depleted and depressed in the first place. We've seen that when rats are put in a situation where they are helpless, their brain norepinephrine will eventually decrease. But first the levels elevate as the rats attempt to escape and to cope. On the other hand, if the brain norepinephrine is artificially depleted in rats first, they display totally helpless behavior from the onset of their stress.

Psychotherapy and psychological methods can help teach you how to assume control over your life, even if you have been surrounded by those who behave helplessly. Helplessness is learned, and so, too, can a sense of control be learned. Take the attitude that something can always actively be done to take control. Certainly you do not have to be in control of all areas of your life—but the overall balance must tip in that direction for you to avoid the biochemical changes caused by chronic helplessness.

PROTEST VERSUS DESPAIR

Along with control or helplessness go the concepts of protest and despair. Protesting isn't complaining but taking control. Despair is the opposite, a passive submission. When baby monkeys are separated from their mothers but still able to see them, they fuss and vocally protest but their body chemistry shows no stress changes. When they are separated from and unable to see their mothers, they seem to despair, are very quiet and show high biological stress responses in their bodies.

I am certainly not urging all of you to go around being cranky and demanding, but studies have indicated that more outspoken, demanding people have tendencies toward longer life spans than passive, dependent types. Those with cancer and other life-threatening illnesses tend to have a better prognosis when they are vocal in and actively participate in the decision-making processes rather than being swept along by the medical machine.

A person who is willing to take some control is usually open to changes. The helpless person, of course, feels change is impossible. If you work to positively change your attitudes, behavior or life in any way great or small, it is well worth your time. The more you know about health and about maximizing your life potentials, the more you are able to implement what is necessary for you. The more you know about yourself and your illness—the more control you have. This mobilizes healing forces.

If you are physically or mentally suffering, you are usually bound to that plane of existence. Taking care of your body and mind machine on the physical plane provides the foundation or launching pad for movement into other spiritual and psychological realms.

Psychological Stressors

This chapter will deal with the psychological aspects of depression. When we use the word "psychological" we are really referring to how you think and how you react emotionally and physiologically to your thoughts.

Some people refuse to consider psychological contributions to illness, others attribute everything to those causes. Either extreme makes understanding impossible. For example, when a highly intelligent forty-year-old woman came for treatment, she told me she had the following symptoms: "I'm rigid and controlling. I can't make any commitments. I avoid all relationships. And I have a lot of trouble getting out of bed in the morning." Testing revealed she suffered from severe depression.

When I explained the biochemical nature and treatment of depression, I could see she didn't buy it at all. She was convinced her problems were purely "psychological," even though her brother had committed suicide, and three other brothers, one uncle and her maternal great-grandfather were alcoholic. This strong family history of depressive symptoms and alcoholism highlighted her own genetic vulnerability, yet despite the evidence and her intelligence she wanted to approach her problems *only* psychologically. Months later, when her symptoms persisted, she finally agreed to combine biochemical nutrient treatment with our psychotherapeutic efforts. Within a few weeks she felt considerably better.

Before psychiatry understood the biochemical causes and changes in depression, the origin of depression was believed to be purely psychological. Some of the numerous psychological theories developed do have some validity, but by no means do they provide all the answers. Psychological factors are only one of numerous variables contributing to mood disturbance. Otherwise, we would expect each person faced with a major loss to become depressed, and this is not the case at all.

Our mental state—everything from general outlook to how we react to everyday stress—can aggravate the development of low moods and depression in those who are vulnerable. But the actual link between psychological reactions and mood changes has not been as distinctly clarified as has the link between biochemistry and mood changes. The only clear psychological link is how we perceive, think and react to stressful events, especially loss.

An article in the June 1986 issue of *Clinical Psychiatry News* proposed a link between psychology and biochemistry. Dr. Paul C. Mohl was quoted as having told the American Psychiatric Association, "Psychotherapy is a biologic treatment that acts through biologic mechanisms on biologic problems," and also, "Medication, dream interpretations and empathy simply become different ways to alter different neurotransmitters, presumably in different parts of the brain."

An effective psychotherapeutic experience may indeed gradually alter brain neurotransmitters, but doesn't it make sense to facilitate the process by directly raising the neurotransmitter concentrations? Psychotherapy can be used simultaneously to provide support, to learn self-care, and to change ingrained negative patterns that otherwise continue to create stress and imbalance.

THEORIES EXPLAINING DEPRESSION

The psychological theories explaining depression actually sound like a partial description of some of the symptoms of depression. This raises the classic chicken/egg question, because those with a *proven biochemical* depression can display the same psychological picture *after* the onset of the depression that others claim was there and caused the depression in the first place. It usually isn't as critical to know which comes first as it is to know they feed into each other. After all, we are complex organisms with all parts interacting and with circular feedback mechanisms operating throughout our bodies.

I have always been struck by how the various psychological

schools seem to use different words to express the same basic phenomena. The psychoanalytic approach describes abnormal grief reaction to loss, individuals with low self-esteem and unrealistic expectations of themselves, and negative feelings about life, the future and the self. Behaviorists believe that people learn helplessness, low energy, dependence and fear of new experiences. Such people are insecure and hypersensitive and have the habit of "learned" negative thinking. Those who take an existentialist view feel that for depressed people there is a *loss* of meaning in living, often accompanied by a sense of nihilism.

Most of these approaches are connected to loss of one kind or another, but since we all experience loss, the important question is: What makes some people more reactive than others to a real loss? And why are some people depressed who have not sustained a real loss at all? We can only conclude that other factors are operating: an inherited biochemical proclivity, nutrient deficiencies, the level of general physical and emotional health, and the amount of support from family and friends.

The same person with the same set of stresses can one day feel well and reasonably happy and a few days later, under the same circumstances, feel down and miserable. The difference has to be caused from a change inside, not outside—a biochemical shift that decreases the communication between the brain cells in the "reward" centers and increases the communication in the "punishment" centers.

The behaviorist approach appeals most to me, professionally, because it holds that we learn or adopt psychological states from others. And once we learn helpless, negative or loss oriented ways of interpreting life we do experience far more stress. But what makes it easier for some people to learn negativity? Are they biologically prone to depression? Why will one child imitate the negative depressive behavior of a parent while two other children in the same family will not? Can all the difference be only psychological? Very unlikely.

LACK OF SOCIAL SUPPORT

The intensity of our stress reactions to upsetting events is powerfully affected by the support we get from other people. Our biochemistry determines whether we'll feel high or low, but life patterns that increase stress will enhance whatever predispositions to depression we may have. By the same token, certain conditions will help us handle the stress and its accompanying biochemical changes much better. If, for example, you have several close loving friends and a supportive family, you are going to be able to handle the death of your spouse far better than if you lead an isolated life. Older depressed people whose family and friends have died and who are isolated by their age are at greater risk for death than those who have loving connections with other people—or even with pets. Studies of the elderly have indicated that good social support systems lower cholesterol and uric acid levels and improve immune function—regardless of the degree of psychological stress. This support, obviously, also helps stave off low moods and depression.

My own Granny lost all of her brothers and sisters and then lost her husband of "fifty-nine years, nine months and five days." She grieved severely and one week later was literally floored when she fell and broke her hip and arm. She recovered until her only son died four years later. Again, in her grief, she fell and broke her thigh. She insisted on returning home to live independently, but was very lonely and didn't know what to do with herself.

Though it seems difficult to believe, when we brought her a dog who needed her love, she was brought back to life. With an artificial steel hip and a steel rod through her leg, she manages to drive around in her 1962 "stick shift" Studebaker and seems younger now at eighty-four than she seemed in the previous seven years.

NEGATIVE ENVIRONMENT

All the influences affecting you at any given moment contribute to your mood by altering your chemistry. Unless you are selective about your environment, much of the input can be stressful. Many people tolerate negative input because they have become desensitized. They've "thickened their skin," so to speak. Sometimes we notice this when we've gotten "away-from-it-all" on vacation and have then felt absolutely bombarded upon returning to our regular daily existence—which we tolerated before.

Some people are highly attuned to the most minute shifts in their surroundings and can adjust the situation when they feel they are responding adversely. Others, who are unaware of all the compounding influences, only experience the end state of a terrible mood and jangled nerves.

HABITUAL NEGATIVE THOUGHT

If you have been depressed for a long time or if you are constantly exposed to someone who is fearful and depressed, you can get into the "habit" of pessimistic negative thinking. This is especially true for children, who are more likely to imitate those around them.

I had one patient who suffered from chronic depression and was also a habitual complainer and fault finder. He'd managed to channel those characteristics into a very successful business but he certainly wasn't happy. We adjusted his nutrients at each monthly appointment, but he continued to complain until his sixth-month visit, when I finally asked him whether the program had helped him at all.

He answered, "Oh, the difference is like night and day! I wouldn't keep coming if it hadn't helped."

This patient, who came from a family with a negative life view, was superstitious and fearful about allowing himself to feel good. This kind of attitude can create depressive character and predispose to depressive illness.

The fact is that research evidence shows that thoughts and emotions influence neurotransmitter production. They absolutely affect the body's secretions, excretions, metabolism, hormones and immune function. Habitual stressful, worrisome thoughts eventually alter the chemistry of the brain and the body to produce physical and psychological symptoms. If you worry about being bitten by a snake, your body's mechanisms will respond accordingly. If your fantasies shift to happy or sexy thoughts, your body responds much more healthily.

An experiment I'd like to conduct is to take baseline measurements of the brain chemicals in a sample of people and then divide the group so that half would be given affirmations and positive thoughts and the other half would focus on all the things that were wrong in their lives. I'll bet that if the brain chemistry was to be reassessed at the end of the study, you would see some startling changes.

In my practice I have found that in order to extricate yourself from the habit of negativity, you must combine chemical and psychological intervention.

For the same reasons, you need to pay attention to the things in the environment that affect you negatively. That does not mean that you have to avoid responsibilities or put your head in the sand. However, a constant diet of murder movies or demoralizing television programs is bound to have an influence on the mechanisms we've been discussing. Taking the responsibility for your own well-being does involve paying attention to what irritates and agitates you and to what calms and elevates you. Restructuring your life toward those positive influences will have valuable physical and biochemical results.

PAST FOCUS

Closely related to this is what I see as the futility of rerunning in your mind, over and over again, past traumas and bad experiences. Rethinking and reliving such life events re-creates and perpetuates the biochemical stress responses in our bodies. If you can't voluntarily release these fixations on the past, you may need professional and spiritual guidance. To end our stress responses to the bad events of our life, we need to let go of what happened or else we will be stuck with the destructive pattern of reliving the past.

ANGER AND GUILT

The guilty person shoulders all the blame—and the power—for the events of daily life and is angry at herself for not measuring up. The angry person feels himself a victim of life's events and is angry with others for putting him in that position. Both these attitudes have biochemical results that seriously affect mood. It's important to release that anger, not necessarily by expressing it but by acknowledging it and then letting it go. Where possible, avoid anger-inducing people and encounters. If you can't, do everything you can to avoid a feeling of helplessness by finding outside supports and fulfillment. In these circumstances, it is particularly important to make sure that the nutrient program is very carefully followed, so as to counteract some of the deleterious effects of the stress of being with difficult people or in situations that add to the burdens of your life.

RESISTANCE TO CHANGE

Accepting, even welcoming, change is another way to avoid physical and psychological stress. Even when such changes seem traumatic, it's important to try to steer the change in positive directions so as to exert whatever control you can over your life at stressful times.

People in low moods seem stuck in a rut. They feel that there is no way out of their current problems or their feelings of depression. Resisting change is, for them, a way of prolonging their illness. Major healing is preceded by a willingness to make necessary changes. Try to list the things that you wish were different and use that list as a guide for growth.

Psychological patterns such as these are common in depressed people. Obviously, you should avoid them if you want to keep yourself out of depression. Nevertheless, the person with normal brain biochemistry will not be mired in these psychological or social difficulties—no matter what. Our behavior and our feelings are clearly contingent upon our brain functions. We have fluctuating brain chemistry that is subject to all sorts of impinging variables. In order to be able to control and direct our thoughts and our lives, it's important that this chemistry be balanced.

Part III

SPECIAL ATTENTION FOR SPECIAL PEOPLE

Time is a great teacher.
Who can live without hope?
In the darkness with a great
bundle of grief the
people march.

—Carl Sandburg,
"The People Will Live On"

Depression is most often overlooked in people under twenty and over sixty-five years old, though it seems obvious that your eight-year-old son and your seventy-year-old mother can become depressed from the hazards we've examined. Both the young and the elderly have so many crises, losses and health changes that we become diverted and miss the depression that may underlie their other problems.

The truth is that in our country depression is a national hazard of youth and old age. Once we learn to recognize its symptoms, this safe, nutritional program works for these people as it does for others.

The Young: Special Attention for Special People

It is hard to accept that young children, sweet, sheltered newcomers to life, are victims of mood disorder. After all, isn't childhood supposed to be a time of innocence and bliss?

Depression in childhood has also been difficult for psychiatrists to accept. When a few daring doctors first documented cases of depressed children forty-five years ago, their observations were promptly rejected. And as late as the 1960's, many psychoanalysts adamantly stated that depression did not and could not exist in children because they believed there must be a certain level of cognitive and emotional development before an individual can experience depression. It seems to me that one might as well say that a person must be full grown before she can sustain a physical injury. Children do not need a fully developed conscience to feel badly about themselves and life. All they need is the kind of disturbed chemistry which gives a "negative set" to perceptions and experiences.

Since the 1970's, psychiatrists have been specifically measuring, clarifying and defining depression in children and adolescents. Denial is—or should be—impossible by now, but since actual depression remains difficult to define, children's "low moods" may be barely noticed, though they can take a devastating toll by interfering with emotional, intellectual and social development.

HOW CAN YOU KNOW A CHILD IS DEPRESSED?

The symptoms in youth may be the same as the ones listed for adult depression in Chapter 2, or they may be masked.

Just as hidden depression in adults often shows itself in physical symptoms, so, too, will the young have their own masks for depression, usually a behavior problem of some sort. Fifteen to twenty-five percent of children treated for behavior disorders are discovered to be depressed. The behavior may range from irritability and hyperactivity to listlessness and underactivity.

Sleep brain wave studies done on certain hyperactive children reveal a subgroup with an abnormal brain wave pattern similar to that in depressed adults.

Other behavioral symptoms of depression in children can include:

Social withdrawal
   Learning difficulties, especially when there is a decline from
      previous functioning
   School phobia
   Anxiety upon separation from the parents
   General anxiety
   Habitual misbehavior
   Excessive dependency
   Chronic anger
   Excess reactivity to loss
   Eating disorders, either overeating, or anorexia

Obviously, any one of these behavior patterns can arise from other causes. A child with learning difficulties may have poor eyesight; a child who refuses to go to school may be right— perhaps the school is awful; there may also be other physical or psycho-social causes for these symptoms. But a child with problems of this type should be evaluated for depression. If you ask a child if she is sad and she says "no," this does not totally rule out depression. Other questions, such as the following, can yield additional useful information:

1. How much do you like yourself?
2. Do you feel things work out for you?
3. Do you have fun very often?
4. Do you think or worry about bad things happening to you?
5. Do you do most things okay or do you do a lot that is wrong?
6. How often do you feel like crying?
7. Do you like being with people?

8. Are you able to make up your mind about things pretty easily?
9. Do you like how you look?
10. Do you have to push yourself to do your school work?
11. Do you have any trouble sleeping?
12. Are you tired a lot?
13. Do you many times feel alone?
14. Do you have plenty of friends?
15. Do you get along with people?
16. Does somebody love you?
17. Do you worry about aches and pains?
18. Do you sometimes wish you were dead?

Of course such questions should not be fired at children in a rat-a-tat-tat fashion, but can be casually brought up over a period of time.

These are adapted from some of the questions in a special scale for measuring depression in children, the Child Depression Inventory, developed by doctors Aaron Beck and Maria Kovacs. It is used in eight- to thirteen-year-old children, and your physician can obtain this scale on request, sending $2.50 to:

Maria Kovacs, Ph.D.
Associate Professor of Psychiatry
Western Psychiatric Institute and Clinic
3811 O'Hara Street
Pittsburgh, PA 15213

If you suspect your child is depressed, seek professional help before implementing the nutrient program.

WHICH CHILDREN BECOME DEPRESSED?

If you are reading this book because you are depressed or have recurrent low moods, the odds of your child having the same problem are increased. If your low moods have been overt, obvious and long-term, your child may not only be affected genetically, but by association as well. This is certainly nothing to feel guilty about, but it will help you to work with the situation if you are aware of it.

Yet, even with no family history, one in every four children needing outpatient psychiatric care is depressed. More and more, it seems to me that nutrition is involved. Prenatal nourishment is the child's "preparation," a balanced nutritional arsenal against all kinds of disorders, including depression. Once born, the child needs to be guided to good nutrition and away from the common addiction to sugar fostered by sweetened infant formulas, Twinkies, sodas and sweetened cereals.

WHAT HAVE WE DISCOVERED ABOUT DEPRESSED YOUTH?

Dr. Kim Puig-Antich and other investigators have presented research indicating that the biological abnormalities in depressed children are similar to those in depressed adults. There are changes in sleep brain wave measures, brain amines, nervous system and hormonal function, brain cell receptor function and other biochemical alterations. All of this suggests that if the causes are the same, the treatment should also be the same.

Prompt treatment is urgently important because, when depression manifests at an early age, it is more likely to be a severe, recurring or even chronic variety.

SUICIDE IN CHILDREN

Younger and younger children are killing themselves—some of them as young as five. They overdose on household pills or poisons, jump from high places, run in front of cars, cut themselves with razor blades and bang their heads against walls. Fortunately they aren't very good at it. There are a great many unsuccessful attempts for every self-inflicted death.

Prior to my fellowship in child psychiatry at UCLA, I had not been exposed to such children, and it was a shock to me when I was assigned a seven-year-old girl who had tried to kill herself by jumping out of a second-story window. She verbalized clear and explicit wishes to die.

Depression can be horrendous enough for mature functional people with developed coping mechanisms. The immature child has to deal with the same oppression and despair, but with far less understanding, less power to cope and a lot less information about possible treatment and relief.

DEPRESSION IN TEENAGERS

"I'm irritated by the sounds of people eating and by loud noises. Little things can send me off into very black moods. Most of the time I feel totally drained and exhausted. This is interspersed with violent anger and destructive rage. I feel 'spaced,' not human, a machine wrapped in gray glass and filled with helium. I have no ambition. I'm very confused."

Sometimes depression in teenagers is clearly articulated, as it was in the sixteen-year-old who told me this story. She was brilliant and wanted to get herself together before starting college in two months. When we talked, I learned that she'd developed a craving for sugar and bread, and had been eating a lot of junk food.

The day after our first meeting Anne started her daily program: L-tyrosine, 3200 mg in the morning, a multivitamin mineral, vitamin B complex 200 mg, 2000 mg of vitamin C, an extra 400 mg of vitamin B_1, 2000 mcg of sublingual vitamin B_{12}, and 150 mg of vitamin B_{15}. She also totally eliminated all sugar and bread.

When I saw her again, six weeks later, there had been a dramatic change. She told me she had no complaints and described her ambition: "To learn and to have fun, to write wild books and play good music; to be outrageous, infamous, and a legend in my own time"—and she may well be.

Her mother, a psychotherapist, said her daughter had improved "one hundred percent. She's totally different. Her moods are so even and she's not emotionally reacting to everything. She's so reasonable and a pleasure to be with."

Though the existence of depression in adolescence has long been acknowledged, the diagnoses of specific cases are often missed. As with children, the symptoms vary widely with the individual. To be safe, any teenager with emotional or behavior problems should be evaluated for depression. The Carroll Test in Chapter 2 is also useful with this age group.

Some teenagers draw attention to themselves by being difficult to manage. Acting-out behavior such as rebellious or antisocial acts, truancy, and alcohol and drug abuse may be the primary signs of adolescent depression. Parents may get caught up in a power struggle with these teenagers and fail to look further for the cause of their misbehavior.

Thirteen-year-old Vance was referred to me because he was about to be rejected from the community group home where he was living. He had been shuffled from home to home because of his extreme restlessness, his agitated provocative behavior and insomnia accompanied by a night-time hyperactivity that totally disrupted everyone in the home. The foster parents were irritated and exhausted, and on the verge of sending Vance to yet another placement. He was intellectually gifted but doing poorly in school and refusing to attend. The strong tranquilizers he had been previously treated with had done nothing but create unpleasant side effects.

During our first interview Vance was very chatty, smiling, and making wisecracks. One would never guess he was depressed— and no one had. When I found out his mother died from an "accidental" barbiturate overdose when he was two years old, I decided to test him for depression. His score revealed severe depression.

He was treated for this and became a different person. He slept well and was no longer disruptive. He went to school, finished his finals and was allowed to continue living at the group home.

Teenage depression can be obscure or combined with all sorts of diversionary actions, but it can also be blatant. I asked a seventeen-year-old boy why he came to see me. He said, "For my depression." I asked, "How long have you been depressed?" And he answered, "Since I was nine years old." Then he proceeded to tell me about his multiple suicide attempts through the years, twice by hanging, several times by overdose, once by wrist slashing. He recounted the details of his hanging attempts—how once the rope had slipped, saving him, how the next time it hurt his neck so much he scrambled back onto the chair from which he had jumped with his neck in a noose.

Two years before seeing me, he had started receiving various psychotherapies and was continuing with this. Occasionally someone would mention antidepressant medication, but no one followed through. As soon as we pursued a biochemical treatment plan, his symptoms cleared and he has continued to do well.

SUICIDE IN ADOLESCENTS

Steel yourself for this: the suicide rate in fifteen- to nineteen-year-olds has doubled in the past twenty years, to become the third leading cause of death in that age group. We read about it in the newspapers, we see television dramas featuring the true stories of such self-inflicted deaths. And still, we resist the idea of profound depression in our young people!

We have been trying to understand why this is happening. All kinds of reasons are proposed: the violence in America, lack of affection in families, family mobility, rootlessness and social disintegration, parental absence and media exposure. Certainly all of these may contribute to the final disregard for life and loss of connectedness in the one who suicides. But the bottom line is still depression. The nondepressed youth will see light at the end of a temporary dark tunnel, while the depressed one sees endless darkness.

Depression is the core activator of suicide, and where suicide is increasing, depression must also be increasing. And could it be that the escalating alcohol abuse, drug abuse and junk food excesses help to produce this condition? Absolutely. All of these tilt the brain's chemistry in the wrong direction.

If you add to these substances poor coping abilities and decreasing social and family support systems, you have a dangerous mix. Romeo and Juliet killed themselves in frustration. Their situation and deaths were entirely romanticized. So it is with many of the sufferings of adolescents. Their suggestibility can lead them to follow suit even in fatal acts. Adolescent suicide is "contagious." It often occurs in clusters where one such act will trigger several more suicides in friends and siblings.

The media adds to this contagion, as do other manufactured elements in the adolescents' environment. Lyrics in punk and heavy-metal music propound nihilism, disillusionment, despondency and anger. Rock groups like the one named "Suicidal Tendencies" don't help the situation, when they sing about mutilated bodies, mass starvation and contaminated water, and then contemplate solving the issue of a threatening future by suicide.

Death is glamorized and presented as a desirable alternative to life. And some surveys show that about 55 percent of college students have considered suicide specifically enough to have decided how they would do it.

Approximately six thousand documented adolescent suicides occurred in the United States in 1984. Professionals who specialize in this area say the real number is closer to twenty-five thousand. But even the six thousand number indicates that every hour and a half a young person somewhere in the United States is choosing and creating his own death.

TREATMENT CONSIDERATIONS

Even though we are beginning to recognize depression in children and adolescents, we are not yet adequately treating them. In fact, the treatment of childhood depression has received little research attention of any kind.

Just as there is limited experience in treating children with the standard antidepressant medications, the same limitations apply with the nutrient treatment detailed in this book. Barring any contraindications, it does seem reasonable and preferable, to use this program rather than medication, following the adjustments and modifications listed for the young.

The treatment for children should begin at one quarter the listed vitamin, mineral and amino acid dosages for adults. The vitamin E in the multivitamin mineral should not exceed thirty IU daily. All prepubertal children should be placed on a full spectrum free from amino acid supplement if they are taking separate amino acids. The dosage is one to two capsules with meals, two to three times daily. Children should not be placed on the amino acids without evaluation and monitoring by a physician, preferably with pretreatment blood and urine amino acid analysis by chromatography.

There is far more antidepressant drug experience with adolescents and also more experience with the nutritional program. Past puberty, the nutritional treatment can be the same as for adults, as listed in Chapter 4.

All of the other sections in the book relating to conditions predisposing to nutrient deficiencies, effects of food allergies, illnesses and unhealthy habits would apply to children and adolescents, as well as to adults.

The Old: Special Attention for Special People

In our country there are about thirty million people over sixty-five, and the number of the elderly increases yearly. Though they comprise 10 percent of our population, old people commit 25 percent of all suicides. A North Carolina study indicated that 14.7 percent of a cross section of the elderly suffered from some form of depressive illness. If we add the number of people with low moods to those with depressive illness, I wouldn't be surprised if 40 to 50 percent of those over sixty-five are feeling "down" at this moment.

Depression is the most widespread and expensive psychiatric illness, and the cost is multiplied in the elderly, whose depression tends to be more chronic, more severe and treatment-resistant.

The tone I'd like to strike is one of *preparation,* because many instances of low mood and depression can be modulated or even avoided if the person begins to prepare psychologically and physically in advance for the possible unpleasant changes that can accompany old age.

REASONS FOR INCREASED DEPRESSION

One half of the depressed elderly experience their *first* episode after sixty, because older age is a stressful, vulnerable time emotionally and physically. The aging brain becomes increasingly sensitive to nutritional and other biochemical changes in the body, and the elderly have up to a 52 percent reduction in neurotransmitters. They also have generally lower blood protein levels and a decreased capacity for binding and utilizing protein. This affects the amino acid levels and contributes to the neurotransmitter shortage. There are innumerable internal physical changes, such as a 25 to 40 percent drop in the production of thyroid, a drop in growth hormones and a 50 percent drop in adrenal function. There is also a drop in the hormones handling glucose, so that older people have greater problems with diabetes, hypoglycemia, general glucose intolerance and disturbed brain functioning.

There are some conditions in older people that predispose them to the brain chemical changes leading to depression. Nutritional deficiencies are among the most important. Poor eating habits, poor food digestion and absorption, mouth and tooth problems—all lead to the kind of imbalance we've noted in people with low moods and low energy. Older people also have more physical illnesses, which can precipitate an associated depression. They use more medicines that can cause depression as a side effect. The amount of the brain enzyme called monoamine oxidase (MAO) increases and tends to destroy the "good mood" chemicals.

For various reasons, stress and its concomitant physiological changes may also increase as we get older. Our friends and loved ones die. We lose our support systems. We may get less exercise —both of the physical and the mental variety.

But depression in the older person is probably more nutritionally connected than for any other age group except, perhaps, adolescence. Many scientific studies have shown the nutritional deficiencies in this age group. The risk is highest in those who live alone, although it often occurs among those living in institutions and receiving a so-called balanced and adequate diet under the supervision of a dietition. The B vitamins are especially deficient, and, of course, they are particularly implicated in depression.

As we've seen, aging decreases food absorption. For this reason it's important to take in larger than usual amounts of nutrients in order for some of them to get through. Yet older people usually eat less.

Of those over sixty-five years old in our country, 10 to 15 percent have a vitamin B_{12} deficiency, 10 to 15 percent have anemia, 15 to 20 percent have thyroid problems and 10 to 12 percent have a folic acid deficiency. All these conditions can be associated with depression.

ATTITUDE AND AGING

Though many of the declines in function that come with aging are related to nutritional deficiencies, others may be attitudinal. Both need attention. Old age becomes what you expect it to be. You gradually prepare yourself to fulfill your attitudes about aging. Whom do you choose to focus on when you take note of people older than you? Do you look at those who are limited, ill and suffering in various ways or do you pay more attention to those who are vitally alive, energetic and have an enthusiasm for life? Do you pay attention to George Burns and Bob Hope? Do you look at the lives of Picasso, Georgia O'Keefe, Joán Miró? Or do you watch with dread the stooped figures who do their lonely painful shuffle down cold, unfriendly streets? Do you think of everlasting independence or are you planning for your convalescent home? Both options are there. Whichever you focus on subtly programs your own subconscious mind to create that later in your life. You are in control.

SENILITY OR DEPRESSION?

A dreaded disease of later years is senility or what is medically called dementia. Many have a deep-seated unconscious or even conscious fear of losing their minds and it is senility, not psychosis, which can truly bring this about. However, once the mind is "lost," it's lost. The key again is preparation, attention to the *process* of getting there.

Alzheimer's disease is a devastating, untreatable, progressively relentless and finally fatal form of brain deterioration. Five percent of those over sixty-five years old have Alzheimer's, and it causes 50 percent of all true senilities. Twenty percent of those over eighty years old have some degree of Alzheimer's. There are other equally disastrous causes of senility such as arteriosclerotic brain disease, multiple blood clots in the brain with destruction of brain tissue, and various degenerative neurological diseases.

Tragically, but understandably, the demented or senile person, who can be difficult to manage, may be separated from her overwhelmed family and carted off to custodial care to vegetate, a shell of her former self. There we only provide her with sedation, food, a bath and bed—and maybe TV. But all cases of so-called senility don't have to be this disastrous. Proper treatment for depression may sometimes strikingly reverse the "senility" symptoms.

EVERY SENILE PERSON SHOULD BE EVALUATED FOR DEPRESSION

Depression often looks like senility in older people. Of those initially diagnosed as senile, approximately 15 percent turned out on later follow-up to have had depression. Even with extensive medical work-ups, the proper diagnosis for this 15 percent had been missed. An even greater number of "senile" people do not have such a thorough evaluation, so we can assume that depression is missed more than 15 percent of the time. Even more problematic and complicated is the fact that 25 to 30 percent of the truly senile also have a superimposed depression which makes their mental deficits seem much worse than they are. In my opinion, there is nothing to lose and possibly a restored mind to gain by treating a senility of unknown origin with antidepressant nutrients according to the recommendations on page 45.

When depression looks like dementia, there can be profound memory loss and intellectual deterioration, a short attention span, changed speech, a sloppy, disheveled appearance and even incontinence.

I once hospitalized a seventy-year-old woman who barely knew her name. She didn't know where she was or the date. She didn't know the name of the president of the United States or what she had eaten for her last meal. She felt her mind was a blank and complained, "I can't remember what any of my relatives look like." She said, "I give up, I surrender, there's no hope, I'm vile, destructive, evil, ruining everyone around me. And the other patients are playing out a scenario against me." She was in anguish, suffering from imaginary guilt for having killed someone. She was exceedingly agitated, wringing her hands and repeating these imagined wrongdoings, over and over.

We put her on an antidepression nutrient program, and this

patient was transformed into a charming, very intelligent, interesting, informed person, with no signs of her previous disordered condition.

TREATMENT CONSIDERATIONS

Treating the older senile or depressed person is much harder than it sounds, harder than for any other group. The elderly metabolize drugs differently and are more prone to side effects. Some of the usual antidepressant medications can complicate certain medical conditions, especially heart disease and heart rhythm problems, an enlarged prostate gland, glaucoma and constipation. Other, safer drugs may have to be used in selected severe cases.

Even with nutrients the situation is more complicated in older people because some patients with heart disease are on what is called beta-blocker medication. The phenylalanine and tyrosine supplements described in Chapters 4 and 5 may not mix well with that medicine, though the rest of the program would be satisfactory.

I have, however, not found this to be a problem. If you are taking medicine for your heart, ask if it is a beta-blocker. If it isn't, you should have no problems. If you are on a beta-blocker, add tyrosine to your daily nutrient plan if the vitamins and tryptophan have not worked after one month's administration. If you do use the tyrosine, start with only one capsule daily and gradually proceed upwards in dosage as needed and tolerated.

Before an older, generally ill person starts the nutritional program, other chapters should be studied to rule out specific causes of the depression such as vitamin B_{12} deficiency or medication side effects. If you are in poor health and are under the care of a physician, it would be useful for your doctor to obtain blood and urine amino acid chromatography tests to determine your amino acid needs more precisely.

In the nutritional treatment program in Chapter 4, I do suggest the elderly start with reduced dosages of some of the nutrients. You can also begin with one new supplement every two to three days and gradually add to the program.

Add the nutrient supplements in this order:

1. Multivitamin mineral
2. Vitamin B complex—some older people may need to double or triple the vitamin B complex dosage if they have many of the symptoms of B vitamin deficiencies listed on the charts on page 45.
3. Vitamin C
4. Tryptophan
5. Tyrosine
6. Mixed amino acid compound

Please see Chapters 4 and 6 for further details on the treatment program. Be sure to follow the precautions on page 42 regarding taking tryptophan if you have a history of high blood pressure. If you are over sixty-five, Chapters 7 and 10 are also very important for you. Review them all and then proceed on your way to a happier mental outlook with each passing day.

THERE IS ALWAYS HOPE

A sixty-eight-year-old patient of mine had had four major depressions in her life. During the depressions she became tearful and agitated, feeling "deadened, unreal and strange, mean and possessed by evil spirits." She was full of guilt and despair, sure that God had totally forsaken her for her imagined wrongdoings and unable to be consoled.

She was in a fulfilling forty-four-year-long marriage when I first met her. During well times, she was involved in golf, gardening, poetry, church and family activities, and she had traveled extensively. Each of her depressions was precipitated by a bout of flu and an associated course of antibiotic treatment. Each required one to two months of psychiatric hospitalization. Part of her treatment clearly involved the nutritional support of her immune system plus doing whatever could be done to avoid catching the flu. We did this and she remained physically and mentally healthy until she became so busy taking care of her sick husband that she neglected herself and stopped following the program. At that point she had a relapse, which further clarified to her the necessity of taking care of herself. She resumed the nutrient program and has continued to remain well.

Old age does not have to be a time of withdrawal, lack of interest, depression and despair. We can always learn and grow by adding new interests and activities. This is especially possible if our brain chemistry is balanced. We are getting to live more years as the life span stretches. This is wonderful when the quality of life is good; it is just marking time with a "life sentence" when you are depressed. The lucky or prepared ones with properly working brain chemicals can enjoy life up to their dying breath. I believe that is how it is meant to be.

Part IV

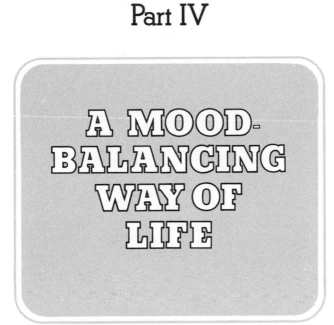

If error is corrected
whenever it is recognized
as such, the path of error
is the path of truth.

—Hans Reichenbach

Even though you follow the biochemical program, if you continue habitual negative thought patterns you will seriously undermine this treatment. Persistent negative attitudes can lead to constriction and bondage, whereas consistent positive thoughts and expectations create expansion and freedom. Someone has said we suffer because we don't see things as *they* are, but as *we* are. Our perceptions are influenced more by our inner world than by the world around us, by our expectations and our "selective focusing."

I can remember marveling at this phenomenon when I was young. For when I decided to selectively notice Chevrolets on the road, it seemed they were everywhere; when I counted the number of overweight people, I could hardly find any slender ones; or, when I drove, trying to avoid jostling my sick mother, a street which had always seemed smooth suddenly had endless bumps. It was as if Chevys, fat people and bumps in the road suddenly materialized when I decided to notice them.

Likewise, if I wake up in the morning saying, "Today is a terrible day," I will selectively seek out and focus on all that supports this position. On the other hand, if I got out of bed eager to greet the day, anticipating interesting, enjoyable experiences, I will be able to find and create them in my day—no matter what lies before me.

We can only learn to see differently by wanting to see differently. We can only unlearn errors in thought and action by replacing them with correct, mood-balancing thought and action. This section presents formulas to help you do this.

15

Improving Mental Habits and Life-styles

Before you can eliminate low moods and depression from your life, you need to decide whether you think it is possible for you. If you believe you can be helped, then you will be more willing to follow whatever path is necessary to create a harmonious and balanced life.

A good treatment will work to some degree regardless of your expectations. For instance, penicillin will attack your strep throat whether you believe in it or not. But your beliefs can facilitate a good treatment, making the healing even faster and more complete. Your beliefs can also modify and interfere with the treatment. If you feel the penicillin is poisoning you or won't help you at all—even if you take it, it may be less effective or you may develop a negative reaction to it.

Do you believe that the nutrition program will change your unhealthy patterns? Do you feel you can follow the program? Do you believe it will help you? The answers to these questions can tell you right now how much you are likely to benefit.

It's natural that the more you experience low moods, the more you expect to respond with additional low moods. The nutrient program can interfere with that cycle by changing your brain chemistry, but the treatment will work much better if you go into it really expecting results.

Even though we may feel that we will follow the program and be benefited, our subconscious expectations may conflict with our conscious desires. If you have difficulty believing you can feel good most of the time, if you have difficulty creating positive expectations for yourself, or if you are sabotaged by your subconscious beliefs, you may need to reprogram your thinking. This is important so that your thoughts do not feed depression and so that your brain biochemistry can do the maximum good work. Otherwise you will keep stressing yourself and having to restart the treatment.

HOW TO REPROGRAM YOUR CONSCIOUS MIND

To reprogram your conscious mind, you must examine and then eliminate negative thoughts about yourself, your world and your future. Stay alert and when you slip, immediately replace the idea with an opposite and positive word, thought or mental picture. Say the correcting statement out loud when possible. For instance, if you find yourself thinking, "I'm so bored, I don't know what to do," you would instead cut off the thought literally in the middle. Make your mind shout over the top of it. Say something like, "My life is full of interesting, stimulating activities." Or, if that phrase doesn't work for you, find one that does. You'll probably initially resist, because you'll say, "But what I'm saying isn't true, because I really *am* bored." That isn't the point. We tend to believe and incorporate what we think and hear over and over again, and, therefore, we must break the negative chain of thoughts by learning and practicing more constructive ones. If I have to walk five miles and I repeatedly say, "I'm so tired I can't make it," my performance and the entire experience becomes very much more difficult than if I'm saying, "I'm full of energy and vitality, this is easy for me," or simply, "I can *do* this."

Some people have specific distressing repetitive negative thoughts which they feel helpless to control. If this is so with you, begin by repeating the word "CANCEL" as soon as the first word of that thought enters your head.

Visualization is an even more powerful tool than word statements. After you think of being bored, for example, mentally see yourself engaged in a specific interesting activity: walking down a lane in a fascinating foreign city, watching people dressed in multicolored garments, watching children play, passing by a colorful marketplace—whatever is interesting to you. There are several good books that discuss this technique, one of which is called *Creative Visualization,* by Shakti Gawain.

What I and many others consider to be the most effective structured psychological treatment for depression is what is called cognitive therapy. It specifically teaches you to recognize your distorted perceptions and negative thoughts and to transform each one into its positive counterpart. Once you have developed the negative thought habit it is difficult to recognize it on your own. It may help to ask your family and friends to signal you when they see signs of its recurrence.

If you learn to think positively you change the stress response and help to improve your brain chemistry. For those with chronic depression and habitual negative perceptions, the ideal treatment may be a combination of the nutritional chemical treatment and cognitive therapy.

SUBCONSCIOUS

If you reprogram your conscious mind, some of the benefits will filter into your subconscious as well. The subconscious is the center of your physical and psychological power and controls all the organic processes of your body. When you are consciously working to change and influence it, you are ready to take charge of yourself.

Subconscious change can be achieved by using a method known as relaxation, or sleep programming. When you are in a totally relaxed state or are asleep, your critical, nonaccepting fixed attitudes and defenses are off guard and you are more open to new input. It is helpful to play tape recordings of corrective positive messages at such times, until you eventually ingrain the new patterns.

There is a list in the appendix of some tapes and books designed to help you develop the skill of thinking and perceiving positively. Generally, they instruct you to play the messages when you go to bed at night, but you can also listen to them anytime you can shut out the world and relax without interruption. If you do this when you retire at night, it doesn't matter whether you fall asleep or not, because your subconscious mind hears the suggestions anyway.

CHANGE YOUR ENVIRONMENT

External changes can also help to improve the way we feel. Be selective about your environment, and change it if necessary so as to expose yourself to uplifting, inspirational and soothing influences.

I can't understand how someone living in a dimly lit, cluttered space with the television blaring day and night, eating sweets, drinking caffeine and alcohol, and staying indoors much of the time would not become hopelessly depressed. Rearrange your life so that you receive regular doses of nature, animals, certain movies and plays, books, beautiful art, color, natural light and meditation. Consider joining groups that promote higher purposes and surround yourself with people with whom you can interact to improve your health and feed your soul. Music also has a powerful effect on the emotions. It can heal, balance and harmonize, or it can irritate, aggravate, disturb and depress you. We've all "got a right to sing the blues," but if you are already overwhelmed and struggling with low moods, make it a point to listen to cheerful, mood-balancing, happy, soothing or at least neutral music.

SELECT YOUR ACTIVITIES

Just as you're implementing the nutrient program in this book to adjust your brain chemistry, you might begin to experiment with activity planning as well. We all have experienced mood slumps associated with inactivity. Conversely, it is well known that exercise is often mood elevating. Several studies have now reported the successful treatment of hospitalized depressed persons by eight hours of daily exercise only. Exercise is believed to increase the brain endorphins and probably creates other neurotransmitter changes as well (though most of us will not be able to devote eight hours a day to it).

Not only is physical movement useful, but anything which absorbs your mind and removes it from worrying or engaging in negative thinking will have antidepressant effects. Creative learning experiences are an important part of the necessary life, mind and mood expanding behavioral repertoire. Try classes in sports, art, music or other interests to improve work-related skills. When our minds are stimulated and our brain cells are firing, the mental activity helps maintain a balanced biochemical environment in our brains. If we are participating in boring, monotonous activities our brain-cell firing slows. A used muscle remains firm and toned, while an unused muscle becomes flabby and wasted. Likewise, it is important that we keep our mental electrochemical pathways in good operating condition to keep them functioning properly.

To see how your activities are affecting your feelings, keep a journal for ten days. Write down the time and a description of all your activities. Rate them as positive, neutral, or negative, by using the following numbers: +3 is very positive, +2 is moderately positive and +1 is slightly positive, 0 is neutral, −1 is slightly negative, −2 is moderately negative and −3 is very negative. Record your moods and the times they occur, using the same numerical scale. At the end of the ten days study the two charts to see how your moods were influenced by what you did. Make it a point to increase the total time you spend in the +2 and + 3 activities and to avoid or decrease your time in the mood-disturbing circumstances as much as possible. If most of your activities are on the minus side, you may need to seek further professional guidance for restructuring your life.

BE HERE NOW

Reading *Be Here Now,* by Baba Ram Dass, several years ago, taught me to discipline myself to remain in the moment as much as possible. Before that, I was future-focused, ahead of myself into what was coming next and missing out on being fully present for what was actually happening. The best way to prepare for the future is to live fully in the present.

People who are prone to guilt or to condemnation of others are often stuck in the past, dwelling on what they did or didn't do and should have done. Those prone to anxiety tend to be caught up in fearful anticipations about the future, worrying about what will happen if something happens to their spouse, if they run out of money, if the car breaks down, and so on.

This is not to say it is never useful to reflect on the past or to make plans for the future. However, reflection and planning need to be done at specified times and then to be released so that we can enter into the moment. For this, we need the conscious use of our will to direct the functioning of our mind. The Eastern philosophies focus on and provide this mental training far more than do the Western philosophies.

Depressed people, especially, tend to focus on remembering or anticipating negative feelings and events, even changing what really happened or what might happen into something worse than the reality. They seem to savor joylessness.

A young woman came to my office complaining that she was consumed with hurt and anger and had pain in many parts of her body. This was related to an assault on her by a female coworker and the ensuing noncooperation from their employer in providing monetary damages. For several sessions she was intense and tearful as she described her trauma. It was new and fresh, invading every part of her being. I was sure it was a recent event. You can imagine my surprise when I learned that the assault had occurred five years previously and that she'd had four and a half years of psychotherapy since that time.

When we become swallowed up by our past, we are lost to ourselves and to others. Be aware of the dangers of excessive retrospection and only look to the past to search for constructive lessons and information you can use to improve your present life. When possible, use data about your past as a neutral, objective, experiential encyclopedia you consult to develop the wisdom and insight necessary to move forward positively into new experiences.

Never use the past to justify or to maintain a current negative position. Observe old negative patterns and change the way you view them. Take from life, even from pain, whatever you can learn from it. This will enable you to cope more positively with whatever is coming next. We all have pain. What differentiates the winners from the losers is how we choose to perceive and cope with our adversities and challenges.

RELEASE ANGER

Chronic anger—whether for a specific reason or for a host of ill-defined ones—hurts no one more than it hurts the one holding on to it. The path of least resistance and greatest health is to learn to forgive others, or to "forgive" a situation, in order to release such consuming feelings. We cannot possibly be angry and happy at the same time. Which will you choose? There are many books and tapes available to help with this process for those who feel stuck in anger. It is also useful to work psychologically and spiritually to move beyond the anger to a position of compassion and forgiveness. Few of us are at this level of development, but it is a liberating goal toward which to aim, and such forgiveness is really an important process by which we gain the integrity of our self.

CULTIVATE A MEANINGFUL, USEFUL, SPIRITUAL PHILOSOPHY

Spiritual faith can sometimes be a deciding factor in whether or not extreme stress tips the balance toward disease and in determining healing once the disease process has set in. By spiritual I do not necessarily mean religious, though the two ideally coincide. Spiritual development can liberate and heal you whereas some religions can bind you by promoting guilt and conflict and by perpetuating judgment and condemnation rather than compassion and forgiveness. This can engender additional suffering in some depressed people who are already prone to guilt and self-condemnation. (Perversely, these people may be drawn to such punitive orientations.)

Be flexible enough to realize when a belief system is not working for you and to search openly for a new one. The fundamental principles of all spiritual pathways are the same, but because of our human differences, a pathway useful for one may be absolutely unworkable for another.

If you have never had any particular kind of spiritual philosophy, explore whether or not you might be happier and enriched if you developed this aspect of yourself. I believe in what works to make us happier and healthier, and I believe that is what a loving God intends for us.

FIND THE LIGHT IN YOURSELF

There's a parable about an old woman who was stitching clothes in her room late one afternoon. She dropped her needle and began to look for it, but the room darkened before she could find it. The woman had to finish her sewing, so she decided to look for the needle outside, where there was more light. Why waste time searching inside where it was dark?

For many of us, happiness—like the old woman's needle—is lost inside, inside our minds and hearts. It is there that we must look to find it. If we search outside ourselves, the happiness we find is often only temporary and illusory. We visit a lovely waterfall and relax and find joy in its environment. Then we notice that there is a charming house on the nearby land and we begin to plan and scheme to buy it. We want to possess the land so that we can keep the happy feeling the waterfall has given us. Real estate agents, roof leaks, tax problems and bad plumbing are the result, and as we sit in the same spot as our first viewing we realize that our former happiness with the waterfall has vanished. We got the outside thing, but not the happiness.

The program in this book will not automatically bring you happiness. It will, however, lead you to the nutrients that are important for influencing your brain chemistry in a positive way. You have also discovered where else to look for the cause and correction of your unpleasant mood changes. This information, combined with careful detective work and follow-through with the program, can help to give you the happiness we all seek.

You now have improved tools for mind control and for becoming aware of and developing your own properties of light and love.

And remember—

> We are not here to experience
> Mental and existential bondage
> We are here to rejoice, to give and receive joy,

To see and experience the true essence
    Not superficial appearances
To perceive beauty, order, and harmony
    Not ugliness, chaos, and discord
To see color, to vibrate and flow with the rhythm
    Of time
To germinate, come to fruition, and ultimately fade
To be swallowed, then spewn into the
Next river of life, new energy, new form
Beyond our current level of reckoning
With unwavering gradual beckoning to cross
The horizon of time
Exchanging dimensions
Expanding and uniting—

                              —Bon voyage

APPENDIXES

Appendix to Chapter 2

More About Diagnosing Depression

The psychiatric diagnostic manual contains several diagnoses that relate to depression. A list of the specific criteria for each type of depression follows:

Major Depressive Episode
This occurs when the patient experiences at least four of the following symptoms for two or more weeks:

1. An appetite change with significant weight gain or loss;
2. Insomnia or excessive sleeping;
3. Physical agitation and nervousness, or slowed, dulled activity;
4. Decreased sex drive and loss of interest or pleasure in usually pleasurable activities;
5. Loss of energy, fatigue;
6. Feelings of worthlessness or self-reproach and excessive or inappropriate guilt;
7. Decreased ability to think and concentrate, or indecisiveness;
8. Recurrent thoughts of death, suicidal thoughts or suicide attempt.

This can include delusions, hallucinations or a totally mute nonresponsive condition. (Condensed from the Diagnostic and Statistical Manual for Mental Disorders, third edition, 1980, p. 121, hereinafter referred to as DSM-III.)

Major depression is recognized by psychiatry as a disorder of brain chemicals and hormone systems. Lesser depressions may be less severe examples of the same physical and biological malfunctioning. In the DSM-III lesser depressions are called dysthymic disorder, atypical depression, or adjustment disorder with depression. They include various combinations of the symptoms listed for major depression.

Dysthymic Disorder

This is a common diagnosis. An adult must have been bothered by depression for at least two years, one year for children. The intensity and severity of symptoms are less than in major depression. The symptoms do not necessarily persist daily and may be separated by periods of normal mood lasting a few days to a few months. During the depressive periods, patients suffer from either low mood or a marked loss of interest in usual activities. At least three of the following symptoms must be present:

1. Insomnia or excessive sleeping;
2. Low energy or chronic exhaustion;
3. Feelings of inadequacy, low self-esteem or self-deprecation;
4. Decreased productivity at school, work, home;
5. Decreased attention, concentration or ability to think clearly;
6. Social withdrawal;
7. Loss of interest in pleasurable activities;
8. Irritability or excessive anger;
9. Inability to respond with pleasure to praise or rewards;
10. Less active or talkative than usual, or feeling slowed down or restless;
11. Pessimistic attitude toward the future, brooding about past, self-pity;
12. Crying;
13. Recurring thoughts of death or suicide.
    (DSM-III, pp. 128–29)

Adjustment Disorder with Depressive Mood

This is a situational depression triggered by psychological stress from such life events as divorce or a job loss, or by physical illness. It usually occurs within three months of the beginning of the stress and its symptoms do not meet many of the criteria of the other forms of depression. The main expressions of the reaction are depressed mood, tearfulness, and feelings of hopelessness. The patient's work and social functioning are often impaired.

Bipolar Disorder (Manic-depressive)

Manic-depressive illness is now called bipolar disorder in the DSM-III. The patient has symptoms of depression that alternate with periods of elevated, expansive or irritable moods.

This manic phase is characterized by at least three of the following symptoms for one or more weeks:

1. Increased restlessness and activity;
2. Increased wordiness, feeling pressure to keep talking;

3. Racing thoughts, mind quickly moving from one idea to another;
4. Inflated self-esteem (may seem "reasonable" or may be delusions of power or influence such as being someone like Jesus or Napoleon;
5. Decreased need for sleep;
6. Easily distracted attention—often to unimportant stimuli;
7. Excessively and impulsively engage in destructive activities like buying sprees, excessive gambling, unwise investments, reckless driving. (DSM-III, pp. 117–18)

Cyclothymic Disorder

This is a milder form of bipolar disorder. The mood swings exist but are not as severe. *Mood Swings* by Ronald Fieve, M.D., is extremely useful in understanding this and bipolar disorder.

Organic Affective Syndrome

The predominant symptom is disturbance in mood, plus at least two of the associated symptoms listed for major depression or for manic disorder. There is no significant loss of intellectual functioning and no evidence of hallucinations or delusions.

It is called "organic" because evidence from the history, physical exam or laboratory tests indicate that a specific organic or physical factor causes the disturbance, such as depression caused by a vitamin B_{12} deficiency, or by hypothyroidism.

Appendix to
Chapter 4

PRODUCT SOURCES FOR HIGH QUALITY SUPPLEMENTS

I can only comment on the amino acid and vitamin manufacturers whose
products I have used in my practice.

Tyson & Associates
  1661 Lincoln
  Suite 300
  Santa Monica, CA 90404
  1-800-367-7744
  in CA (213) 452-7844

A leader in researching the medical and psychiatric applications of
amino acids, this company provides the full range of pharmaceutical
grade amino acids as well as select vitamin-mineral formulations. They
are one of the few companies to provide enteric coated pyridoxal-5-
phosphate (the active form of vitamin B_6).

These products are sold nationwide in pharmacies and health food
stores under the label Integrated Health, or your doctor can order their
products by telephoning Tyson.

USA International
  4820 Adohr Lane
  Camarillo, CA 93010
  in CA 1-800-554-6682
  out of CA 1-800-428-6682

They provide a full range of pharmaceutical grade amino acids, the
pyridoxal-5-phosphate form of vitamin B_6, and the basic vitamins and
minerals. They are not directly available to the consumer, but you can

ask your pharmacist to stock their products or your doctor can order them for you.

Cardiovascular Research Ltd.
  1061-B Shary Circle
  Concord, CA 94518
  1-800-351-9429
  in CA & HA (415) 827-2636

Their products are available at your doctor's request.

Vitamin Research Products
  2044-A Old Middlefield Way
  Mountain View, CA 94043-9971
  1-800-541-1623
  CA only call 1-800-541-8536

They distribute a full range of amino acid and vitamin products. You can telephone for their catalogue and order by mail.

L & H Vitamins
  38-01 35th Avenue
  Long Island City, New York 11101
  1-800-221-1152

This is a mail order company providing products at a 20 percent discount. You can write or phone for a catalogue.

The Vitamin Trader
  3021-B Harbor Blvd.
  Costa Mesa, CA 92626
  1-800-334-9310
  in CA 1-800-334-9300

This is a mail order company that supplies products from most of the major companies at 15 to 25 percent discounts. You can write or telephone for a catalogue.

RESOURCES FOR LITERATURE RELATED TO ORTHOMOLECULAR TREATMENT

Biosocial Publications
   P. O. Box 1174
   Tacoma, WA 98401

They will provide a list and synopsis of current nutritional books that can be ordered through them.

SAGW
   Wheaton Plaza Office Building North #404
   Wheaton, MD 20902
   (301) 949-8282

They will provide a list of available audio tapes on various orthomolecular therapies that relate to many emotional and physical symptoms.

Huxley Institute for Biosocial Research Inc.
   900 North Federal Highway
   Boca Raton, FLA 33432
   1-800-847-3802
   (305) 393-6167

They have complete book lists, pamphlets, audio tapes, order forms and referral lists of doctors who use orthomolecular methods.

Wright/Gaby Research Library
   Wright/Gaby Nutrition Institute
   6931 Fieldcrest Road
   Baltimore, MD 21215
   (301) 764-3471, 685-7767

The library is being computerized for use as a nutrition data base. It may only be available to your physician.

Bio-ecologic Research Center, Inc.
   312 Carpenter Road
   Defiance, OH 43512

Food Allergy Update Newsletter
  Immuno-nutritional Clinical Laboratory
  6700 Valjean Avenue
  Van Nuys, CA 91406
  1-800-344-4646
  in CA (818) 780-4720

NUTRITIONALLY ORIENTED RESOURCE ORGANIZATIONS FOR DOCTOR REFERRALS

Huxley Institute for Biosocial Research, Inc.
900 North Federal Highway
Boca Raton, FLA 33432
1-800-847-3802
(305) 393-6167

American Academy of Environmental Medicine
Box 16106
Denver, CO 80216
(303) 662-9755

Feingold Association of the United States
6808 Stoneybrooke Lane
Alexandria, VA 22306
(703) 281-7728

Human Ecology Action League (Heal)
P. O. Box 1369
Evanston, IL 60204
(312) 864-0995

Institute for Child Behavior Research
4758 Edgeware Road
San Diego, CA 92216
(619) 281-7165

International Association of Cancer Victims and Friends
7740 West Manchester, Suite 110
Playa del Rey, CA 90291
(213) 822-5032

Nutrition for Optimal Health Association (Noah)
P. O. Box 380
Winnetka, IL 60093
(312) 835-5030

Linus Pauling Institute of Science and Medicine
440 Page Mill Road
Palo Alto, CA 94306
(415) 327-4064

Northwest Academy of Preventive Medicine
15615 Bellevue-Redmond Road
Bellevue, WA 98008
(206) 881-9660

The American Holistic Medical Association
6932 Little River Turnpike
Annandale, VA 22003
(703) 642-5880

The International Academy of Preventive Medicine
Box 5832
Lincoln, NE 68505
(402) 467-2716

Appendix to Chapter 5

THE SYNTHESIS OF SEROTONIN AND NOREPINEPHRINE

The following technical material explains how amino acids ultimately become neurotransmitters. Since each amino acid has multiple metabolic processes and breakdown products, I have simplified to avoid confusion.

A quick glance down the left side of the following chart will give you an overview of how tryptophan changes into serotonin and vitamin B₃. Normally, only 3 percent of our dietary tryptophan is converted to serotonin. Much of the rest becomes vitamin B_3. If the body has enough B_3, it will use the tryptophan more efficiently for producing serotonin.

Notice that several B vitamins are involved as coenzymes. All the listed enzymes and coenzymes have to be present in sufficient quantities for the reaction to occur. If any are low, the reaction is impaired.

THE SYNTHESIS OF SEROTONIN

PRECURSOR:	IN THE PRESENCE OF:
L-tryptophan	the enzyme tryptophan hydroxylase and the coenzyme folic acid and vitamin C
becomes: 5-hydroxytryptophan and niacin and then: 5-hydroxytryptophan	the coenzyme biotin and 5-hydroxytryptophan decarboxylase and the coenzyme vitamin B_6
becomes: serotonin	

THE SYNTHESIS OF NOREPINEPHRINE AND EPINEPHRINE

PRECURSOR:	IN THE PRESENCE OF:
L-phenylalanine	The enzyme phenylalanine hydroxylase, the coenzyme folic acid, sufficient magnesium, iron, copper, manganese, zinc, pancreatic enzymes and vitamin C
becomes:	
L-tyrosine	the enzyme tyrosine hydroxylase and the coenzyme folic acid
becomes either:	
L-dopa, or else combines with iodine in the thyroid gland to form thyroxine	
and then:	
L-dopa	the enzyme dopa decarboxylase and the coenzyme vitamin B_6
becomes:	
dopamine	the enzyme dopamine B-hydroxylase and the coenzyme vitamin C
becomes:	
norepinephrine	
becomes:	
epinephrine	

L-dopa may form thyroid hormones or go on to form the neurotransmitters. In Chapter 10 we saw the association of low thyroid levels with depression.

The body also uses phenylalanine for processes other than the production of tyrosine. Because tyrosine precursor loading is one chemical step closer to the desired norepinephrine than phenylalamine, and because the body tolerates it better, I usually prescribe tyrosine. The times when phenylalanine may be necessary or preferable are detailed in Chapter 4.

When you look at the information on the synthesis of norepinephrine from tyrosine, bear in mind that the 60 to 70 percent response rates mentioned in research reports on tyrosine are obtained by giving only tyrosine. Obviously those results can be increased by adding the other ingredients needed for norepinephrine formation and by adding the tryptophan to produce serotonin.

Appendix to Chapter 7

VITAMIN B$_1$ (THIAMINE)

SYMPTOMS OF DEFICIENCY	RISK OR DEPLETING FACTORS	AUGMENTING OR SYNERGISTIC NUTRIENTS	BEST FOOD SOURCES
			High:
Depression	Alcohol	B complex vitamins	Wheat germ and bran
Chronic fatigue and apathy	Excess sugar Tobacco	Vitamin C	Brewers' yeast
Irritability	Stress	Vitamin E	Blackstrap molasses
Memory loss	White rice and flour	Manganese	Soybeans
Confusion	Caffeine	Magnesium	Organ meats
Personality changes (including aggression)	Raw clams and oysters	Sulfur	Pork
Emotional instability	Heavy exercise		
Insomnia	Pregnancy		*Medium:*
Anxiety and feelings of impending doom	Nursing		
Restlessness	Aging		Liver
Night terrors	Food processing and cooking		
Sensitivity to noise	Surgery		Nuts
Appetite loss	Fever		Beans

197

SYMPTOMS OF DEFICIENCY	RISK OR DEPLETING FACTORS	AUGMENTING OR SYNERGISTIC NUTRIENTS	BEST FOOD SOURCES
Indigestion (especially constipation)	Sulfa drugs		Poultry
Abdominal pains	Birth control pills		Milk
Nausea and vomiting	Hyperthyroidism		Oatmeal
Weak sore muscles			
Atrophy of leg muscles			
Numbness and tingling or burning in hands and feet			
Headaches			
Heart palpitations and irregularities			
Circulation problems			
Shortness of breath			
Increased sensitivity to pain			

Severe deficiency diseases are beriberi, polyneuritis, Wernicke-Korsakoffs syndrome.

VITAMIN B$_2$ (RIBOFLAVIN)

SYMPTOMS OF DEFICIENCY	RISK OR DEPLETING FACTORS	AUGMENTING OR SYNERGISTIC NUTRIENTS	BEST FOOD SOURCES
			High:
Depression	Stress	B Complex vitamins	Liver
Insomnia	Alcohol	Vitamin C	Tongue
Mental sluggishness	Excess Protein	Iron	Kidney
Dizziness	Excess Carbohydrates	Vitamin A	*Medium:*
Dermatitis	Excess Sugar	Copper	
Oily skin with scaling around nose, forehead, and ears	Vegetarianism	Phosphorus	Wheat germ
Cracks and sores at corners of mouth	Pregnancy		Brewers' yeast
Dry chapped-looking lips	Nursing		Blackstrap molasses
Increased aging lines around the mouth	High energy expenditures		Fish
Red sore tongue	Liver disease		Meats
Narrowing upper lip	Antibiotics		Beans
Itching burning eyes	Fever		Dairy products

SYMPTOMS OF DEFICIENCY	RISK OR DEPLETING FACTORS	AUGMENTING OR SYNERGISTIC NUTRIENTS	BEST FOOD SOURCES
Bloodshot eyes	Hyperthyroidism		Nuts
Crusty burning eyelids	Exposure of food to sunlight		Green leafy vegetables
Sensitivity to light			Asparagus
Cataracts			Currants
Trembling			Avocados
Vaginal itching			
Digestive disturbances			
Hair and eyebrow loss			
Tiny visible blood vessels on skin			

VITAMIN B₃ (NIACIN)

SYMPTOMS OF DEFICIENCY	RISK OR DEPLETING FACTORS	AUGMENTING OR SYNERGISTIC NUTRIENTS	BEST FOOD SOURCES
			High:
Depression	Stress	B complex vitamins	Peanuts
Mental fatigue	Alcohol	Vitamin C	Rice bran
Poor concentration	Caffeine	Phosphorus	Liver and heart
Memory loss	Corn	Tryptophan	Turkey and chicken
Nervous disorders (anxiety, fear, worry, apprehension, suspicion)	Sugar	Adequate protein diet	Tuna, halibut, and swordfish
Irritability	Refined carbohydrates	Chromium	Brewers' yeast
Insomnia	Antibiotics	Zinc	
Amoral behavior	Illness	Vitamin D	*Medium:*
Indigestion, gas	Injury		
Abdominal pains	Physical exercise		Avocados
Appetite loss			
Nausea			Asparagus
Diarrhea			
Sore mouth			Beans
Painful swollen gums			Potatoes
Halitosis			Nuts
Coated tongue but red-tipped			Grains
Canker sores			Meats
Muscle weakness			Mushrooms
Skin eruptions and dermatitis			
Burning sensations any where on body			

Severe deficiency leads to disease of pellagra.

VITAMIN B₅ (PANTOTHENIC ACID)

SYMPTOMS OF DEFICIENCY	RISK OR DEPLETING FACTORS	AUGMENTING OR SYNERGISTIC NUTRIENTS	BEST FOOD SOURCES
			High:
Depression	Stress	B complex vitamins	Organ meats
Sullenness	Tobacco	Vitamin C	Brewers' yeast
Quarrelsomeness	Caffeine	Chromium	Peanuts
Fatigue	Aging	Zinc	Wheat germ
Restlessness	Illness		Liver
Weakness	Injury		Eggs
Muscle cramps	Sulfa drugs		Herring
Diarrhea	Estrogen		
Vomiting	Food processing		*Medium:*
Duodenal ulcers			
Eczema			Beans
Allergies			Peas
Hypoglycemia			Meats
Poor wound healing			Salmon, clams and mackerel
Digestive disorders			Walnuts
Constipation			Whole grains
Arthritis			Mushrooms
Hair loss			Cheese
Kidney disorders			Spinach
Premature aging			Brown rice
Cramping in arms and legs			Broccoli
Sore or burning feet			Cauliflower
Infection susceptibility with frequent respiratory illness			Carrots
Adrenal insufficiency			Avocados
Low blood pressure			

VITAMIN B$_6$ (PYRIDOXINE)

SYMPTOMS OF DEFICIENCY	RISK OR DEPLETING FACTORS	AUGMENTING OR SYNERGISTIC NUTRIENTS	BEST FOOD SOURCES
Depression	Stress	B complex vitamins	*High:*
Irritability	Alcohol	Vitamin C	Brewers' yeast
Nervousness	Birth control pills	Vitamin E	Blackstrap molasses
Insomnia	Tobacco	Magnesium	Liver
Slow learning	Excess sugar	Zinc	Herring
Poor dream recall	Pregnancy	Chromium	
Dizziness	Nursing	Cobalt	Salmon
Premenstual tension	Exposure to radiation	Sodium	Nuts
Increased sensitivity to sound	High protein diet	Potassium	Brown rice
Muscular weakness	Food processing and cooking	Copper	*Medium:*
Temporary limb paralysis	Isoniazide (drug)	Phosphorus	Meats
Numbness and tingling in limbs	Penicillamine (drug)	Linoleic acid	Other fish
Carpal-tunnel syndrome	Heart failure		Soybeans
Neuritis			Eggs
Water retention			Butter
Decreased resistance to infection			Vegetables
Poor appetite and morning nausea			Bananas
Hair loss			Avocados
Cracks around mouth and eyes			Grapes
Dermatitis and acne			Pears
Dental cavities			

SYMPTOMS OF DEFICIENCY	RISK OR DEPLETING FACTORS	AUGMENTING OR SYNERGISTIC NUTRIENTS	BEST FOOD SOURCES
Low blood sugar and low glucose tolerance			
Arthritis			
Anemia			
Convulsions			
Stillbirths if deficiency during pregnancy			

VITAMIN B$_{12}$

SYMPTOMS OF DEFICIENCY	RISK OR DEPLETING FACTORS	AUGMENTING OR SYNERGISTIC NUTRIENTS	BEST FOOD SOURCES
			High:
Depression	Stress	B complex vitamins (except niacin) especially folic acid	Kidney
Mental apathy	Vegetarianism	Calcium	Liver
Nervousness	Alcohol	Iron	Brain
General weakness	Pregnancy	Copper	
Fatigue	Nursing	Phosphorus	**Medium:**
Poor memory and concentration	Aging	Vitamin A	
Mood swings	Estrogens	Vitamin E	Heart
Intolerance to noise or light	Dilantin (drug)	Vitamin C	Egg yolk
Confusion	Excess vitamin C	Choline	Clams
Sore tongue	Intestinal malabsorption and digestion problems	Inositol	Sardines
Loss of menstruation	Laxatives	Potassium	Salmon
Disturbed digestion	Loss of stomach "intrinsic factor"	Sodium	Crabs
Numbness and tingling	Gastrectomy		Oysters
Hair loss	Cooking		Herring
Hallucinations	Hypothyroidism		
Paranoia			
Psychosis			
Rapid heart beat			
Anemia			
Chest pain			
Degeneration of long nerve tracts in spinal cord			
Walking and speaking difficulties			

Severe deficiency can lead to pernicious anemia and death

FOLIC ACID

SYMPTOMS OF DEFICIENCY	RISK OR DEPLETING FACTORS	AUGMENTING OR SYNERGISTIC NUTRIENTS	BEST FOOD SOURCES
			High:
Depression	Stress	B complex vitamins, especially B_{12}	Liver
Mental lethargy	Alcohol	Vitamin C	Asparagus
Withdrawal	Caffeine	Iron	Spinach
Irritability	Birth control pills	Copper	Brewers' yeast
Poor memory	Methotrexate (drug)		Dry beans: lentils limas navy
Sore tongue	Aminopterin (drug)		
Lesions at corners of the mouth	Antibiotics		*Medium:*
Graying hair	Dilantin (drug)		Kidney
Increased sensitivity to pain	Phenobarbital (drug)		Green vegetables
Lowered resistance to infection	Pregnancy		Almonds
Digestive disturbances	Nursing		Filberts
Diarrhea			
Low white blood cell count	Cooking and food processing losses are great		Peanuts
Anemia	Illness		Walnuts
Toxemia of pregnancy	Aging		Oats
Premature births			Rye Wheat

BIOTIN

SYMPTOMS OF DEFICIENCY	RISK OR DEPLETING FACTORS	AUGMENTING OR SYNERGISTIC NUTRIENTS	BEST FOOD SOURCES
			High:
Depression	Stress	B complex vitamins	Brewers' yeast
Extreme lassitude and sleepiness	Avidin (in raw egg whites)	Manganese	Royal Bee jelly
Anxiety	Antibiotics	Vitamin C	Liver
Hallucinations			
Grayish skin color			*Medium:*
Appetite loss			Wheat
Muscular pain			Brown rice
Scaly dermatitis			Chick peas
Dry skin			Corn
Chest pain			Lentils
Slight anemia			Oats
Hair loss			Soybeans
			Barley
			Eggs
			Chicken
			Mushrooms
			Nuts
			Mackerel
			Salmon
			Sardines

VITAMIN C (ASCORBIC ACID)

SYMPTOMS OF DEFICIENCY	RISK OR DEPLETING FACTORS	AUGMENTING OR SYNERGISTIC NUTRIENTS	BEST FOOD SOURCES
			High:
Depression	Stress	B complex vitamins	Broccoli
Weakness	Alcohol	Vitamin A	Brussel sprouts
Fatigue	Tobacco	Vitamin E	Collards
Listlessness	Pregnancy	Zinc	Horse radish
Confusion	Nursing	Iron	Kale
Rough skin	Aging	Vitamin K	Parsley
Aching joints	High copper	Calcium	Green peppers
Easy bruising	Excessive iron	Magnesium	Turnip greens
Dental cavities	Antibiotics	Manganese	Rose hips
Bleeding gums	Estrogens	Bioflavonoids	Black currants
Nosebleeds	Barbiturates		Guava
Allergies	Long-term dieting		
Poor digestion	Heavy metal intoxication		*Medium:*
Edema	Irradiation		Lemons
Poor wound healing	Trauma		Oranges
Low resistance to infection	Air, food and water pollution		Papayas
	High protein diet		Strawberries
	Surgery		Cabbages
	Infections		Tomatoes
	Burns		Cauliflower
	Food processing and cooking		Watercress
	Street drugs		Spinach
	Cortisone		
	High fever		
	Hyperthyroidism		

Severe deficiency leads to illness of scurvy, with brittle bones and weak blood vessels, hemorrhage into the muscles and skin, tender aching joints, lethary, anemia, loss of teeth, severe bruising, drug, kidney trouble and death.

MAGNESIUM

SYMPTOMS OF DEFICIENCY	RISK OR DEPLETING FACTORS	AUGMENTING OR SYNERGISTIC NUTRIENTS	BEST FOOD SOURCES
			High:
Depression	Alcohol	Vitamin B₆	Wheat germ and bran
		Vitamin C	
Fatigue	Excess sugar	Vitamin D	Almonds
Insomnia	Aging	Potassium	Cashews
Anxiety	Cooking in water	Calcium	Blackstrap molasses
Nervousness	Low protein diet	Phosphorus	Brewers' yeast
Confusion	Long-term dieting	Protein	Brazil nuts
Hyperactivity	Irradiation		
Disorientation	Soil deficiencies		*Medium:*
Learning disability	Birth control pills		
Easily aroused anger	Excess protein, fat, calcium and vitamin D		Nuts
Increased sense of hearing and startled response	Diuretics		Soybeans
Tremors	Burns		Sesame seeds
Muscle twitching	Surgery		Parsnips
Numbness and tingling			Wild rice
Appetite loss			Oats
Rapid pulse			Rye
Heart irregularities			Millet
Kidney stones			Barley
High blood pressure			Corn
			Peas
			Carrots
			Beet greens

Severe deficiency can induce visual hallucinations, delerium and seizures.

ZINC

SYMPTOMS OF DEFICIENCY	RISK OR DEPLETING FACTORS	AUGMENTING OR SYNERGISTIC NUTRIENTS	BEST FOOD SOURCES
			High:
Depression	Stress	Vitamin B_6	Oysters
Apathy	Alcohol	Vitamin E	Herring
Fatigue	Excess calcium intake	Vitamin A	Liver
Loss of sense of taste and smell	Excess copper intake	Calcium	Sunflower seeds
Poor dream recall	Pregnancy		Pumpkin seeds
Appetite loss	Nursing		Cheese
Oily skin	Surgery		Wheat germ and bran
Prolonged wound healing	Burns		Brewers' yeast
Stretch marks on the skin	Depleted soils		*Medium:*
Failure of growth	Food processing		Seafood
Brittle nails	High phytate diet		Meats
White spots on nails	Birth control pills		Peanuts
Poor hair growth	Excess iron		Cashews
Acne			Other grains
Menstrual irregularities			Avocados
Prostate disorders			Vegetables
Painful knees and hips especially in teenagers and children			
Cold extremities with poor circulation			

IRON

SYMPTOMS OF DEFICIENCY	RISK OR DEPLETING FACTORS	AUGMENTING OR SYNERGISTIC NUTRIENTS	BEST FOOD SOURCES
			High:
Depression	Vegetarianism	Vitamin C	Blackstrap molasses
Fatigue	Caffeine	Vitamin E	Brewers' yeast
Listlessness	Pregnancy	Vitamin B$_{12}$	Liver
Impaired learning	Nursing	Folic acid	Kidneys
Poor memory and attention span	Excessive zinc, calcium or phosphorus	Calcium	Clams
Headache	Aging	Copper	Oysters
Irritability	Illness	Amino acids	Caviar
Hair loss	Copper deficiency	Alcohol	Red wine
Dizziness	Antacid use		Sesame, sunflower and pumpkin seeds
Weakness	Boiling food		Walnuts, almonds, pistachio, and pine nuts
Sore or burning tongue	High phytate diet		Millet
Brittle, flattened or spoon-shaped nails	Tetracyclines (drugs)		Soybeans
Longitudinal ridges in nails			Parsley
Constipation			Wheat germ and bran
Heart palpitation on exertion			Brown rice
Shortness of breath			*Medium:*
Difficulty swallowing			Seafood
Cold extremities			Meats
Decreased resistance to infection			Other nuts and seeds
Anemia			Vegetables
Numbness and tingling			Cheese
			Raisins

MANGANESE

SYMPTOMS OF DEFICIENCY	RISK OR DEPLETING FACTORS	AUGMENTING OR SYNERGISTIC NUTRIENTS	BEST FOOD SOURCES
			High:
Depression (not yet well studied and delineated)	Pregnancy	Lecithin	Snails
	Nursing	Choline	Coconuts
Dizziness	Depleted soils	Alcohol	Sunflower seeds
Impaired glucose tolerance	Excess dietary calcium, zinc, phosphorus, soyprotein, iron and cobalt	Vitamin K	Nuts
Disc degeneration	Phenothiazine tranquilizers (drugs)	Vitamin B_1	Barley
Birth defects	Food processing	Vitamin E	Rye
Reduced fertility	Long-term dieting		Buckwheat
			Split peas
			Whole wheat
			Walnuts
			Spinach
			Peanuts
			Oats
			Raisins
			Blueberries
			Olives
			Avocados

BLOOD TESTS FOR VITAMINS

There is growing evidence that the vitamin and mineral levels in our blood do not accurately reflect overall nutritional status. In one study comparing blood levels of vitamin B_{12} with cerebrospinal fluid levels, three out of forty-nine patients with organic mental disorders had low blood B_{12} levels, but thirty had low cerebrospinal fluid levels. The low spinal levels went up with vitamin B_{12} treatment and the symptoms improved.

Few vitamin-assay laboratories can accurately perform the tests that measure vitamin levels in blood. Make sure your doctor chooses a lab that uses protozoan-based methods for determining vitamin levels. If you have recently eaten foods high in the vitamins or taken supplements, your blood tests will be normal to high. This can happen even if your actual body cells are chronically low in the vitamin. For this reason indirect blood measures of the vitamins are taken. Each test measures a substance in the blood that is dependent on normal concentrations of the vitamin.

This method of testing is sometimes inaccurate because it depends on the presence of enough protein, zinc and magnesium in the blood. Determining the level of each separate vitamin is also costly and is therefore not done except under special circumstances.

TESTS FOR AMINO ACIDS

Serum and twenty-four-hour urine amino acid levels should be measured by amino acid chromatography using the Beckman Amino Acid Analyzer model 6300 or 7300. Serum levels reflect tissue pools, and urine levels reflect how the body is using the amino acids.

Amino acid analysis not only indirectly measures protein intake and

VITAMIN	BLOOD TEST
Thiamine (B_1)	Erythrocyte transketolase
Riboflavin (B_2)	Erythrocyte glutathione reductase
Niacin (B_3)	-1-N-Methylnicotinamide
Pyridoxine (B_6)	Kynurenic and xanthurenic acids or pyridoxal-5-phosphate level
Folic acid	Formininoglutamic acid (FIGLU)
Vitamin C	Vitamin C levels in the white blood cells
Vitamin B_{12}	Methylmalonic acid

metabolism, it also indicates the presence of enzyme deficiencies and inactivations caused by vitamin or mineral deficiencies. These enzyme abnormalities, in turn, cause blockages in the metabolic pathways of various amino acids. These blocks result either in the accumulation of various amino acid metabolites that cannot be processed further or in the accumulation of abnormal amino acid metabolites.

Stress, alcoholism, protein intolerance, malabsorption syndromes, rheumatoid arthritis, burns, cancer, kidney failure, vitamin and mineral deficiencies, and many other disease conditions can all lead to amino acid imbalances in the blood and urine.

USEFUL BOOKS ON NUTRITION

Body, Mind and Sugar, E.M. Abrahamson, M.D., and P.W. Pezet

The Doctors' Book of Vitamin Therapy, by H. Rosenberg, M.D., and A.N. Feldzman, M.D., Putnam, 1974.

Dr. Cott's Help for Your Learning Disabled Child: The Orthomolecular Treatment, Allan Cott, M.D., Ph.D.

Dr. Wright's Book of Nutritional Therapy, by Jonathan V. Wright, M.D.

Fighting Depression, by Harvey Ross, M.D.

Food For Nought: The Decline in Nutrition, by Roose Hume Hall (Chairman of Dept. of Biochemistry, McMasters University in Canada)

How to Live Longer and Feel Better, by Linus Pauling, Ph.D.

Hypoglycemia, A Better Approach, Paavo Airola

Improving Your Child's Behavior Chemistry, by Lendon Smith, M.D.

Kids Are What They Eat, by Betty Kamen and Sy Kamen

Life Extension, by Durk Pearson and Sandy Shaw

Low Blood Sugar and You, Carlton Fredericks, Ph.D. and Henry Goodman, M.D.

Mega-Nutrition, The Prescription For Maximum Health, Energy and Longevity, by Richard A. Kunin, M.D.

Megavitamin Therapy: In Reply to the APA Task Force Report on Megavitamin and Orthomolecular Therapy in Psychiatry, by Abram Hoffer, M.D. and H. Osmond, M.D.

Mental and Elemental Nutrients, by Carl Pfeiffer, Ph.D., M.D.

Modern Nutrition in Health and Disease, 6th edition, edited by Robert S. Goodhart, M.D., D.M.S. and Maurice E. Shils, M.D., Sc.D.

Nutrition and Brain Development, by Govind A. Dhopesheurkar

Nutrition and the Brain, Vol. 1–6, edited by Richard S. Wurtman, M.D. and Judith J. Wurtman, Ph.D.

Nutrition, Stress and Toxic Chemicals, by Arthur J. Vander, M.D.

The Orthomolecular Approach to Learning Disabilities, by Allan Cott, M.D., Ph.D.

Orthomolecular Nutrition, by Abram Hoffer, M.D., Ph.D.

A Physician's Handbook on Orthomolecular Medicine, by Roger J. Williams, Ph.D., and Dwight Kalita, Ph.D.

Psychodietetics, by Manual Cheraskin, M.D., D.M.D., and W.M. Ringsdorf, Jr., D.M.D., MS.

Psychonutrition, by Carlton Fredericks, Ph.D.

The Roots of Orthomolecular Medicine—A Tribute to Linus Pauling, Edited by Richard P. Huemer, M.D.

Sugar Blues, by Howard Dufty

Supernutrition, by Richard Passwater, Ph.D.

Total Nutrition, by Carl Pfeiffer, M.D., Ph.D.

The Vitamin Robbers, by Earl Mindell, Ph.D., and William Lee, Ph.D.

Your Personal Vitamin Profile, by Michael Colgan, Ph.D.

Appendix to
Chapter 8

ALLERGY TESTS

1. *The RAST Test.* This is a generally accepted blood test for food and inhalant allergies. It measures only the IGE allergies, not food sensitivities related to IGM, A or G.
2. *Enzyme-Linked Immunosorbent Assay (ELISA).* This is a new blood test that measures IGA, G, and M immunoglobulins—the delayed reaction food sensitivities. Since it is done by machine, the test is standardized and reproducible.
3. *Food Immune Complement Assay (FICA).* This is a new blood test to measure the Ig G immune complexes. It is automated, standardized and reproducible.
4. *Cytotoxic Test.* This is a blood test that has been in use for several years, measuring the toxicity or damage to your white blood cells. It is a subjective test, but when it is evaluated correctly, it is very reliable.
5. *Skin Testing.* This test is outdated and only 50 percent accurate, and may cause an allergic response.
6. *Challenge Testing.* There is also a risk of allergic reaction with this test. To test for a reaction to a certain food, the patient is instructed to avoid the food for three to four days, then to eat a large amount of that food by itself, first thing in the morning, on an empty stomach. If a reaction follows, it indicates a food allergy.
7. *Sublingual Testing.* Concentrated drops of an allergen are put under the tongue to absorb into the blood stream. If allergic, the patient will react immediately. This test's value is limited because it can precipitate a severe allergic reaction. In addition, this and the challenge test can only measure one substance at a time.
8. *Cellular Immune Response Assay.* This new blood test for food sen-

sitivities measures swelling of certain white blood cells. When a
sensitivity exists, it is reproducible with 90 percent accuracy.

SELF-HELP ALLERGY BOOKS

Brain Allergies, The Psychonutrient Connection, by William Philpott, M.D.
An Alternative Approach to Allergies, by Theron Randolph, M.D.
Dr. Mandell's 5-Day Allergy Relief System, by Marshall Mandell, M.D. and Lynn
   Waller Scanlon
Tracking Down Hidden Food Allergies, by William Crook, M.D.
The Food Sensitivity Diet, by D.A. Kaufman, Freundlich, 1984
Do-It-Yourself Allergy Analysis Handbook, by Kate Ludeman, Ph.D.
The Food Connection, by David Sheinkin, M.D., and Michael Schacter, M.D.
How to Control Your Allergies, by Robert Forman, Ph.D.

Appendix to
Chapter 15

Sources for Audio Tapes for Relaxation and Positive Reprogramming

If this approach appeals to you, these catalogues will provide a comprehensive range for self-improvement through reprogramming.

1. "Discoveries Through Inner Quests" catalogue from:
   Institute of Human Development
   P. O. Box 1616
   Ojai, CA 93023
   1-800-443-0100 ext. 356

   Tapes such as:
   1 Coping with Emotions (six tape set)
   2 Stress Reduction (three tape set)
   3 Intuitive Decision Making (three tape set)
   4 Pathways for Mastership (twelve tape set)
   5 Building a Positive Self-Image (three tape set)
   6 Coping with Divorce (three tape set)
   7 Health Imaging Video Tape
   8 Defeat Discouragement
   9 Helping Yourself to Happiness
   10 Increased Love and Affection
   11 Letting Go of the Past
   12 Freedom from Alcohol/Drugs
   13 How to Live with a Negative Person
   14 Pain Reduction
   15 Peak Learning
   16 Controlling Anger and Temper
   —and many other effective tapes.

2. *The Healing Brain* brochure from:
   ISHK Book Service, Dept. T9
   P. O. Box 1062
   Cambridge, MA 02238
   (617) 497-4124

   Tapes such as:
   1. Controlling Depression Through Cognitive Therapy

3. Effective Learning Systems, Inc.
   5221 Edina Ind. Blvd.
   Edina, Minnesota 55435
   (612) 893-1680

   Tapes such as:
   1 How to be Positive
   2 Developing Enthusiasm
   3 Decision Making
   4 Coping with the Death of a Loved One
   5 Concentration
   6 Energy
   7 Guilt Free
   8 How to be Happy
   9 Managing Stress
   10 Overcoming Worry
   11 Motivation
   12 Self-Image Programming
   13 Spiritual Healing
   14 Surviving Separation

4. Self-Help Update
   Valley of the Sun Publishing
   Box 38, Malibu, CA 90265

   Tapes such as:
   1 Love Yourself
   2 Positive Thinking
   3 Eliminating Fear and Worry
   4 Canceling Out Fear Thoughts
   5 Surviving Separation or Divorce
   6 Coping with Grief
   7 Peace of Mind
   8 Increasing Self Confidence

     9 Intensifying Creative Ability
   10 High Energy and Enthusiasm Personality
     Transformation

5. Sybervision Catalogue from:
   Sybervision
   Fountain Square
   6066 Civic Terrace Avenue
   Newark, CA 94560-3747
   1-800-227-0600

   Tapes such as:
   1 The Neuropsychology of Weight Control
   2 The Neuropsychology of Achievement
   3 The Neuropsychology of Self-Discipline

6. The Soundworks Corp.
   Customer Service
   P. O. Box 75890
   Washington, D.C. 20013-5890

   Tapes such as:
   1 Peak Performance (four tape set)
   2 Tapes on relationships
   3 Various spiritual tapes
   4 Tapes on stress management, meditation and guided imagery

7. Mind Communication, Inc.
   2620 Remico S.W.
   P. O. Box 9429
   Grand Rapids, MI 49509-0429
   1-800-237-1974
   1-800-531-9972

Bibliography

"119% Rise in U.S. Youth Suicide Between '65, '77." *Clinical Psychiatry News*, 13:8 (1985), pp. 1, 13.

"15–20% of U.S. Population Over 65 Have Alzheimer's Symptoms." *Clinical Psychiatry News*, 13:2 (1985), p.9.

Abraham, G.E. "Bioavailability of Selected Nutrients from a Dietary Supplement." *Journal of Applied Nutrition*, 37:2 (1985), pp. 61–77.

———. "The Calcium Controversy." *Journal of Applied Nutrition*, 34(1982), pp. 69–73.

——— "Magnesium Deficiency in Premenstrual Tension." *Magnesium Bulletin*, 4 (1982), p. 68.

———. "Nutrition and the Premenstrual Tension Syndromes." *Journal of Applied Nutrition*, 36:2 (1984), pp. 103–17.

———. "Nutritional Factors in the Etiology of the Premenstrual Tension Syndromes." *The Journal of Reproductive Medicine*, 28:7 (1983) pp. 445–60.

———. *Premenstrual Blues*. Costa Mesa, CA: Optimox Corp., 1980.

———, and M. N. Lubran. "Serum and Red Cell Magnesium Levels in Patients with Premenstrual Tension." *American Journal of Clinical Nutrition*, 34 (1981), p. 2364.

———, et al. "Effect of Vitamin B_6 on Plasma and Red Blood Cell Magnesium Levels in Premenopausal Women." *Annals of Clinical and Laboratory Science*, 11 (1981), p. 333.

Abramowitz, E.S., et al. "Onset of Depressive Psychiatric Crises and the Menstrual Cycle." *American Journal of Psychiatry*, 139:4 (1982), pp. 475–77.

Adams, P.W., et al. "Effect of Pyridoxine Hydrochloride (Vit B_6) upon Depression Associated with Oral Contraception." *Lancet*, 1 (1973), pp. 897–904.

Adams, R., and F. Murray. *The Vitamin B_6 Book*. New York: Larchmont Books, 1980.

Aero, R., and E. Weiner. *The Mind Test*. Great Neck, NY: Morrow, 1981.

Affective Disorders in Childhood and Adolescence, an Update, ed. Dennis Cantwell and Gabrielle Carlson. New York: SP Medical and Scientific Books, 1983.

Ahles, S., et al. "Comparative Cardiac Effects of Maprotiline and Doxepin in Elderly Depressed Patients." *Journal of Clinical Psychiatry*, 45:11 (1984), pp. 460–65.

Aihara, K., et al. "Zinc, Copper, Manganese, and Selenium Metabolism in Thyroid Disease." *American Journal of Clinical Nutrition,* 40 (1984), pp. 26–35.

Aikawa, J.W. "Effects of Pyridoxine and Desoxypyridoxine on Magnesium Metabolism in the Rabbit." *Proceedings of the Society Exp. Biol. Med.,* 104 (1960), p. 461.

Akiskal, H.S. "Dysthymic Disorder: Psychopathology of Proposed Chronic Depressive Subtypes." *American Journal of Psychiatry,* 140:1 (1983), pp. 11–20.

Alexopoulos, G.S., et al. "Platelet MAO Activity and Age at Onset of Depression in Elderly Depressed Women." *American Journal of Psychiatry,* 141:10 (1984), pp. 1276–78.

Allen, R.E., and F. N. Pitts. "Dexamethasone Suppression in Depressed Elderly Outpatients." *Journal of Clinical Psychiatry,* 45:9 (1984), pp. 397–98.

Alvarado, F. "Transport of Sugars and Amino Acids in the Intestine: Evidence for a Common Carrier." *Science,* 151 (1966), pp. 1010–13.

Amino Acid and Protein Metabolism, Report of the Thirtieth Ross Conference on Pediatric Research, ed. S. J. Fomon. Columbus, Ohio: Ross Laboratories, 1959.

Ammon, H.P.T., et al. "Effect of Alcohol and Acetaldehyde on Coenzyme A," in *The Biological Aspects of Alcohol,* ed. M. K. Roach. Austin: University of Texas Press, 1971, pp. 185–211.

Ananth, J.V., and R. Yassa. "Magnesium in Mental Illness." *Comprehensive Psychiatry,* 20:5 (1979), pp. 475–82.

Ananth, J.V., et al. "Potentiation of Therapeutic Effects of Nicotinic Acid by Pyridoxine in Chronic Schizophrenics." *Canadian Psychiatric Association Journal,* 18 (1973), pp. 377–82.

Anderson, D.J., et al. "A Comparison of Panic Disorder and Generalized Anxiety Disorder." *American Journal of Psychiatry,* 141:4 (1984) pp. 572–75.

Anderson, G.H., and J. L. Johnston. "Nutrient Control of Brain Neurotransmitter Synthesis and Function." *Canadian Journal of Physiology and Pharmacology,* 61 (1983) pp. 271–81.

Anderson, R.W., and A. Lev-Ran. "Hypoglycemia: The Standard and the Fiction." *Psychosomatics,* 26:1 (1985), pp. 38–47.

Aneshensel, C.S., and J. D. Stone. "Stress and Depression: A Test of the Buffering Model of Social Support." *Archives of General Psychiatry,* 39 (1982), pp. 1392–96.

Arieti, S., and J. R. Bemporad. "The Psychological Organization of Depression." *American Journal of Psychiatry,* 137:11 (1980), pp. 1360–65.

Asberg, M., et al. "Therapeutic Effects of Serotonin Uptake Inhibitors in Depression." *Journal of Clinical Psychiatry,* 47:4, Suppl. (1986), pp. 23–35.

Ashcroft, G.W., et al. "Modified Amine Hypothesis for the Aetiology of Affective Illness. *Lancet,* 2 (1972), pp. 573–77.

Ayd, F.J. "Update Pharmacotherapy for Depressed Parkinsonian Patients." *Psychiatric Annals,* 14:9 (1984).

―――. "Update Pharmacotherapy for Psychotic Depression." *Psychiatric Annals,* 15:8 (1985), p. 506.

Baer, R.K., et al. "Clinical Psychiatry Conference: Biological and Family Indicators in Depression." *Journal of Clinical Psychiatry,* 44:10 (1983), pp. 372–78.

Baker, H. "Functional Enzyme Analyses Versus Blood Vitamin Analyses as Indicators of Vitamin Status." *Anabolism*, 4:1 (1985) pp. 9–10.

Baker, H., and O. Frank. "A Vitamin Profile of Metabolic Disturbances." *Journal of Applied Nutrition*, 33:1 (1981), pp. 3–18.

Baker, J.P., et al. "Nutritional Assessment: A Comparison of Clinical Judgment and Objective Measurements." *New England Journal of Medicine*, 306:16 (1982), pp. 969–72.

Bakwin, R.M. "Suicide in Children and Adolescents." *JAMWA*, 28:12 (1973) pp. 643–50.

Baldessarini, R.J. *Biomedical Aspects of Depression and Its Treatment.* Washington, D.C.: American Psychiatric Press, 1983.

Balfour, D.J.K., et al. "The Effects of Nicotine on Brain Neurotransmitter Systems," in *Nicotine and the Tobacco Smoking Habit*, ed. D.J.K. Balfour. New York: Pergamon Press, 1984.

Ban, T. "Chronic Disease and Depression in the Geriatric Population." *Journal of Clinical Psychiatry*, 45:3 (1984), pp. 18–23.

Banki, C., et al. "Cerebrospinal Fluid Magnesium and Calcium Related to Amine Metabolites, Diagnosis, and Suicide Attempts." *Biological Psychiatry*, 20 (1985), pp. 163–71.

Barnes, B.O. *Hypothyroidism: The Unsuspected Illness.* New York: Harper & Row, 1976.

Basu, T.K., and C. J. Schorah. *Vitamin C in Health and Disease.* Westport, CT: AVI, 1982.

Bateman, N.E. "Vitamin B_6: Comparative Absorption Studies." *International Clinical Nutrition Review*, 5:3 (1985), pp. 130–34.

Baumblatt, M.J., and F. Winston. "Pyridoxine and the Pill." *Lancet*, 1 (1970) p. 832.

Beck, A.T., and R. W. Beck. "Screening Depressed Patients in Family Practice." *Postgraduate Medicine*, 52:6 (1972), pp. 81–85.

——, et al. *Cognitive Therapy of Depression.* New York: Guilford Press, 1980.

——, et al. "An Inventory for Measuring Depression." *Archives of General Psychiatry*, 4 (1961), pp. 561–71.

Beckmann, H., et al. "D,L-Phenylalanine Versus Imipramine: A Double Blind Controlled Study." *Archiv fur Psychiatre und Nerven Krankheiten* (Berlin), 227:1 (1979), pp. 49–58.

Beecher, G., et al. Amino Acid Uptake and Levels: Influence of Endurance Training." *Biochemical Medicine*, 21 (1978), pp. 196–97.

Behar, D., et al. "Depression in the Abstinent Alcoholic." *American Journal of Psychiatry*, 141:9 (1984), pp. 1105–7.

Bender, D.A. *Amino Acid Metabolism.* New York: John Wiley & Sons, 1975.

Benedict, C.R., et al. "Effect of Oral Tyrosine and Tryptophan on Plasma Catecholamines." *American Journal of Clinical Nutrition*, 38 (1983), pp. 429–35.

"Bereavement Tied to Psychiatric, Medical Ills, Early Death in Some." *Clinical Psychiatry News*, November 1984, pp. 2, 34.

Bernstein, J.G. "Pharmacotherapy of Geriatric Depression." *Journal of Clinical Psychiatry*, 45:10 (1984), pp. 30–34.

Berry, I.R., and L. Borkan. "Phosphatidyl Choline—Its Use in Neurological and

Psychiatric Syndromes." *Journal of Orthomolecular Psychiatry*, 12:2 (1983), pp. 129–41.

――. "Precursor Therapy with Orthmolecular Nutrition." *Journal of Orthomolecular Psychiatry*, 13:3 (1984), pp. 179–92.

Bickers, W., and M. Woods. "Premenstrual Tension: Its Relation to Abnormal Water Storage." *New England Journal of Medicine*, 245 (1951), p. 453.

Bidzinska, E.J. "Stress Factors in Affective Diseases." *British Journal of Psychiatry*, 144 (1984), pp. 161–64.

Biere, J.G. "Vitamin E Levels in the Diet." *Nutrition Review*, 33 (1975), p. 161.

Biggs, J.T., et al. "Validity of the Zung Self-Rating Depression Scale." *British Journal of Psychiatry*, 132 (1978), pp. 381–85.

Biochemical and Medical Aspects of Tryptophan Metabolism. ed. O. Hayaishi, et al. New York: Elsevier, 1980.

Biskind, M.S. "Nutritional Deficiency in the Etiology of Menorrhagia, Cystic Mastitis and Premenstrual Tension, Treatment with Vitamin B Complex." *Journal of Clinical Endocrinology and Metabolism*, 3 (1943), pp. 227–34.

Biskind, M.S., and G. R. Biskind. "Effect of Vitamin B Complex Deficiency on Inactivation of Estrone in the Liver." *Endocrinology*, 31 (1942), pp. 109–14.

Blackburn, G.I., et al. "Criteria for Choosing Amino Acid Therapy in Acute Renal Failure." *American Journal of Clinical Nutrition*, 31:10 (1978) pp. 1841–53.

Blackwell, B. "Adverse Effects of Antidepressant Drugs: Part 1: Monoamine Oxidase Inhibitors and Tricyclics." *Drugs*, 21 (1981), pp. 201–19.

――. "Adverse Effects of Antidepressant Drugs: Part 2: 'Second Generation' Antidepressants and Rational Decision Making in Antidepressant Therapy." *Drugs*, 21 (1981), pp. 273–82.

Blackwood, U.B. "Can Nutrients Restore Mental Health?" *Journal of Orthomolecular Psychiatry*, 4:2, pp. 132–41.

Bland, J. "Endocrinology and Adolescent Nutrition." *Journal of Applied Nutrition*, 33:2 (1981), pp. 156–59.

――. *Digestive Enzymes.* New Canaan, CT: Keats, 1983.

――. *The Justification for Vitamin Supplementation.* Bellevue, WA: Northwest Diagnostic Services, 1981.

――. *Medical Applications of Clinical Nutrition.* New Canaan, CT: Keats, 1983.

Blazer, D.G. "Impact of Late-Life Depression on the Social Network." *American Journal of Psychiatry*, 140:2 (1983), pp. 162–66.

Blinder, B.J., et al. "Brain Iron, Dopamine Receptor Sensitivity, and Tardive Dyskinesia." *American Journal of Psychiatry*, 143:2 (1986), pp. 277–78.

Blumer, D., et al. "Antidepressant Treatment of the Pain-Prone Disorder." *Psychopharmacology Bulletin*, 20:3 (1984), pp. 531–35.

Bolton, S., et al. "Caffeine: Its Effects, Uses and Abuses." *Journal of Applied Nutrition*, 33:1 (1981), pp. 35–53.

Borer, M.S., and V. K. Bhanot. "Hyperthyroidism: Neuropsychiatric Manifestations." *Psychosomatics*, 26:7 (1985) pp. 597–601.

Boublik, J.H., et al. "Coffee Contains Potent Opiate Receptor Binding Activity." *Nature*, 301 (1983), pp. 246–48.

Braithwaite, S.S., and F. Ellyin. "Hypothyroidism: Current concepts." *Current Prescribing*, 3 (1979), pp. 39–49.

Branchey, L., et al. "Relationship Between Changes in Plasma Amino Acids and Depression in Alcoholic Patients." *American Journal of Psychiatry*, 141:10 (1984) pp. 1212–15.

Breier, A., et al. "The Diagnostic Validity of Anxiety Disorders and Their Relationship to Depressive Illness." *American Journal of Psychiatry*, 142 (1985), pp. 787–97.

Bremer, H.J., et al. *Disturbances of Amino Acid Metabolism*. Baltimore: Urban and Schwarzenberg, 1981.

Bressier, R. "Treating Geriatric Depression." *Drug Therapy*, September, 1984, pp. 35–50.

Brewerton, T.D., and V. I. Reus. "Lithium Carbonate and L-Tryptophan in the Treatment of Bipolar and Schizoaffective Disorders." *American Journal of Psychiatry*, 140:6 (1983), pp. 757–60.

Briggs, M.H. "Plasma Tryptophan and Oral Contraceptives." *Lancet*, 1 (1974) p. 460.

Brodie, B.B., et al. "Interrelationships of Catecholamines with Other Endocrine Systems." *Pharmacol. Rev.*, 19 (1966), pp. 273–89.

Brodie, H.K.H., et al. "Clinical Studies of L-5-Hydroxytryptophan in Depression," in *Serotonin and Behavior*, ed. J. Barchas and E. Usdin. New York: Academic Press, 1973, pp. 549–59.

Brotman, A.W., et al. "Antidepressant Treatment of Bulimia: The Relationship Between Bingeing and Depressive Symptomology." *Journal of Clinical Psychiatry*, 45 (1984) pp. 7–9.

Brown, J.H., and F. Paraskevas. "Cancer and Depression: Cancer Presenting with Depressive Illness: An Autoimmune Disease?" *British Journal of Psychiatry*, 141 (1982), pp. 227–32.

———, et al. "Is It Normal for Terminally Ill Patients to Desire Death?" *American Journal of Psychiatry*, 143:2 (1986), pp. 208–11.

Brown, R. "The Prescription of Exercise for Depression." *Physician and Sportsmedicine*, 6 (1978), pp. 34–49.

———, et al. "Differences in Nocturnal Melatonin Secretion Between Melancholic Depressed Patients and Control Subjects." *American Journal of Psychiatry*, 142 (1985), pp. 811–16.

Buist, R.A. "Drug-Nutrient Interactions—An Overview." *International Clinical Nutrition Review*, 4:3 (1984), pp. 114–21.

———. "Vitamin Toxicities, Side Effects and Contraindications." *International Clinical Nutrition Review*, 4:4 (1984) pp. 159–71.

———. "Who Needs Vitamin Supplements?" *International Clinical Nutrition Review*, 5:3 (1985), pp. 107–9.

Bunn, N.T., et al. "Receptors for Amino Acid in Neural Function." *Neurosciences Research Program Bulletin*, 10:2 (1971), pp. 123–251.

Bunney, W.E., and B. L. Garland. "Selected Aspects of Amine and Receptor Hypotheses of Affective Illness." *Journal of Clinical Psychopharmacology*, 1:6 (1981), pp. 3s–11s.

———, and D. L. Murphy. "Strategies for the Study of Neurotransmitter Receptor Function in Man," in *Pre and Post Synaptic Receptors*, ed. E. Usdin and W. E. Bunney. New York: Marcel Dekker, 1975.

Burch, E.A. "Primary Care Management of the Depressed Hypertensive Patient." *Psychosomatics,* 24:4 (1983), pp. 389–94.

Burke, P.M., et al. "Correlation Between Serum and Salivary Cortisol Levels in Depressed and Nondepressed Children and Adolescents." *American Journal of Psychiatry,* 142:9 (1985), pp. 1005–67.

"Caffeine Consumption Increases the Urinary Excretion of Calcium, Magnesium and Sodium." *Nutrition Research,* 4 (1984), pp. 43–50.

"Candida Albicans: Nutritional Management Considerations." *Nutraletter,* 3:1 (1985), pp. 1–4.

Carlson, G.C., and D. P. Cantwell. "Suicidal Behavior and Depression in Children and Adolescents." *Journal of the American Academy of Child Psychiatry,* 21 (1982), pp. 361–68.

Carr, D.B., et al. "Rate-Sensitive Inhibition of ACTH Release in Depression." *American Journal of Psychiatry,* 141:4 (1984), pp. 590–92.

Carroll, B.J. "Monoamine Precursors in the Treatment of Depression." *Clinical Pharmacology and Therapeutics,* 12 (1971), pp. 743–61.

———, et al. "The Carrol Rating Scale for Depression I. Development, Reliability, and Validation." *British Journal of Psychiatry,* 138 (1981), pp. 194–200.

———, et al. "Cholinergic Reversal of Manic Symptoms." *Lancet,* 1 (1973), pp. 427–28.

———, et al. "Depression Rating Scales: A Critical Review." *Archives of General Psychiatry,* 23 (1973), pp. 361–66.

———, et al. "Sequential Comparison of L-Tryptophan with ECT in Severe Depression." *Lancet,* 1 (1970), pp. 967–69.

Cartwright, R.D. "Rapid Eye Movement Sleep Characteristics During and After Mood Disturbing Events." *Archives of General Psychiatry,* 40 (1983), pp. 197–201.

Cavanaugh, S.V. "Diagnosing Depression in the Hospitalized Patient with Chronic Medical Illness." *Journal of Clinical Psychiatry,* 45:3 (1984), pp. 13–16.

Cavanaugh, S.V. "Use of Desipramine in the Medically Ill." *Journal of Clinical Psychiatry,* 45:10, Sec. 2 (1984), pp. 23–27.

Chaitow, L. *Amino Acids in Therapy.* New York: Thorson, 1985.

Chakmakjian, Z.H., et al. "The Effect of a Nutritional Supplement, Optivite@ for Women, on Premenstrual Tension Syndromes: Effect on Symptomatology, Using a Double Blind Cross-Over Design." *Journal of Applied Nutrition,* 37:1 (1985), pp. 12–17.

Chambers, C.A., and G. J. Taylor. "A Controlled Trial of L-Tryptophan in Mania." *British Journal of Psychiatry,* 132 (1978), pp. 555–59.

Chanarin, I. "Distribution of Folate Deficiency," in *Folic Acid in Neurology, Psychiatry, and Internal Medicine,* ed. M. I. Botez and E. H. Reynolds. New York: Raven Press, 1979.

Chandra, R.K. "Excessive Intake of Zinc Impairs Immune Responses." *Journal of the American Medical Association,* 252:11 (1984), pp. 1443–46.

Chen, C.N., et al. "Plasma Tryptophan and Sleep." *British Medical Journal,* 4 (1974), pp. 564–66.

Cheraskin, E., and W. M. Ringsdorf. "Prevalence of Possible Lead Toxicity as

Determined by Hair Analysis." *Journal of Orthomolecular Psychiatry*, 8:2 (1979), pp. 82–83.

———. *Psychodietetics*. New York: Bantam, 1974.

———, et al. "The Psychotherapeutic Implications of Cytotoxic Testing." *Journal of Orthomolecular Psychiatry*, 14:2 (1985), pp. 128–35.

———, et al. *The Vitamin C Connection*. New York: Harper & Row, 1983.

Chess, S., et al. "Depression in Childhood and Adolescence: A Prospective Study of Six Cases." *Journal of Nervous and Mental Disorders*, 171 (1983), pp. 411–20.

Chouinard, G., et al. "A Controlled Clinical Trial of L-Tryptophan in Acute Mania." *Biological Psychiatry*, 20 (1985), pp. 546–57.

———, et al. "Potentiation of Lithium by Tryptophan in a Patient with Bipolar Illness." *American Journal of Psychiatry*, 136:5 (1979), pp. 719–20.

———, et al. "Tryptophan Dosage Critical for Its Antidepressant Effect." *Lancet*, 1 (1976).

Christensen, L. "Hypoglycemia: Implications and Suggestions for Research." *Journal of Orthomolecular Psychiatry*, 10:2 (1981), pp. 77–92.

Clemis, J.D. "Inner Ear Diseases, an Allergic Reaction." *Journal of the American Medical Association*, 218 (1971), p. 1634.

Cochrane, N. "A Contribution from the Field of Psychodynamics to the Controversy over Reactive and Endogenous Depression." *British Journal of Medical Psychology*, 50 (1977), pp. 87–94.

Cohen, B.M., et al. "Lecithin in Mania: A Preliminary Report." *American Journal of Psychiatry*, 137 (1980), pp. 242–43.

———, et al. "Lecithin in the Treatment of Mania: Double-Blind, Placebo-Controlled Trials." *American Journal of Psychiatry*, 139 (1982), pp. 1162–64.

Cohen, E.L., and R. J. Wurtman. "Brain Acetylcholine: Increase after Systemic Choline Administration." *Life Sciences*, 16 (1975), pp. 1095–102.

———. "Brain Acetylcholine Synthesis: Control by Dietary Choline." *Science*, 191: (1976), pp. 1095–102.

Colby-Morley, E. "Neurotransmitters and Nutrition." *Journal of Orthomolecular Psychiatry*, 12:1 (1983), pp. 38–43.

———. "An Orthomolecular Approach to Malnutrition and the Brain." *Journal of Orthomolecular Psychiatry*, 12:2 (1983), pp. 82–88.

Coleman, M., et al. "A Preliminary Study of the Effect of Pyridoxine Administration in a Subgroup of Hyperkinetic Children: A Double-Blind Crossover Comparison with Methylphenidate." *Journal of Biological Psychiatry*, 14:5 (1979), pp. 741–51.

Colgan, M. *Your Personal Vitamin Profile*. Great Neck, NY: Morrow, 1982.

Colimore, B., and S. Colimore. *Nutrition and Your Body*. Los Angeles: Light Wave Press, 1974.

Comprehensive Textbook of Psychiatry, ed. H. I. Kaplan and B. J. Sadock. Baltimore: Williams and Wilkins, 1985.

Coppen, A., et al. "Potentiation of the Antidepressant Effect of a Monoamine-Oxidase Inhibitor by Tryptophan." *Lancet*, 1 (1963), pp. 79–81.

———, et al. "Tryptophan Metabolism in Depressive Illness." *Psychological Medicine*, 4 (1974), pp. 164–73.

Coryell, W., et al. "Bipolar I, Bipolar II, and Nonbipolar Major Depression Among the Relatives of Affectively Ill Probands." *American Journal of Psychiatry,* 142 (1985), pp. 817–21.

Covington, S.S. "Nutritional Factors Affecting Alcoholism." *Anabolism,* 4:1 (1985), pp. 4, 8.

Crapo, P.A., et al. "Plasma Glucose and Insulin Responses to Orally Administered Simple and Complex Carbohydrates." *Diabetes,* 25 (1976), pp. 741–47.

Crook, W.G. "Depression Associated with Candida Albicans Infections." *Journal of the American Medical Association,* 251:22 (1984), pp. 2928–29.

———. *Tracking Down Hidden Food Allergy.* Jackson, TN: Professional Books, 1980.

———. *The Yeast Connection.* Jackson, TN: Professional Books, 1983.

Crowder, M.K., and J. K. Pate. "A Case Report of Cimetidine-Induced Depressive Syndrome." *American Journal of Psychiatry,* 137:11 (1980), p. 1451.

Cumming, C. "Kidney Stones." *Anabolism,* 4:1 (1985), pp. 3, 8.

———. "Sweet but Controversial." *Anabolism,* 2:5 (1983), p. 3.

Cundall, R.L., et al. "Plasma and Erythrocyte Magnesium Levels in Affective Disorders." Lancet, 2 (1972), pp. 281–85.

Current Perspectives on Major Depressive Disorders in Children, ed. E. B. Weller and R. A. Weller. Washington, D.C.: American Psychiatric Press, 1984.

Curzon, G. "Relationships Between Plasma, CSF and Brain Tryptophan." *Journal of Neural Transmission,* Suppl. 15 (1979), pp. 81–92.

———. "Tryptophan Pyrrolase—a Biochemical Factor in Depressive Illness?" *British Journal of Psychiatry,* 115 (1969), pp. 1367–74.

Cutler, P. "Pyridoxine and Trace Element Therapy in Selected Clinical Cases." *Journal of Orthomolecular Psychiatry,* 3:2 (1973), pp. 89–95.

Cutting, W.C. *Handbook of Pharmacology.* New York: Meredith, 1964.

d'Elia, G., et al. "L-Tryptophan and 5-Hydroxytryptophan in the Treatment of Depression." *Acta Psychiatrica Scandinavica,* 57 (1978), pp. 239–52.

Dackis, C.A., et al. "Specificity of the TRH Test for Major Depression in Patients with Serious Cocaine Abuse." *American Journal of Psychiatry,* 142:9 (1985), pp. 1097–99.

"Data Accumulating to Support Concept That Psychotherapy Is Biologic Treatment." *Clinical Psychiatry News,* 14:6 (1986), pp. 1, 28.

Davidson, J.R.T. "The Newcastle Endogenous Depression Diagnostic Index (NEDDI): Validity and Reliability." *Acta Psychiatrica Scandinavica,* 69 (1984), pp. 220–30.

———, et al. "Comparative Diagnostic Criteria for Melancholia and Endogenous Depression." *Archives of General Psychiatry,* 41 (1948), pp. 506–11.

Davies, B., et al. "A Comparative Study of Four Depression Rating Scales." *Australian and New Zealand Journal of Psychiatry,* 9 (1975), pp. 21–24.

Davies, S. "Assessment of Zinc Status." *International Clinical Nutrition Review,* 4:3 (1984), pp. 122–29.

Davis, J.M., et al. "Acetylcholine and Mental Disease," in *Neuroregulators and Psychiatric Disorders,* eds. U. E. Hamburg and J. D. Barchas. New York: Oxford Press, 1977.

———, et al. "Cholinergic Mechanisms in Schizophrenia, Mania and Depression," in *Cholinergic Mechanisms and Psychopharmacology*, ed. D. J. Jenden. New York: Plenum Press, 1975.

Davis, K.L., et al. "Age and the Dexamethasone Suppression Test in Depression." *American Journal of Psychiatry*, 141:7 (1984), pp. 872–74.

———, et al. "Cholinergic Mechanisms in Neurological and Psychiatric Disorders," in *Neuroregulators and Psychiatric Disorders*, eds. U. E. Hamburg and J. D. Barchas. New York: Oxford Press, 1977.

DeFeudis, F.V. "Amino Acids as Central Neurotransmitters." *Annual Review of Pharmacology*, 15 (1975), pp. 105–27.

DeLiz, A.J. "Large Amounts of Nicotinic Acids and Vitamin B_{12} in the Treatment of Apparently Irreversible Psychotic Conditions Found in Patients with Low Levels of Folic Acid." *Journal of Orthomolecular Psychiatry*, 8:2 (1979), pp. 63–65.

Denson, R. "The Value of Nicotinamide in the Treatment of Schizophrenia." *Diseases of the Nervous System*, 23 (1962), pp. 167–72.

Devanand, D., and J. C. Nelson. "Concurrent Depression and Dementia: Implications for Diagnosis and Treatment." *Journal of Clinical Psychiatry*, 46:9 (1985), pp. 389–92.

Dhopeshearkar, G.A. *Nutrition and Brain Development.* New York: Plenum, 1983.

Diamond, S. "Tricyclics Becoming Agents of Choice in Treating Chronic Pain." *Clinical Psychiatry News*, 13:5 (1985), p. 26.

"Dietary Intake of Certain Amino Acids Linked to Brain Function." *Clinical Psychiatry*, 8:10 (1980), pp. 1, 20.

Dietz, A.S. "The Vitamins: Thiamine, the First B Vitamin." *Anabolism*, 2:5 (1983), p. 4.

Dilsauer, S.C., et al. "Antidepressant Withdrawal Symptoms Treated with Anticholinergic Agents." *American Journal of Psychiatry*, 140:2 (1983), pp. 249–51.

———, and K. White. "Affective Disorders and Associated Psychopathology: A Family History Study." *Journal of Clinical Psychiatry.* 47:4 (1986), pp. 162–69.

Dorfman, W. "Depression: Its Expression in Physical Illness." *Psychosomatics*, 19:11 (1978), pp. 702–8.

Douglass, W.C. "Candida Albicans: The Great Undiagnosed Disease of Women." *Health Freedom News*, June, 1984.

Dreyfus, P.M. "Transketolase Activity in the Nervous System," in *Thiamine Deficiency*, eds. G.E.W. Wolstrenholme and M. O'Connor. London: Ciba Foundation Study Group. No. 28., (1967), pp. 103–11.

Dunner, D.L. "Anxiety and Panic Relationship to Depression and Cardiac Disorders." *Psychosomatics*, 26:11 (1985), pp. 18–22.

———, and F. K. Goodwin. "Effect of L-Tryptophan on Brain Serotonin Metabolism in Depressed Patients." *Archives of General Psychiatry*, 26 (1972), pp. 364–66.

———, and R. R. Fieve. "Affective Disorder: Studies with Amine Precursors." *American Journal of Psychiatry*, 132 (1975), pp. 180–83.

———, et al. "Heritable Factors in Severity of Affective Illness." *Sci. Proceedings of the American Psychiatric Association*, 123 (1970).

———, et al. "Plasma and Erythrocyte Magnesium Levels in Patients with Primary

Affective Disorder during Chronic Lithium Treatment." *Acta Psychiatrica Scandinavica,* 51 (1975), pp. 104–9.

Dye, L. "Victims of Rare Illness Allergic to Everything." *Los Angeles Times,* October 30, 1983, pp. 1, 3, 34.

Edwin, E., et al. "Vitamin B_{12} Hypovitaminosis in Mental Diseases." *Acta Medica Scandinavica,* 177:6 (1965), pp. 689–99.

Egeland, J.A., and A. M. Hostetter. "Amish Study, I: Affective Disorders Among the Amish, 1976–1980." *American Journal of Psychiatry,* 140:1 (1983), pp. 56–61.

———, et al. "Amish Study, III: The Impact of Cultural Factors on Diagnosis of Bipolar Illness." *American Journal of Psychiatry,* 140:1 (1983), pp. 67–71.

Ellis, R.E., et al. "Incidence of Osteoporosis in Vegetarians and Omnivores." *American Journal of Clinical Nutrition,* 25 (1972), pp. 555–58.

Enna, S.J., and D. A. Kendall. "Interaction of Antidepressants with Brain Neurotransmitter Receptors." *Journal of Clinical Psychopharmacology,* 1:6 (1981), pp. 12s–16s.

Eriksson, N.E. "Food Sensitivity Reported by Patients with Asthma and Hay Fever." *Allergy,* 33:4 (1978), pp. 189–96.

Evans, M. "Treatment of Unipolar Depression." (Letters) *Lancet,* 1 (1976), pp. 90–91.

Extein, I., and M. S. Gold. "Psychiatric Applications of Thyroid Tests." *Journal of Clinical Psychiatry,* Supplement. 47:1 (1986), pp. 13–16.

———, et al. "Does Subclinical Hypothyroidism Predispose to Tricyclic-Induced Rapid Mood Cycles?" *Journal of Clinical Psychiatry,* 43 (1982), pp. 290–91.

"Eye Opening Facts." *NCA-LA Newsletter.* Los Angeles: National Council on Alcoholism, 1986, p. 3.

Faelten, S. *The Complete Book of Minerals for Health.* Emmaus, PA: Rodale, 1981.

Falk, D.E. "Identifying Individuals at Risk for Suicidal Behavior." *Clinical Psychiatry News,* 13:12 (1985), pp. 1, 11.

Farkas, T., et al. "L-Tryptophan in Depression." *Biological Psychiatry,* 11:3 (1976), pp. 295–301.

Fawcett, J., et al. "Evaluation of Lithium Therapy for Alcoholism." *Journal of Clinical Psychiatry,* 45:12 (1984), pp. 494–99.

Fein, G.G., et al. "Environmental Toxins and Behavioral Development." *American Psychologist,* November, 1983, pp. 1188–97.

Feinberg, M., et al. "The Carroll Rating Scale for Depression II. Factor Analyses of the Feature Profiles." *British Journal of Psychiatry,* 138 (1981), pp. 201–4.

———, et al. "The Carroll Rating Scale for Depression III. Comparison with Other Rating Instruments." *British Journal of Psychiatry,* 138 (1981), pp. 205–9.

Feinberg, T., and B. Goodman. "Affective Illness, Dementia, and Psuedodementia." *Journal of Clinical Psychiatry,* 45:3 (1984), pp. 99–103.

Fernstrom, J.D. "Diet-Induced Changes in Plasma Amino Acid Pattern: Effects on the Brain Uptake of Large Neutral Amino Acids, and on Brain Serotonin Synthesis." *Journal of Neural Transmission,* Suppl. 15 (1979), pp. 55–67.

———, and R. J. Wurtman. "Brain Serotonin Content: Physiological Dependence on Plasma Tryptophan Levels." *Science,* 173 (1971), pp. 149–52.

———, et al. "Acute Reduction of Brain Serotonin and 5-HIAA Following Food Consumption. Correlation with the Ratios of Serum Tryptophan to the Sum of

Competing Neutral Amino Acids." *Journal of Neural Transmission*, 36, pp. 113–21.

Ferrannini, E., et al. "Sodium Elevates the Plasma Glucose Response to Glucose Ingestion in Man." *Journal of Clinical Endocrinology and Metabolism*, 54 (1982), p. 455.

Fincher, J. "Sunlight May Be Necessary for Your Health." *Smithsonian*, 16:3 (1985), pp. 70–76.

Fine, B.P., et al. "Influence of Magnesium on the Intestinal Absorption of Lead." *Environmental Research*, 12 (1976), p. 224.

Fishbein, D. "The Contribution of Refined Carbohydrate Consumption to Maladaptive Behaviors." *Journal of Orthomolecular Psychiatry*, 11:1 (1982), pp. 17–25.

Fitten, L.J., et al. "L-Tryptophan as a Hypnotic in Special Patients." *Journal of the American Geriatric Society*, 33 (1985), p. 294.

Foreman, R.E. "Candida Albicans: A Lingering Problem." *Let's Live Magazine*, February, 1984.

Fouad, M.T. "Factors Influencing Dietary Zinc Bioavailability." *Journal of Applied Nutrition*, 35:1 (1983), pp. 1–5.

Fox, A., and B. Fox. *DLPA to End Chronic Pain and Depression*. New York: Pocket Books, 1985.

Frances, R.J., et al. "Outcome Study of Familial and Nonfamilial Alcoholism." *American Journal of Psychiatry*, 141:11 (1984), pp. 1469–71.

Fraser, W., et al. "Effect of L-Tryptophan on Growth Hormone and Prolactin Release in Normal Volunteers and Patients with Secretory Pituitary Tumors." *Hormone and Metabolic Research*, 11 (1979), pp. 149–55.

Freeman, E.W., et al. "PMS Treatment Approaches and Progesterone Therapy." *Psychosomatics*, 26:10 (1985), pp. 811–16.

Frizel, D., et al. Plasma Magnesium and Calcium in Depression." *British Journal of Psychiatry*, 115 (1969), pp. 1375–77.

Fuchs, N., et al. "The Effect of a Nutritional Supplement, Optivite@ for Women, on Premenstrual Tension Syndromes: Effect on Blood Chemistry and Serum Steroid Levels During the Midluteal Phase." *Journal of Applied Nutrition*, 37:1 (1985), pp. 1–11.

Fuller, R.W. "Pharmacologic Modification of Serotonergic Function: Drugs for the Study and Treatment of Psychiatric and Other Disorders." *Journal of Clinical Psychiatry*, 47:4, Suppl. (1986), pp. 4–8.

Gaby, A. *The Doctor's Guide to Vitamin B_6*. Emmaus, PA: Rodale, 1984.

Gallagher, D.W., et al. "Chronic Benzodiazepine Treatment Decreases Postsynaptic GABA Sensitivity." *Nature*, 308 (1984), pp. 74–77.

Galland, L. "Vitamin B_6, Magnesium and Essential Fatty Acid Deficiencies in Patients with Candidiasis." *Journal of Orthomolecular Psychiatry*, 14:1 (1984), pp. 50–60.

Gardner, E.R., and R.C.W. Hall. "Medical Screening of Psychiatric Patients." *Journal of Orthomolecular Psychiatry*, 9:3 (1980), pp. 207–15.

Garfinkel, B.D., et al. "Suicide Attempts in Children and Adolescents." *American Journal of Psychiatry*, 139:10 (1982), pp. 1257–61.

Garrison, R. *Lysine, Tryptophan and Other Amino Acids*. New Canaan, CT: Keats, 1982.

Garvey, M.J., et al. "Migraine Headaches and Depression." *American Journal of Psychiatry*, 141:8 (1984), pp. 986–88.

Geissler, C.A., and J. E. Bates. "Nutritional Effects of Tooth Loss." *American Journal of Clinical Nutrition*, 39 (1984), pp. 478–89.

Gelenberg, A.J., et al. "Tyrosine for the Treatment of Depression." *American Journal of Psychiatry*, 137:5 (1980), pp. 622–23.

Gerner, R.H., et al. "CSF Neurochemistry of Women with Anorexia Nervosa and Normal Women." *American Journal of Psychiatry*, 141:11 (1984), pp. 1441–44.

———, et al. "Treatment of Geriatric Depression with Trazodone, Imipramine, and Placebo: A Double-Blind Study." *Journal of Clinical Psychiatry*, 41:6 (1980), pp. 216–20.

Gerrard, J.W. "Food Intolerance." *Lancet*, 2 (1984), p. 413.

Gershon, E.S., et al. "Clinical Findings in Patients with Anorexia Nervosa and Affective Illness in Their Relatives." *American Journal of Psychiatry*, 141:11 (1984), pp. 1419–22.

Giannini, A.J., et al. "Prevalence of Mitral Valve Prolapse in Bipolar Affective Disorder." *American Journal of Psychiatry*, 141:8 (1984), pp. 991–92.

———, et al. "Reversibility of Serotonin Irritation Syndrome with Atmospheric Anions." *Journal of Clinical Psychiatry*, 47:3 (1986), pp. 141–43.

Gibson, C.J., and A. Gelenberg. "Tyrosine for the Treatment of Depression." *Management of Depressions with Monoamine Precursors*, eds. J. Mendlewicz and H. M. van Praag. New York: S. Karger, 1983.

Gibson, C.J., and R. J. Wurtman. "Physiological Control of Brain Catechol Synthesis by Brain Tyrosine Concentration." *Biochemical Pharmacology*, 26 (1977), pp. 1137–42.

———. "Physiological Control of Brain Norepinephrine Synthesis by Brain Tyrosine Concentration." *Life Sciences*, 22 (1978), pp. 1399–406.

Gillin, J.C., et al. "Clinical Effects of Tryptophan in Chronic Schizophrenic Patients." *Biological Psychiatry*, 11:5 (1976), pp. 635–39.

Gitelman, H.J., and L. G. Welt. "Magnesium Deficiency." *Annual Review of Medicine*, 20 (1969), pp. 233–42.

Glaeser, B.S., et al. "Elevation of Plasma Tyrosine after a Single Dose of L-Tyrosine." *Life Sciences*, 25 (1979), pp. 265–72.

Glassner, B., and C. V. Haldipur. "Life Events and Early and Late Onset of Bipolar Disorder." *American Journal of Psychiatry*, 140:2 (1983), pp. 215–17.

Goei, G.S., et al. "Dietary Patterns of Patients with Premenstrual Tension." *Journal of Applied Nutrition*, 34 (1982), p. 4.

Goff, D.C. "Two Cases of Hypomania Following the Addition of L-Tryptophan to a Monoamine Oxidase Inhibitor." *American Journal of Psychiatry*, 142:12 (1985), pp. 1487–88.

Goldbeck, N. *How to Cope with Menstrual Problems—A Wholistic Approach.* New Canaan, CT: Keats, 1983.

Goldberg, I. "Tyrosine in Depression." *Lancet*, 2 (1980), p. 364.

Goldin, B.R., et al. "Estrogen Excretion Patterns and Plasma Levels in Vegetarian and Omnivorous Women." *New England Journal of Medicine*, 307 (1982), pp. 1542–47.

"Good News about Premenstrual Blues." *Drug Therapy*, April, 1982, pp. 57–59.

Goodwin, F.K., et al. "Potentiation of Antidepressant Effects by L-Triiodothyronine in Tricyclic Nonresponders." *American Journal of Psychiatry,* 139 (1982), pp. 34–38.

Gottlieb, B. "Brain Food." *Prevention,* September, 1979, pp. 181–87.

Greenstein, J.P., and M. Winitz. "Tyrosine," in *Chemistry of the Amino Acids.* Melbourne, FL: Krieger, 3 (1961), pp. 2348–65.

Greger, J.L., and M. J. Baier. "Effect of Dietary Aluminum on Mineral Metabolism." *American Journal of Clinical Nutrition,* 38 (1983), pp. 411–19.

Greist, J.H., and J. W. Jefferson. *Depression and Its Treatment: Help for the Nation's #1 Mental Problem.* Washington, D.C.: American Psychiatric Press, 1984.

———, et al. "Antidepressant Running." *Psychiatric Annals,* 9:3 (1979), pp. 134–40.

———, et al. "Running as Treatment for Depression." *Comprehensive Psychiatry,* 20:1 (1979), pp. 41–54.

Growden, J.H. "Neurotransmitter Precursors in the Diet," in *Nutrition and the Brain,* eds. R. J. Wurtman, et al. New York: Raven Press, 1979, pp. 117–81.

———, and R. J. Wurtman. "Contemporary Nutrition: Nutrients and Neurotransmitters." *New York State Journal of Medicine,* 80:10 (1980), pp. 1638–39.

———. "Dietary Influences on the Synthesis of Neurotransmitters in the Brain." *Nutrition Reviews,* 37:5 (1979), pp. 129–36.

———. "Treatment of Brain Disease with Dietary Precursors of Neurotransmitters." *American International Medicine,* 86 (1977), pp. 337–39.

———, et al. "Treatment of Brain Disease with Dietary Precursors of Neurotransmitters." *Annals of Internal Medicine,* 86:3 (1977), pp. 337–39.

Guenther, R.M. "Role of Nutritional Therapy in Alcoholism Treatment." *International Journal for Biosocial Research,* 4:1 (1983), pp. 5–18.

Ha, H., et al. "The Dexamethasone Suppression Test in Adolescent Psychiatric Patients." *American Journal of Psychiatry,* 141 (1984), pp. 421–23.

Hackett, T.P. "Depression Following Myocardial Infarction." *Psychosomatics,* 26:11 (1985), pp. 23–30.

Halaris, A.E., and E. M. DeMet. "Studies of Norepinephrine Metabolism in Manic and Depressive States," in *Catecholamines: Basic and Clinical Frontiers,* eds. E. Usdin, et al. New York: Pergamon Press, 1979.

Hale, H., et al. "Human Amino Acid Excretion Patterns During and Following Prolonged Multistressor Tests." *Aviation, Space and Environmental Medicine,* February, 1975, pp. 173–78.

Hall, K. "Allergy of the Nervous System: A Review." *Annals of Allergy,* 36:1 (1976), pp. 49–64.

Hall, R.C. "Psychiatric Manifestations of Hashimoto's Thyroiditis." *Psychosomatics,* 23:4 (1982), pp. 337–42.

Hamilton, J.A., et al. "Premenstrual Mood Changes: A Guide to Evaluation and Treatment." *Psychiatric Annals,* 14:6 (1984), pp. 426–35.

Hamilton, M. "Rating Depressive Patients." *Journal of Clinical Psychiatry,* 41:12, Sec. 2. (1980), pp. 21–24.

Hamilton, Max. "A Rating Scale for Depression." *Journal of Neurol. Neurosurg. Psychiat.,* 23 (1960), pp. 56–62.

Handbook of Affective Disorders, ed. E. S. Paykel. New York: Guilford Press, 1982.

Hanna, S., et al. "Hypomagnesemia: Physical and Psychiatric Symptoms." *Journal of the American Medical Association,* 224 (1973), pp. 1749–51.

Harrison, T.S. "Adrenal Medullary and Thyroid Relationships." *Physiol. Rev.,* 44 (1964), pp. 161–85.

Harrison, W.M. "Psychiatric Evaluation of Premenstrual Changes." *Psychosomatics,* 26:10 (1985), pp. 789–99.

Hartmann, E. "L-Tryptophan: An Effective Hypnotic." *Current Psychiatric Therapies,* 1977, pp. 165–69.

―――. "L-Tryptophan: A Rational Hypnotic with Clinical Potential." *American Journal of Psychiatry,* 134:4 (1977), pp. 366–70.

―――, and R. Chung. "Sleep Inducing Effects of L-Tryptophan." *Journal of Pharmacy and Pharmacology,* 24 (1972), pp. 252–53.

―――, and J. Cravens. "Effects of Long-Term Administration of L-Tryptophan on Human Sleep," (abstract) in *Sleep Research,* Vol. 4, eds. M. H. Stern, et al. Los Angeles: UCLA Brain Information Service/Brain Research Institute, 1975, p. 76.

―――, and R. Elion. "The Insomnia of 'Sleeping in a Strange Place': Effects of L-tryptophan." *Psychopharmacology,* 53:2 (1977), pp. 131–33.

―――, and C. L. Spinweber. "Sleep Induced by L-Tryptophan: Effect of Dosages within the Normal Dietary Intake." *Journal of Nervous and Mental Disease,* 1979, pp. 497–99.

―――, et al. "L-Tryptophan and Sleep." *Psychopharmacologia,* 19 (1971), pp. 114–27.

―――, et al. "Effect of Amino Acids on Quantified Sleepiness." *Nutrition and Behavior,* 1 (1983), pp. 179–83.

Hawkins, D.R., et al. "Extended Sleep (Hypersomnia) in Young Depressed Patients." *American Journal of Psychiatry,* 142:8 (1985), pp. 905–10.

Hedlund, J.L., and B. W. Vieweg. "The Hamilton Rating Scale for Depression: A Comprehensive Review." *Journal of Operational Psychiatry,* 10:2 (1979), pp. 149–65.

―――. "The Zung Self-Rating Depression Scale: A Comprehensive Review." *Journal of Operational Psychiatry,* 10:1 (1979) pp. 52–64.

Heller, B., et al. "Parkinson's Disease, Depression, and Amino Acid Therapy." *Drug Research,* 26 (1976), p. 577.

Hemila, H.O. "A Critique of Nutritional Recommendations." *Journal of Orthomolecular Psychiatry,* 14:2 (1985), pp. 88–91.

Hendler, Nelson. "Depression Caused by Chronic Pain." *Journal of Clinical Psychiatry,* 45:3 (1984), pp. 30–36.

Heroux, O., et al. "Long-Term Effect of Suboptimal Dietary Magnesium." *Journal of Nutrition,* 107 (1977), p. 1640.

Hertz, D., and F. G. Sulman. "Preventing Depression with Tryptophan." *Lancet,* 1 (1968), p. 531.

Herzberg, L., and B. Herzberg. "Mood Change and Magnesium: A Possible Interaction Between Magnesium and Lithium." *Journal of Nervous and Mental Disease,* 165 (1977), pp. 423–26.

Himmelhoch, J.M., et al. "The Dilemma of Depression in the Elderly." *Journal of Clinical Psychiatry*, 43:9 (Sec. 2) (1982), pp. 26–32.

Hirsch, M.J., et al. "Lecithin Consumption Increases Acetylcholine Concentrations in Rat Brain and Adrenal Gland." *Science*, 202 (1978), pp. 223–25.

Hirschfeld, R.M.A., and G. L. Klerman. "Personality Attributes and Affective Disorders." *American Journal of Psychiatry*, 136:1 (1979), pp. 67–70.

———, et al. "Assessing Personality: Effects of the Depressive State on Trait Measurement." *American Journal of Psychiatry*, 140:6 (1983), pp. 695–99.

The History of Depression, eds. A. T. Beck, et al. New York: Insight Communications, 1977.

Hoes, M.J. "L-Tryptophan in Depression and Strain." *Journal of Orthomolecular Psychiatry*, 11:4 (1982), pp. 231–42.

———, et al. "Hyperventilation Syndrome, Treatment with L-Tryptophan and Pyridoxine; Predictive Values of Xanthurenic Acid Excretion." *Journal of Orthomolecular Psychiatry*, 10:1 (1981), pp. 7–15.

Hoffer, A. "Allergy, Depression and Tricyclic Antidepressants." *Journal of Orthomolecular Psychiatry*, 9:3 (1980), pp. 164–70.

———. "Editorial: Mega Amino Acid Therapy." *Journal of Orthomolecular Psychiatry*, 9:1 (1980), pp. 2–5.

———. "Natural History and Treatment of Thirteen Pairs of Identical Twins: Schizophrenic and Schizophrenic-Spectrum Conditions." *Journal of Orthomolecular Psychiatry*, 5:2 (1976), pp. 101–22.

———. "Obsessions and Depression." *Journal of Orthomolecular Psychiatry*, 8:2 (1979), pp. 78–81.

———, and M. Walker. *Nutrients to Age Without Senility*. New Canaan, CT: Keats, 1980.

Hoffer, J. *Orthomolecular Therapy: An Examination of the Issues*. Regina, Saskatchewan: Canadian Schizophrenia Foundation, 1974.

"Holiday Blues a Reality, But Rise in Suicides, Hospitalization a Myth." *Medical Tribune*, November 7, 1984, p. 7.

Holland, A.J., et al. "Anorexia Nervosa: A Study of 34 Twin Pairs and One Set of Triplets." *British Journal of Psychiatry*, 145 (1984), pp. 414–19.

Holmes, T.H. "Life Situations, Emotions, and Disease." *Psychosomatics*, 19:12 (1978), pp. 747–54.

Honore, P., et al. "Lithium + L-Tryptophan Compared with Amitriptyline in Endogenous Depression." *Journal of Affective Disorders*, 4:1 (1982), pp. 79–82.

Horton, R., and E. G. Biglieri. "Effect of Aldosterone on the Metabolism of Magnesium." *Journal of Clinical Endocrinology*, 22 (1962), p. 1187.

Hostetter, A.M., et al. "Amish Study, II: Consensus Diagnoses and Reliability Results." *American Journal of Psychiatry*, 140:1 (1983), pp. 62–66.

Huggins, H.A. "Mercury: A Factor in Mental Disease." *Journal of Orthomolecular Psychiatry*, 11:1 (1982), pp. 3–16.

Hughes, John, and Dorothy Hatsukami, et al. "Prevalence of Smoking among Psychiatric Outpatients." *American Journal of Psychiatry*, 143:8 (1986), pp. 993–97.

Hunter, B.T. *The Sugar Trap: And How to Avoid It.* New York: Houghton Mifflin, 1982.

Hussein, M.A., et al. "Daily Fluctuation of Plasma Amino Acid Levels in Adult Men: Effect of Dietary Tryptophan Intake and Distribution of Meals." *Journal of Nutrition*, 101 (1971), pp. 61–70.

Ingber, D. "The Science of Emotion." *American Health*, 6:3 (1984), pp. 19–21.

Insel, T.R., et al. "Possible Development of the Serotonin Syndrome in Man." *American Journal of Psychiatry*, 139:7 (1982), pp. 954–55.

"Iron and Copper Excess: Update." *Nutraletter*, 2:1 (1984), pp. 1–4.

Iron Deficiency: Brain Biochemistry and Behavior, eds. E. Pollitt and R. L. Liebel. New York: Raven, 1982.

Iversen, Leslie L. "Neurotransmitters and CNS Disease." *Lancet*, 1 (1982), pp. 914–18.

Jacobs, B.L., and A. Gelperin. *Serotonin Neurotransmission and Behavior*. Boston: MIT Press, 1981.

Jampala, V.C. "Anorexia Nervosa: A Variant Form of Affective Disorder." *Psychiatric Annals*, 15:12 (1985), pp. 698–703.

Janowsky, D.S., et al. "Acetylcholine and Depression." *Psychosomatic Medicine*, 36 (1974), 248–57.

——, et al. "A Cholinergic-Adrenergic Hypothesis of Mania and Depression." *Lancet*, 1 (1972), pp. 632–35.

——. "Pseudodementia in the Elderly: Differential Diagnosis and Treatment." *Journal of Clinical Psychiatry*, 43:9 (Sec. 2) (1982), pp. 19–25.

Jarvik, L.P. "Antidepressant Therapy for the Geriatric Patient." *Journal of Clinical Psychopharmacology*, 1:6 (1981), pp. 55S–61S.

Jefferson, J.W. "Biologic Treatment of Depression in Cardiac Patients." *Psychosomatics*, 26:11 (1985), pp. 31–38.

Jenike, M.A. *Alzheimer's Disease: Diagnosis, Treatment and Management, Clinical Perspectives on Aging, Number 1*. Philadelphia: Wyeth Laboratories, 1985.

Jensen, L.S., and D. V. Maurice. "Influence of Sulfur Amino Acids on Copper Toxicity in Chicks." *Journal Nutr.*, 109:1 (1979), pp. 91–97.

Johansson, G. "Magnesium and Renal Stone Disease." *Acta Medica Scandinavica Supplementum*, 661 (1982), pp. 13–18.

Jones, V.A., et al. "Food Intolerance: A Major Factor in the Pathogenesis of Irritable Bowel Syndrome." *Lancet*, 2 (1982), p. 8308.

Jurnovoy, J., and D. Jenness. "The Tragic Impulse: Teenage Suicide." *American Health*, 6:3 (1984), pp. 3–5.

Jyotirmayananda, S. "Where Is Happiness?" *Integral Light*, 1:2 (1985), p. 1.

Kashani, J.H., et al. "Depression and Depressive-Like States in Preschool-Age Children in a Child Development Unit." *American Journal of Psychiatry*, 141:11 (1984), pp. 1397–402.

Katon, Wayne. "Depression: Relationship to Somatization and Chronic Medical Illness." *Journal of Clinical Psychiatry*, 45:3 (1984), pp. 4–11.

Katya-Katya, M., et al. "The Effect of Zinc Supplementation on Plasma Cholesterol Levels." *Nutrition Research*, 4 (1984), pp. 633–38.

Katz, I.R. "Is There a Hypoxic Affective Syndrome?" *Psychosomatics*, 23:8 (1982), pp. 846–53.

Katz, J.L., et al. "Is There a Relationship Between Eating Disorder and Affective

Disorder? New Evidence from Sleep Recordings." *American Journal of Psychiatry*, 141 (1984), pp. 753–59.

Katz, M.M., and G. L. Klerman. "Introduction: Overview of the Clinical Studies Program." Special Section: The Psychobiology of Depression—NIMH—Clinical Research Branch Collaborative Program. *American Journal of Psychiatry*, 136:1 (1979), pp. 49–51.

Kaufmann, D.A. *The Food Sensitivity Diet.* New York: Freundlich, 1984.

Kaufmann, Michael W., et al. "Use of Psychostimulants in Medically Ill Depressed Patients." *Psychosomatics*, 23:8 (1982), pp. 817–19.

Keeler, M.H., et al. "Are All Recently Detoxified Alcoholics Depressed?" *American Journal of Psychiatry*, 136:4B (1979), pp. 586–88.

Keiffer, E. "Premenstrual Syndrome." *Family Circle*, April 6, 1982, pp. 30–31.

Keller, M.B., and R. W. Shapiro. " 'Double Depression': Superimposition of Acute Depressive Episodes on Chronic Depressive Disorders." *American Journal of Psychiatry*, 139:4 (1982), pp. 438–42.

———, et al. "Double Depression": Two Year Follow-Up." *American Journal of Psychiatry*, 140:6 (1983), pp. 689–94.

———, et al. "Long-Term Outcome of Episodes of Major Depression: Clinical and Public Health Significance." *Journal of the American Medical Association*, 252:6 (1984), pp. 788–92.

———, et al. "Recovery in Major Depressive Disorder." *Archives of General Psychiatry*, 39 (1982), pp. 905–10.

Kellner, R., et al. "Hyperprolactinemia, Distress, and Hostility." *American Journal of Psychiatry*, 141:6 (1984), pp. 759–63.

Ketcham, K., and L. A. Mueller. *Eating Right to Live Sober.* Seattle: Madonna Publishers, 1983.

Khan, A.U. "Sleep Latency in Hyperkinetic Boys." *American Journal of Psychiatry*, 139:10 (1982), pp. 1358–60.

Khanna, J.M., et al. "Role of Serotonin (5-HT) in Tolerance to Ethanol and Barbiturates." *Advances in Medical Biology*, 126 (1980), pp. 181–95.

Kim, J.C.S. "Effects of Nutrition on Disease and Life Span." *Journal of Applied Nutrition*, 37:1 (1985), pp. 41–42.

King, R.B. "Pain and Tryptophan." *Journal of Neurosurgery*, 53:1 (1980), pp. 44–52.

Kirstein, L., et al. "Clinical Correlates of the TRH Infusion Test in Primary Depression." *Journal of Clinical Psychiatry*, 43:5 (1982), pp. 191–94.

Kishimoto, H., and Y. Hama. "The Level and Diurnal Rhythm of Plasma Tryptophan and Tyrosine in Manic-Depressive Patients." *Yokohama Medical Bulletin*, 27 (1976), p. 89.

Kline, N.S. "Depression: Its Diagnosis and Treatment," in *Modern Problems of Pharmacopsychiatry*, Vol. 3. New York: S. Karger, Basel, 1969.

———. "The Endorphins Revisited." *Psychiatric Annals*, 11:4 (1981), pp. 137–42.

———, and W. Sacks. "Relief of Depression Within One Day Using a MAO Inhibitor and Intravenous 5-HTP." *American Journal of Psychiatry*, 120 (1963), pp. 274–75.

Knesevich, J.W., et al. "Preliminary Report on Affective Symptoms in the Early Stages of Senile Dementia of the Alzheimer Type." *American Journal of Psychiatry*, 140:2 (1983), pp. 233–35.

Knesevich, J.W., et al. "Validity of the Hamilton Rating Scale for Depression." *British Journal of Psychiatry*, 131 (1977), pp. 49–52.

Knox, W.E. "The Regulation of Tryptophan Pyrrolase Activity by Tryptophan." *Advances in Enzyme Regulation*, 4 (1966), pp. 287–97.

Kolata, G.B. "Brain Biochemistry: Effects of Diet." *Science*, 192 (1976), p. 41.

Kosky, R. "Childhood Suicidal Behavior." *Journal of Child Psychology and Psychiatry*, 24 (1983), pp. 457–68.

Kovacs, M. "The Efficacy of Cognitive and Behavior Therapies for Depression." *American Journal of Psychiatry*, 137:12 (1980), pp. 1495–501.

———. "Rating Scales to Assess Depression in School-Aged Children." *Acta Paedopsychiatry*, 46 (1980/81), pp. 305–15.

———, et al. "Depressive Disorders in Childhood I: A Longitudinal Prospective Study of Characteristics and Recovery." *Archives of General Psychiatry*, 41 (1984), pp. 229–37.

———, et al. "Depressive Disorders in Childhood II." *Archives of General Psychiatry*, 41 (1984), pp. 643–49.

Kraemer, G.W., and W. T. McKinney. "Interactions of Pharmacological Agents Which Alter Biogenic Amine Metabolism and Depression." *Journal of Affective Disorders*, 1 (1979), pp. 33–54.

Krall, A.R., et al. "Effects of Magnesium Infusions on the Metabolism of Calcium and Lead," in *Magnesium in Health and Disease*, eds. M. Cantin and M. S. Seelig. New York: SP Medical and Scientific Books, 1980.

Krippner, S., and S. Fischer. "A Study of Organization Procedures and Megavitamin Treatment for Children with Brain Dysfunction." *Journal of Orthomolecular Psychiatry*, 1:2 and 3 (1972), pp. 121–32.

Krog-Meyer, I., et al. "Prediction of Relapse with the TRH Test and Prophylactic Amitriptyline in 39 Patients with Endogenous Depression." *American Journal of Psychiatry*, 141:8 (1984), pp. 945–48.

Kronfol, Z., et al. "Application of Biological Markers in Depression Secondary to Thyrotoxicosis." *American Journal of Psychiatry*, 139:10 (1982), pp. 1319–22.

Kueppers, H. *The Basic Law of Color Therapy*. New York: Barron, 1982.

Kupinsel, R. "Mercury Amalgam Toxicity, a Major Common Denominator of Degenerative Disease." *Journal of Orthomolecular Psychiatry*, 13:4 (1984), pp. 240–57.

Kutner, S.J., and W. L. Brown. "Types of Oral Contraceptives, Depression, and Premenstrual Symptoms." *Journal of Mental and Nervous Disease*, 155:3 (1972), pp. 153–62.

Kutsky, R. *Handbook of Vitamins, Minerals and Hormones*. New York: Van Nostrand, 1981.

Lake, C.R., and M. G. Ziegler. *Catecholamines in Psychiatric and Neurolologic Disorders*. Stoneham, MA: Butterworth, 1985.

———, et al. "High Plasma Norepinephrine Levels in Patients with Major Affective Disorder." *American Journal of Psychiatry*, 139:10 (1982), pp. 1315–18.

Laker, M. "On Determining Trace Element Levels in Man: The Uses of Blood and Hair." *Lancet*, 2 (1982), p. 260.

Lark, S.M. "Natural Rx for PMS." *Yoga Journal*, May/June 1985, pp. 7–8.

Lauersen, N.H. *Premenstrual Syndrome and You*. Hamden, CT: Fireside, 1983.

Lebowitz, M.R., et al. "Psychopharmacologic Validation of Atypical Depression." *Journal of Clinical Psychiatry,* 45:7 (1984), pp. 22–25.

"Lecithin and Memory." *Lancet,* 1 (1980), p. 293.

Leevy, C.M. "Red Cell Transketolase as an Indicator of Nutritional Deficiency." *American Journal of Clinical Nutrition,* 33 (1982), p. 260.

Lehman, H.E. "The Clinician's View of Anxiety and Depression." *Journal of Clinical Psychiatry,* 44:8 (1983), pp. 3–7.

Lehmann, J. "Tryptophan Malabsorption in Levodopa-Treated Parkinsonian Patients." *Acta Medica Scandinavica,* 194 (1973), pp. 181–89.

Lerer, B. "Alternative Therapies for Bipolar Disorder." *Journal of Clinical Psychiatry,* 46 (1985), pp. 309–16.

Lesser, M. *Nutrition and Vitamin Therapy.* New York: Random House, 1980.

Lester, M.L., et al. "Refined Carbohydrate Intake, Hair Cadmium Levels, and Cognitive Functioning in Children." *Nutrition and Behavior,* 1 (1982), pp. 3–13.

Levine, S., et al. "Behavioral and Hormonal Responses to Separation in Infant Rhesus Monkeys and Mothers." *Behavioral Neuroscience,* 99:3 (1985), pp. 399–410.

Lewis, A., and M. Hoghughi. "An Evaluation of Depression as a Side Effect of Oral Contraceptives." *British Journal of Psychology,* 115 (1969), pp. 698–701.

Lewis, J.L., and G. Winokur. "The Induction of Mania." *Archives of General Psychiatry,* 39 (1982), pp. 303–6.

Lieberman, H.R., et al. "Use of Nutrients That Are Neurotransmitter Precursors to Modify Behaviors: The Effects of Tryptophan and Tyrosine on Human Mood and Performance." *Psychopharmacology Bulletin,* 20:3 (1984), pp. 595–98.

Lim, M.L., and S.B.J. Ebrahim. "Depression After a Stroke: A Hospital Treatment Survey." *Postgraduate Medical Journal,* 59 (1983), pp. 489–91.

"Link Between Substance Abuse and Suicide Substantiated, At Least in People Under 30." *Clinical Psychiatry News,* 13:8 (1985), pp. 1, 13.

Lion, J.R., and L. M. Conn. "Self-Mutilation: Pathology and Treatment." *Psychiatric Annals,* 12:8 (1982), pp. 782–87.

Lipman, A.G. "Nutritional Deficiencies: Which to Blame on Alcohol Abuse." *Modern Medicine,* April 30, 1980, pp. 77–78.

London, R.S., et al. "Premenstrual Syndrome (PMS) and Vitamin E." *Journal of the American College of Nutrition,* 2 (1983), pp. 115–22.

Lonsdale, D. "Thiamine." *Journal of Orthomolecular Psychiatry,* 13:3 (1984), pp. 197–209.

Lovenberg, W. "Action of Antihypertensive Drugs in the Central Nervous System." *Clinical and Experimental Hypertension, Part A.* 4:1–2 (1982), pp. 201–8.

Luchins, D. "Biogenic Amines and Affective Disorders: A Critical Analysis." *International Pharmacopsychiatry,* 11 (1976), pp. 135–49.

Lukaski, H.C., et al. "Maximal Oxygen Consumption as Related to Magnesium, Copper, and Zinc Nutriture." *American Journal of Clinical Nutrition,* 37 (1983), pp. 407–15.

Lyle, H.L. "The Uses of the Hypoglycemic Diet in the Treatment of Emotional Disturbances: A Recent History." *Journal of Applied Nutrition,* 33:1 (1981), pp. 54–62.

McClure, G.M.G. "Recent Trends in Suicide Amongst the Young." *British Journal of Psychiatry,* 144 (1984), pp. 134–38.

MacIntyre, I., et al. "Intracellular Magnesium Deficiency in Man." *Clinical Science,* 20 (1961), pp. 297–305.

McKean, C.M., et al. "The Influence of High Phenylalanine and Tyrosine on the Concentration of Essential Amino Acids in the Brain." *Journal of Neurochemistry,* 15 (1908), pp. 235–41.

Mackenzie, T.B. "Hypoglycemia and Alcoholism." *Psychosomatics,* 20:1 (1979), pp. 39–42.

McKinney, W.T. "Primate Separation Studies: Relevance to Bereavement." *Psychiatric Annals,* 16:5 (1986).

Makipour, H. "Effects of L-Tryptophan on Sleep in Hospitalized Insomniac Patients," (Abstract) in *Sleep Research,* Vol. 1, eds. M. H. Stern, et al. Los Angeles: UCLA Brain Information Service/Brain Research Institute, 1972, p. 65.

Mandell, M., and L. W. Scanlon. *Dr. Mandell's 5-Day Allergy Relief System.* New York: Pocket, 1979.

Mann, J., et al. "D-Phenylalanine in Endogenous Depression." *American Journal of Psychiatry,"* 137:12 (1980), pp. 1611–12.

Marano, H.E. "Aminos Meet the Acid Test." *American Health,* 11:1 (1983), p. 32.

Marier, J.R. "Quantitative Factors Regarding Magnesium Status in the Modern-Day World. *Magnesium,* 1 (1982), pp. 3–15.

Maris, R. *Biology of Suicide.* New York: Guilford Press, 1986.

Marlowe, M., et al. "Lead and Mercury Levels in Emotionally Disturbed Children." *Journal of Orthomolecular Psychiatry,* 12:4 (1983), pp. 260–67.

Martin, H.E. "Clinical Magnesium Deficiency." *Annals of the New York Academy of Science,* 162:2 (1969), pp. 891–900.

Martin, H.E., and F. K. Bauer. "Magnesium 28 Studies in the Cirrhotic and Alcoholic." *Proceedings of the Royal Society of Medicine,* 55 (1962), pp. 912–14.

———, et al. "Electrolyte Disturbance in Acute Alcoholism with Particular Reference to Magnesium." *American Journal of Clinical Nutrition,* 7 (1959), pp. 191–96.

Massey, L., and K. Wise. "Effect of Dietary Caffeine on Mineral Status." *Nutrition Research,* 4 (1984), pp. 43–50.

Massie, Mary Jane, and Jimmie C. Holland. "Diagnosis and Treatment of Depression in the Cancer Patient." *Journal of Clinical Psychiatry,* 45:3 (1984), pp. 25–28.

Mathew, R.J., et al. "Cerebral Flow in Depression." *American Journal of Depression,* 137:11 (1980), pp. 1449–50.

———. "Vegetative Symptoms in Anxiety and Depression." *British Journal of Psychiatry,* 141 (1982), pp. 162–65.

Mawson, A.R. "Gout and Hypervitaminosis." (Letter) *Lancet,* 1 (1984), p. 1181.

Mayeux, R., et al. "Clinical and Biochemical Features of Depression in Parkinson's Disease." *American Journal of Psychiatry,* 143:6 (1986), pp. 756–59.

Meister, A. *Biochemistry of the Amino Acids.* 2nd Edition. New York: Academic Press, 1965.

Melby, C.L., et al. "The Rationale for Incorporating Nonpharmacologic Therapy in the Treatment of Borderline-Mild Hypertension." *Journal of Applied Nutrition,* 36:2 (1984), pp. 63–80.

Meltzer, H.L. *The Chemistry of Human Behavior.* Chicago: Nelson Hall, 1979.

Meltzer, H.Y., et al. "Effect of Serotonin Precursors and Serotonin Agonists on Plasma Hormone Levels," in *Serotonin in Biological Psychiatry*, eds. B. T. Ho et al. New York: Raven Press, 1982.

Mendels, J., and A. Frazer. "Brain Biogenic Amine Depletion and Mood." *Archives of General Psychiatry*, 30 (1974), pp. 447–51.

Mendels, J., et al. "Amine Precursors and Depression." *Archives of General Psychiatry*, 32 (1975), pp. 22–30.

Mendelshon, J.H., et al. "Effects of Alcohol Ingestion and Withdrawal on Magnesium States of Alcoholics: Clinical and Experimental Findings." *Annals of the New York Academy of Science*, 162 (1969), pp. 918–33.

"Mercury Amalgams." *Complementary Medicine*, 1:2 (1985), pp. 14–17.

Merikangas, K.R., et al., "Familial Transmission of Depression and Alcoholism." *Archives of General Psychiatry*, 42 (1985), pp. 367–72.

Metcalfe, D.D., and M. A. Kaliner. "What Is Food to One . . ." *New England Journal of Medicine*, 311:6 (1984), pp. 399–400.

Milakofsky, L., et al. "Rat Plasma Levels of Amino Acids and Related Compounds During Stress." *Life Sciences*, 36 (1985), pp. 753–61.

Miller, A. "A Comparative Trial in the Treatment of Hayfever." *Clinical Allergy*, (1976), p. 556.

Miller, R.D. "Hypochodriasis, Masked Depression, and Electroconvulsive Therapy." *Psychosomatics*, 23:8 (1982), pp. 862–64.

Milne, D.B., et al. "Effect of Oral Folic Acid Supplements on Zinc, Copper, and Iron Absorption and Excretion." *American Journal of Clinical Nutrition*, 39 (1984), pp. 535–39.

Milner, G. "Ascorbic Acid in Chronic Psychiatric Patients: A Controlled Trial." *British Journal of Psychiatry*, 109 (1963), pp. 294–99.

Mindell, E. *Earl Mindell's Vitamin Bible*. New York: Rawson, Wade Publishers, 1979.

————, and W. H. Lee. *The Vitamin Robbers*. New Canaan, CT: Keats, 1983.

Mitchell, James E., et al. "The Dexamethasone Suppression Test in Patients with Bulimia." *Journal of Clinical Psychiatry*, 45:12 (1984), pp. 508–11.

Modern Nutrition in Health and Disease, 6th Ed., eds. R. S. Goodhart and M. E. Shils. Philadelphia: Lea & Febiger, 1980.

Modlinger, R.S., et al. "Adrenocorticotropin Release by Tryptophan in Man." *Journal of Clinical Endocrinology and Metabolism*, 50 (1980), p. 360.

Moir, A.T.B., and D. Eccleston. "The Effect of Precursor Loading in the Cerebral Metabolism of 5-Hydroxyindoles." *Journal of Neurochemistry*, 15 (1968), pp. 1093–108.

Moller, S.E. "Effect of Oral Contraceptives on Tryptophan and Tyrosine Availability: Evidence for a Possible Contribution to Mental Depression." *Neuropsychobiology*, 7:4 (1981), pp. 192–200.

Moller, S.E. "Tryptophan and Tyrosine Availability and Oral Contraceptives." *Lancet*, 2 (1979), p. 472.

————, et al. "Plasma Amino Acid as an Index for Subgroups in Manic Depressive Psychosis: Correlation to Effect Tryptophan." *Psychopharmacology*, 49 (1976), pp. 205–13.

Monte, W.C., and S. H. Ashoor. "Caffeine Content of Selected Soft Drinks." *Journal of Applied Nutrition*, 37:1 (1985), pp. 43–45.

Moos, R.H., et al. "Fluctuations in Symptoms and Moods During the Menstrual Cycle." *Journal of Psychosomatic Research*, 13 (1969), p. 37.

Morgan, R. "Tryptophan Overdose." (Correspondence) *British Journal of Psychiatry*, 131 (1977), p. 548.

Morgan, W.P., et al. "Psychological Effects of Chronic Physical Activity." *Med. Sci. Sports*, 2 (1970), pp. 213–17.

Morstyn, R., et al. "Depression Vs. Pseudodepression in Dementia." *Journal of Clinical Psychiatry*, 43:5 (1982), pp. 197–99.

Mountjoy, C.Q., et al. "A Double-Blind Crossover Sequential Trial of Oral Thyrotrophin-Releasing Hormone in Depression." *Lancet*, 2 (1974), pp. 958–60.

Mountokalakis, T.D. "Diuretic-Induced Magnesium Deficiency." *Magnesium*, 2 (1983), pp. 57–61.

Moynahan, E.J. "Zinc Deficiency and Disturbances of Mood and Visual Behavior." *Lancet*, 1 (1976), p. 89.

Murer, H., et al. "On the Mechanism of Sugar and Amino Acid Interaction in Intestinal Transport." *Journal of Biological Chemistry*, 250 (1975), pp. 7392–96.

Murphy, D.L. "Introduction: Serotonin Neurochemistry and Psychopharmacology in 1986." *Journal of Clinical Psychiatry*, 47:4, Suppl. (1986), p. 3.

———, et al. "L-Tryptophan in Affective Disorders: Indolamine Changes and Differential Clinical Effects." *Psychopharmacologia*, 34 (1974), pp. 11–20.

———, et al. "Use of Serotonergic Agents in the Clinical Assessment of Central Serotonin Function." *Journal of Clinical Psychiatry*, 47:4, Suppl. (1986), pp. 9–15.

Murphy, E. "The Prognosis of Depression in Old Age." *British Journal of Psychiatry*, 142 (1983), pp. 111–19.

Naranjo, C.A., et al. "Modulation of Ethanol Intake by Serotonin Uptake Inhibitors." *Journal of Clinical Psychiatry*, Suppl., 47:4 (1986), pp. 16–22.

Naylor, G.J., et al. "Plasma Magnesium and Calcium Levels in Depressive Psychosis." *British Journal of Psychiatry*, 120 (1972), pp. 683–84.

Nelson, W.H., et al. "Hypothalamic-Pituitary-Adrenal Axis Activity and Age in Major Depression." *Journal of Clinical Psychiatry*, 45:3 (1984), pp. 120–21.

Nemeroff, C.B., et al. "Antithyroid Antibodies in Depressed Patients." *American Journal of Psychiatry*, 142 (1985), pp. 840–43.

Nestoros, J.N., et al. "Levels of Anxiety and Depression in Spinal Cord-Injured Patients." *Psychosomatics*, 23:8 (1982), pp. 823–30.

"A New Attack on Alcoholism." *NCA-LA Newsletter*. Los Angeles: National Council on Alcoholism, 1986, pp. 3–4.

"A New Treatment for Depression." *Lancet*, 2 (1980), p. 364.

Newbold, H.L., et al. "Psychiatric Syndromes Produced by Allergies: Ecologic Mental Illness." *Journal of Orthomolecular Psychiatry*, 2:84 (1973).

Newey, H., and D. H. Smyth. "Effects of Sugars on Intestinal Transfer of Amino Acids." *Nature*, 202 (1964), pp 400–401.

Nicholson, A.N., and B. M. Stone. "L-Tryptophan and Sleep in Healthy Man." *Electroencephalography and Clinical Neurophysiology*, 47 (1979), pp. 539–45.

Nolan, K.R. "Copper Toxicity Syndrome." *Journal of Orthomolecular Psychiatry,* 12:4 (1983), pp. 270–82.

Nutrition Almanac. Nutrition Search, Inc., J. D. Kirschman, Director. New York: McGraw-Hill, 1984.

Nutrition and the Brain, Vol. 1–6, eds. R. J. Wurtman et al. New York: Raven, 1977–86.

Nutrition Education in U.S. Medical Schools. Washington, D.C.: National Academy Press, 1985.

"NYPD Counseling Service." *Alcoholism Update,* 7:4 (1984), pp. 2, 3.

O'Banion, D.R. *The Ecological and Nutritional Treatment of Health Disorders.* Springfield, IL: Charles C. Thomas, 1981.

Okada, F. "Depression after Treatment with Thiazide Diuretics for Hypertension." *American Journal of Psychiatry,* 142:9 (1985), pp. 1101–2.

Orten, J.M., and O. W. Neuhaus. *Human Biochemistry.* St. Louis: C. V. Mosby, 1982.

Osmond, H., and A. Hoffer. "Massive Niacin Treatment in Schizophrenia: Review of a Nine-Year Study." *Lancet,* 1 (1962), pp. 316–20.

———. "Naturally Occurring Endogenous Major and Minor Tranquilizers." *Journal of Orthomolecular Psychiatry,* 9:3 (1980), pp. 198–206.

Ostroff, Robert, et al. "Neuroendocrine Risk Factors of Suicidal Behavior." *American Journal of Psychiatry,* 139 (1982), pp. 1323–25.

Ostrow, D.G., et al. "Biologic Markers and Antidepressant Response." *Journal of Clinical Psychiatry,"* 44:9 (1983), pp. 10–13.

———. "Ion Transport and Andregenic Function in Major Affective Disorder." *Biological Psychiatry,* 17 (1982), pp. 971–80.

———. "State Dependence of Noradrenergic Activity in a Rapidly Cycling Bipolar Patient." *Journal of Clinical Psychiatry,* 45:7 (1984), pp. 306–9.

"Ovarian Insufficiency, Depression Linked." *Clinical Psychiatry News,* 7:11 (1979), p. 1.

Pagnelli, R., et al. "Detection of Specific Antigen Within Circulating Immune Complexes: Validation of the Assay and Its Application to Food Antigen-Antibody Complexes Formed in Healthy and Food-Allergic Subjects." *Clinical and Experimental Immunology,* 46:1 (1981), pp. 4644–53.

Pallis, D.J., et al. "Estimating Suicide Risk Among Attempted Suicides: I. The Development of New Clinical Scales." *British Journal of Psychiatry,* 141 (1982), pp. 37–44.

Pandey, G., et al. "Beta-Adrenergic Receptor Function in Affective Illness." *American Journal of Psychiatry,* 136:5 (1979), pp. 675–78.

Pardridge, W. "Regulation of Amino Acid Availability to the Brain," in *Nutrition and the Brain,* Vol. I, eds. R. J. Wurtman et al. New York: Raven Press, 1977, pp. 141–204.

Pare, C.M.B. "Potentiation of Monoamine-Oxidase Inhibitors by Tryptophan." *Lancet,* 2 (1963), p. 527.

Parker, S.D. "Research on Magnesium, Protein Synthesis, and Memory." *Anabolism,* 5:1 (1986), p. 4.

Parsons, J.M., and A. T. Sapse. "Significance of Hypercortisolism in Anorexia Nervosa." *Journal of Orthomolecular Psychiatry,* 14 (1985), pp. 13–18.

Passwater, R.A., and E. Cranton. *Trace Elements, Hair Analysis and Nutrition.* New Canaan, CT: Keats, 1983.

Paterson, E.T. "Aspects of Hypoglycemia." *Journal of Orthomolecular Psychiatry,* 11:3 (1982), pp. 151–56.

Patterson, W.M., et al. "Evaluation of Suicidal Patients: The SAD PERSONS scale." *Psychosomatics,* 24:4 (1983), pp. 343–48.

Paykel, E.S., et al. "Life Events and Depression." *Archives of General Psychiatry,* 21 (1969), pp. 753–60.

———. "Scaling of Life Events." *Archives of General Psychiatry,* 25 (1971), 340–47.

———. "Self-Report and Clinical Interview Ratings in Depression." *Journal of Nervous and Mental Disease,* 156:3 (1973), pp. 166–82.

Pearson, D., and S. Shaw. "How to Prevent Jet Lag." *Anti-Aging News,* 13 February (1981), p. 12.

———. *Life Extension.* New York: Warner Books, 1982.

Permutt, M.A. "Hypoglycemia: The Condition You Miss, Scoff At, or Diagnose Too Often." *Modern Medicine,* January 15–30, 1979, pp. 49–56.

Perry, P.J., et al. "Treatment of Unipolar Depression Accompanied by Delusions: ECT versus Tricyclic Antidepressant-Antipsychotic Combinations." *Journal of Affective Disorders,* 4 (1982), pp. 195–200.

Peterson, C.M. "Problems of Iron Imbalance." *Drug Therapy,* (1979), pp. 128–42.

Petti, T.A., and A. Unis. "Imipramine Treatment of Borderline Children: Case Reports with a Controlled Study." *American Journal of Psychiatry,* 138:4 (1981), pp. 515–18.

Pfeffer, C.R., et al. "Suicidal and Assaultive Behavior in Children: Classification, Measurement, and Interrelations." *American Journal of Psychiatry,* 140:2 (1983), pp. 154–57.

———. "Suicidal Behavior in Child Psychiatric Inpatients and Outpatients and in Nonpatients." *American Journal of Psychiatry,* 143:6 (1986), pp. 733–38.

———. "Suicidal Behavior in Normal School Children: A Comparison with Child Psychiatric Inpatients." *Journal of American Academy of Child Psychiatry,* 23 (1984), pp. 416–23.

Pfeiffer, C. *Mental and Elemental Nutrients.* New Canaan, CT: Keats, 1975.

Phillips, M.E., et al. "Oral Essential Amino Acid Supplementation in Patients on Maintenance Hemodialysis." *Clinical Nephrology,* 9:6 (1978), pp. 241–48.

Philpott, W., and D. K. Kalita. *Brain Allergies, the Psycho-Nutrient Connection.* New Canaan, CT: Keats, 1980.

"Physician's Guide to Nutrigenic Amino Acids." Sivad BioResearch Co., Inc., #129 Nutrigenic Amino Acid Formula.

Pies, R. "Change in Depression Score During Mononucleosis." *Psychosomatics,* 24:8 (1983), pp. 766–67.

Piesse, J.W. "Nutrition Factors in the Premenstrual Syndrome." *International Advances in Clinical Nutrition,* 4 (1984), pp. 54–81.

Pintar, J.E., et al. "Gene for Monamine Oxidase Type A Assigned to the Human X Chromosome." *Journal of Neuroscience,* 1 (1981), p. 166.

Plotkin, D.A., et al. "Subjective Memory Complaints in Geriatric Depression." *American Journal of Psychiatry,* 142:9 (1985), pp. 1103–5.

Podell, R.N. "Is Migraine a Manifestation of Food Allergy?" *Migraine*, 75:4 (1984), p. 221.

Pomerleau, O.F., et al. "Neuroendocrine Reactivity to Nicotine in Smokers." *Psychopharmacology*, 81 (1983), pp. 61–67.

Poulos, C.J. "What Effects Do Corrective Nutritional Practices Have on Alcoholics?" *Journal of Orthomolecular Psychiatry*, 10:1 (1981), pp. 61–64.

Poznanski, E.O. "The Clinical Phenomenology of Childhood Depression." *American Journal of Orthopsychiatry*, 52:2 (1982), pp. 308–13.

————, et al. "Diagnostic Criteria in Childhood Depression." *American Journal of Psychiatry*, 142 (1985), pp. 1168–73.

Prakash, R., and W. M. Petrie. "Psychiatric Changes Associated with an Excess of Folic Acid." *American Journal of Psychiatry*, 139:9 (1982), pp. 1192–93.

Prange, A.J., and P. T. Loosen. "Some Endocrine Aspects of Affective Disorders." *Journal of Clinical Psychiatry*, 41:12 (1980), pp. 29–34.

————, et al. "Enhancement of Imipramine Antidepressant Activity by Thyroid Hormone." *American Journal of Psychiatry*, 126:4 (1969), pp. 458–69.

Pratt, O.E. "Kinetics of Tryptophan Transport Across the Blood-Brain Barrier." *Journal of Neural Transmission*, Suppl., 15 (1979), pp. 29–42.

Progress in Tryptophan and Serotonin Research, eds. H. G. Schlossberger, et al. New York: Walter de Gruyer, 1984.

Prusoff, B.A., et al. "Concordance Between Clinical Assessments and Patients' Self-Report in Depression." *Archives of General Psychiatry*, 26 (1972), pp. 546–52.

Psychiatric Presentations of Medical Illness, ed. R. Hall. New York: SP Medical and Scientific Books, 1980.

Puig-Antich, J. "Sleep Architecture and REM Sleep Measures in Prepubertal Major Depressives." *Archives of General Psychiatry*, 40 (1983), pp. 187–92.

Rabey, J.M., et al. "L-Tryptophan Administration in L-Dopa-Induced Hallucinations in Elderly Parkinsonian Patients." *Gerontology*, 23 (1977), pp. 438–44.

Rabin, P.L. "Effects of Dietary Lecithin on Hormonal and Neurobehavioral Profiles in Normal Subjects." *Journal of Clinical Psychiatry*, 44:4 (1983), pp. 136–38.

Rancurello, M.D. "Clinical Applications of Antidepressant Drugs in Childhood Behavioral and Emotional Disorders. *Psychiatric Annals*, 15:2 (1985), pp. 88–100.

Randolph, T.G., and R. W. Moss. *An Alternative Approach to Allergies*. New York: Lippincott and Crowell, 1980.

Raskin, A., et al. "Replication of Factors of Psychopathology in Interview, Ward Behavior and Self-Report Ratings of Hospitalized Depressives." *Journal of Nervous and Mental Disease*, 148:1 (1969), pp. 87–98.

Rasmussen, S.A. "Lithium and Tryptophan Augmentation in Clomipramine-Resistant Obsessive-Compulsive Disorder." *American Journal of Psychiatry*, 141:10 (1984), pp. 1283–85.

————, and M. T. Tsuang. "The Epidemiology of Obsessive Compulsive Disorder." *Journal of Clinical Psychiatry*, 45:11 (1984), pp. 450–57.

Reading, C.M. "X-Linked Dominant Manic-Depressive Illness." *Journal of Orthomolecular Psychiatry*, 8:2 (1979), pp. 68–77.

Recent Developments in Alcoholism, Vol. III, ed. M. Galanter. New York: Plenum, 1985.

Recent Vitamin Research, ed. M. H. Briggs. Boca Raton, FL: CRC Press, 1984.

"Recovery in Major Depressive Disorder: Analysis with the Life Table and Regression Models." *Archives of General Psychiatry,* 39 (1982), pp. 905–10.

Redmond, D.E. "A Historical and Biological Overview: Brain Transmitters, Receptors, Single Cells, and a New Treatment for Opiate Addiction." *Journal of Clinical Psychiatry,* 43:6 (1982), pp. 4–8.

Reid, R.L. "Premenstrual Syndrome: A Therapeutic Enigma." *Drug Therapy,* April, 1982, pp. 33–43.

Reinis, S., and J. M. Goldman. *The Chemistry of Behavior: A Molecular Approach to Neuronal Plasticity.* New York: Plenum, 1982.

Reisberg, B., et al. "The Global Deterioration Scale for Assessment of Primary Degenerative Dementia." *American Journal of Psychiatry,* 139:9 (1982), pp. 1136–39.

Reynolds, C.F., et al. "Depressive Psychopathology in Male Sleep Apneics." *Journal of Clinical Psychiatry,* 45:7 (1984), pp. 287–90.

Richelson, E. "Are Receptor Studies Useful for Clinical Practice?" *Journal of Clinical Psychiatry,"* 44:9 (1983), pp. 4–9.

Rimland, B. "High Dosage of Certain Vitamins in the Treatment of Children with Severe Mental Disorders," in D. Hawkins and L. Pauling, *Orthomolecular Psychiatry.* San Francisco: W. H. Freeman, 1973.

Ripley, Herbert S., and Theodore L. Dorpat. "Life Change and Suicidal Behavior." *Psychiatric Annals,* 11:6 (1981), pp. 32–47.

Risch, S.C., et al. "Neurochemical Mechanisms in the Affective Disorders and Neuroendocrine Correlates." *Journal of Clinical Psychiatry,* 1 (1981), pp. 180–85.

———. "Plasma Levels of Tricyclic Antidepressants and Clinical Efficacy: Review of the Literature." *Journal of Clinical Psychiatry,* 40 (1979), pp. 4–16.

Rivinus, T.M., et al. "Anorexia Nervosa and Affective Disorders: A Controlled Family History Study." *American Journal of Psychiatry,* 141:11 (1984), pp. 1414–18.

Roberts, R.E., and S. W. Vernon. "The Center for Epidemiologic Studies Depression Scale: Its Use in a Community Sample." *American Journal of Psychiatry,* 140:1 (1983), pp. 41–46.

Robinson, J.W.L., and F. Alvarado. "Interaction between the Sugar and Amino Acid Transport Systems at the Small Intestinal Brush Border: A Comparative Study." *Pflugers Arch.-European Journal of Physiology,* 326 (1971), pp. 48–75.

———. "Interactions Between Tryptophan, Phenylalanine and Sugar Transport in the Small Intestinal Mucosa." *Journal of Neural Transmission,* Suppl. 15 (1979), pp. 125–37.

Robinson, R.G., et al. "Diagnosis and Clinical Management of Post-Stroke Depression." *Psychosomatics,* 26:10 (1985), pp. 769–78.

Robinson, R.G., et al. "A Two Year Longitudinal Study of Mood Disorders Following Stroke: Prevalence and Duration at Six Months Follow-up." *British Journal of Psychiatry,* 144 (1984), pp. 256–62.

Rodgers, L.L., and R. B. Pelton. "Effect of Glutamine on I.Q. Scores of Mentally Deficient Children." *Texas Reports on Biology and Medicine,* 15 (1957), pp. 84–90.

Rodin, G., and K. Voshart. "Depression in the Medically Ill: An Overview." *American Journal of Psychiatry*, 143:6 (1986), pp. 696–705.

Roe, D.A. *Drug-Induced Nutritional Deficiencies.* Westport, CT: AVI, 1978.

———. *Geriatric Nutrition.* Englewood Cliffs, NJ: Prentice-Hall, 1983.

"Role of Hormones in Affective Disorders Being Studied." *Clinical Psychiatry News*, 6:4 (1978), p. 16.

Rose, D.P., and F. McGinty. "The Influence of Adrenocortical Hormones and Vitamins upon Tryptophan Metabolism in Man." *Clinical Science and Molecular Medicine*, 35 (1968), pp. 1–9.

Rose, W.C. "II. The Sequence of Events Leading to the Establishment of the Amino Acid Needs of Man." *American Journal of Public Health*, 58:11 (1968), pp. 2020–27.

———. "The Nutritive Significance of the Amino Acids." *Physiotherapy Review*, 18 (1958), pp. 109–36.

Rosenberg, G., and K. Davis. "Use of Cholinergic Precursors in Neuropsychiatric Diseases." *American Journal of Clinical Nutrition*, 36 (1982), pp. 709–20.

Rosenberg, H., and A. N. Feldzamen. *The Doctors' Book of Vitamin Therapy.* New York: G. P. Putnam, 1974.

Rosenblatt, S. "Amino Acids in Bipolar Affective Disorders: Increased Glycine Levels in Erythrocytes." *American Journal of Psychiatry*, 136:5 (1979), pp. 672–74.

Rosenthal, N., et al. "Antidepressant Effects of Light in Seasonal Affective Disorder." *American Journal of Psychiatry*, 142 (1985), pp. 163–70.

Rosenthal, P.A., and S. Rosenthal. "Suicidal Behavior by Preschool Children." *American Journal of Psychiatry*, 141:4 (1984), pp. 520–25.

Ross, H.M. "Vitamin Therapy." *Journal of Orthomolecular Psychiatry*, 12:2 (1983), pp. 149–53.

Rothschild, J. "The Role of Carnitine in Medicine and Biological Systems." *Journal of International Academy of Preventive Medicine*, 8:5 (1984), pp. 10–16.

Roy, A. "Family History of Suicide in Affective Disorder Patients." *Journal of Clinical Psychiatry*, 46 (1985), pp. 317–19.

———. "Risk Factors for Suicide in Psychiatric Patients." *Archives of General Psychiatry*, 39 (1982), pp. 1089–95.

———, and J. Glaister. "Suicide in Psychiatric Patients." *Psychiatric Journal of the University of Ottawa*, 9 (1984), pp. 42–44.

Roy-Byrne, Peter, et al. "Possible Antidepressant Effect of Oral Contraceptives: Case Report." *Journal of Clinical Psychiatry*, 45:8 (1984), pp. 350–52.

Ruenwongsa, P., and S. Pattanavibag. "Decrease in the Activities of Thiamine Pyrophosphate Dependent Enzymes in Rat Brain after Prolonged Tea Consumption." *Nutrition Reports International*, 27:4 (1983), pp. 713–21.

Rush, A.J., et al. "Comparison of the Effects of Cognitive Therapy and Pharmacotherapy on Hopelessness and Self-Concept." *American Journal of Psychiatry*, 139:7 (1982), pp. 862–66.

Russell, R.M., et al. "Acceleration of Folic Acid Excretion by Alcohol." *American Journal of Clinical Nutrition*, 38 (1983), pp. 64–70.

Saad, A.A., et al. "Relationship Between Pyridoxal Phosphate and Some Synthetic Oestrogens." *Biochemical Pharmacology*, 23 (1974), pp. 999–1013.

Sabelli, H.C., et al. "Clinical Studies on the Phenylethylamine Hypothesis of Affective Disorder: Urine and Blood Phenylacetic Acid and Phenylalanine Dietary Supplements." *Journal of Clinical Psychiatry,* 47:2 (1986), pp. 66–70.

Saller, C.F., and L. A. Chiodo. "Glucose Suppresses Basal Firing and Haloperidol-Induced Increases in the Firing Rate of Central Dopaminergic Neurons." *Science,* 210 (1980), pp. 1269–71.

Saltman, P., et al. "For the Want of a Nail . . . , Trace Elements in Health and Disease," in *Metabolism of Trace Metals in Man, Development Aspects,* Vol. I, eds. O. M. Rennert and W. Y. Chan. Boca Raton, FL: CRC Press, 1984.

Sampson, H.A., and P. L. Jolie. "Increased Plasma Histamine Concentrations after Food Challenges in Children with Atopic Dermatitis." *New England Journal of Medicine,* 311:6 (1984), pp. 372–76.

Sandler, R.S. "Diet and Cancer: Food Additives, Coffee and Alcohol." *Nutrition and Cancer,* 4 (1983), pp. 273–78.

Sangdee, C., and D. N. Franz. "Lithium Enhancement of Central 5-HT Transmission Induced by 5-HT Precursors." *Biological Psychiatry,* 15:1 (1980), pp. 59–75.

Schatzberg, A.F. *Common Treatment Problems in Depression.* Washington, D.C.: American Psychiatric Press, 1985.

———. "Discussion: Controversies in Antidepressant Therapy." *Journal of Clinical Psychiatry,"* 44:9 (1983), pp. 29–30.

———, et al. "A Corticosteroid/Dopamine Hypothesis for Psychotic Depression and Related States." *Journal of Psychiatric Research,* 19 (1985), pp. 57–64.

———. "The Dexamethasone Suppression Test: Identification of Subtypes of Depression." *American Journal of Psychiatry.* 140:1 (1983), pp. 88–91.

———. "Toward a Biochemical Classification of Depressive Disorders, V: Heterogeneity of Unipolar Depressions." *American Journal of Psychiatry,* 139:4 (1982), pp. 471–74.

Schilldkraut, J.J. "The Catecolamine Hypothesis of Affective Disorders: A Review of Supporting Evidence." *American Journal of Psychiatry,* 122 (1965), p. 509.

Schneider, M.A. *Alcohol and Nutrition.* Santa Ana, CA: MAS, 1982.

Schneider-Helmert, D. "Interval Therapy with L-Tryptophan in Severe Chronic Insomniacs." *International Pharmaco-Psychiatry,* Switzerland, 16: (1981), pp. 162–73.

Schreier, H.A. "Mania Responsive to Lecithin in a 13-Year-Old Girl." *American Journal of Psychiatry,* 139 (1982), pp. 108–10.

Schuckit, M. "Alcoholic Patients with Secondary Depression." *American Journal of Psychiatry,* 140:6 (1983), pp. 711–14.

———. "Genetic and Clinical Implications of Alcoholism and Affective Disorder." *American Journal of Psychiatry,* 143:2 (1986), pp. 140–47.

Schwab, J.J., et al. "A Study of the Somatic Symptomology of Depression in Medical Inpatients." *Psychosomatics,* 6 (1965), pp. 273–77.

Scrimshaw, N.S. "Functional Consequences of Iron Deficiency in Human Populations." *Journal of Nutritional Science and Vitaminology,* 30 (1984), pp. 47–63.

Scriver, C.R., and L. E. Rosenberg. *Major Problems in Clinical Pediatrics, Vol. X, Amino Acid Metabolism and Its Disorders,* ed. Alexander J. Schaffer. Philadelphia: W. B. Saunders, 1973.

———. "Phenylalanine," in *Amino Acid Metabolism and Its Disorders.* Philadelphia: W. B. Saunders, 1973.

Seelig, M. *Magnesium Deficiency in the Pathogenesis of Disease.* New York: Plenum Medical Book Company, 1980.

———. "Magnesium Requirements in Human Nutrition." *Magnesium Bulletin,* 1a (1981), pp. 26–47.

Shafii, Mohammad, et al. "Psychological Autopsy of Completed Suicide in Children and Adolescents." *American Journal of Psychiatry,* 142:9 (1985), pp. 1061–64.

Shalita, B., and S. Dikstein. "Tyrosine Prevents Hypertension in DOCA-Saline Treated Uninephrectomized Rats." *Pflugers Archive,* 379 (1979), p. 245.

Shamoian, C.A. *Biology and Treatment of Dementia in the Elderly.* Washington, D.C.: American Psychiatric Press, 1984.

Shank, R.P., and M. H. Aprison. "Present Status and Significance of the Glutamine Cycle in Neural Tissue." *Life Sciences,* 28 (1981), pp. 837–42.

Sharaf, A., and N. Gomaa. "Interrelationship Between Vitamins of the B-Complex Groups and Oestradiol." *Journal of Endocrinology,* 62 (1974), pp. 241–44.

Shaw, D.M., et al. "Distribution of Tryptophan and Tyrosine in Unipolar Affective Disorders as Defined by Multicompartmental Analysis." *Journal of Neural Transmission,* Suppl. 15 (1979), pp. 197–207.

———. "Tryptophan Affective Disorder and Stress." *Journal of Affective Disorders,* 2:4 (1980), pp. 321–25.

Sheard, M.H., and J. L. Marini. "Treatment of Human Aggressive Behavior: Effect of Lithium." *Comprehensive Psychiatry,* 19 (1978), pp. 37–46.

Sheinkin, D., et al. *Food, Mind and Mood.* New York: Warner, 1979.

Shils, M.E. "Experimental Human Magnesium Depletion." *Medicine,* 48 (1969), pp. 61–85.

Shore, D., and R. J. Wyatt. "Aluminum and Alzheimer's Disease." *Journal of Nervous and Mental Disease,* 171:9 (1983), pp. 553–57.

Shulman, R. "An Overview of Folic Acid Deficiency and Psychiatric Illness," in *Folic Acid in Neurology, Psychiatry, and Internal Medicine,* eds. M. I. Botez and E. H. Reynolds. New York: Raven Press, 1979.

Sicuteri, F. "The Ingestion of Serotonin Precursors (L-5 Hydroxy-Tryptophan and L-Tryptophan) Improves Migraine Headache." *Headache,* 13 (1973), pp. 19–22.

Siever, L.J., and K. L. Davis. "Overview: Toward a Dysregulation Hypothesis of Depression." *American Journal of Psychiatry,* 142 (1985), pp. 1017–31.

Silberfarb, P.M., et al. "Psychosocial Aspects of Neoplastic Disease: II. Affective and Cognitive Effects of Chemotherapy in Cancer Patients." *American Journal of Psychiatry,* 137:5 (1980), pp. 597–601.

Simonson, Melvin. "L-Phenylalanine." *Journal of Clinical Psychiatry,* 46:8 (1985), p. 355.

Simpson, George, and Kerrin White. "Monoamine Oxidase Inhibitors: Their Use in Clinical Practice." *Hospital & Community Psychiatry,* 33 (1982), pp. 615–16.

Singh, N.P., et al. "Intake of Magnesium and Toxicity of Lead: An Experimental Model." *Archives of Environmental Health,* 34 (1979), p. 168.

Siris, S.G., et al. "Course-Related Depressive Syndromes in Schizophrenia." *American Journal of Psychiatry,* 141:10 (1984), pp. 1254–57.

Smedes, L.B. *Forgive and Forget.* New York: Pocket Books, 1984.

Smith, B., and D. J. Prockop. "Central-Nervous-System Effects of Ingestion of L-Tryptophan by Normal Subjects." *New England Journal of Medicine,* 267:26 (1962), pp. 1338–41.

Smith, R.C., et al. "Cardiovascular Effects of Therapeutic Doses of Tricyclic Antidepressants: Importance of Blood Monitoring." *Journal of Clinical Psychiatry,* 41:12 (1980), pp. 57–63.

Sohler, A., et al. "Blood Aluminum Levels in a Psychiatric Outpatient Population: High Aluminum Levels Related to Memory Loss." *Journal of Orthomolecular Psychiatry,* 10:1 (1981), pp. 54–60.

Sondheimer, S.J., et al. "Hormonal Changes in Premenstrual Syndrome." *Psychosomatics,* 26:10 (1985), pp. 803–10.

Sourlles, T.L. "Toxicology of Serotonin Precursors." *Advances in Biological Psychiatry,* 10 (1983), pp. 160–75.

Speer, F. "Multiple food allergy." *Annals of Allergy,* 34:2 (1975), p. 71.

Spinweber, C., et al. "L-Tryptophan: Effect on Daytime Sleep Latency and the Waking EEG." *Electroencephalography and Clinical Neurophysiology,* 55 (1983), pp. 652–61.

"Spotlight: James F. Devine, NYPD." *Alcoholism Update,* 7:4 (1984), pp. 1, 6.

Stahl, S.M. "Regulation of Neurotransmitter Receptors by Desipramine and Other Antidepressant Drugs: The Neurotransmitter Receptor Hypothesis of Antidepressant Action." *Journal of Clinical Psychiatry,* 45:10, Sec. 2 (1984), pp. 37–44.

————, et al. "Hyperserotonemia and Platelet Serotonin Uptake and Release in Schizophrenia and Affective Disorders." *American Journal of Psychiatry,* 140:1 (1983), pp. 26–30.

Stanley, M., and J. J. Mann. "Increased Serotonin-2 Binding Sites in Frontal Cortex of Suicide Victims." *Lancet,* 2 (1983), pp. 214–16.

Stebbing, J.B., et al. "Reactive Hypoglycemia and Magnesium." *Magnesium Bulletin,* 4 (1982), p. 131.

Stein, L. et al. "Memory Enhancement by Central Administration of Norepinephrine." *Brain Research,* 84:2 (1975), pp. 329–35.

Stending-Lindberg, G. "Hypomagnesaemia in Alcohol Encephalopathies." *Acta Psychiatrica Scandinavica,* 50 (1974), pp. 465–80.

Stern, S.L., et al. "Toward a Rational Pharmacotherapy of Depression." *American Journal of Psychiatry,* 137:5 (1980), pp. 545–52.

————. "Affective Disorder in the Families of Women with Normal Weight Bulimia." *American Journal of Psychiatry,* 141:10 (1984), pp. 1224–1227.

Sternbach, H.A., et al. "Identifying Depression Secondary to Lithium-Induced Hypothyroidism." *Psychosomatics,* 25:11 (1984), pp. 864–66.

Sternberg, D.E. "Testing for Physical Illness in Psychiatric Patients." *Journal of Clinical Psychiatry,* 47:1, Suppl. (1986), pp. 3–9.

Stevens, L.J. *The Complete Book of Allergy Control.* New York: Macmillan, 1983.

Stoll, Christopher. "I Can't Eat That!" *American Health,* 6:3 (1984), pp. 15–16.

"Stress." Research Bulletin No. 530. Phoenix, AZ: American Society of Nutritional Research, n.d.

Sudak, H. *Suicide in the Young.* Littleton, MA: PSG Publishing, 1984.

Suggerman, A.A., et al. "A Study of Antibody Levels in Alcoholic, Depressive and Schizophrenic Patients." *Annals of Allergy,* 48:3 (1982), pp. 166–71.

Sydenstricker, V.P., and H. M. Cleckly. "The Effect of Nicotinic Acid in Stupor, Lethargy and Various Other Psychiatric Disorders." *American Journal of Psychiatry,* 98 (1941), pp. 83–92.

Tamminga, C., et al. "Depression Associated with Oral Choline." *Lancet,* 2 (1976), p. 905.

Targum, S.D. "The Application of Serial Neuroendocrine Challenge Studies in the Management of Depressive Disorder." *Biological Psychiatry,* 18:1 (1983), pp. 3–20.

―――, et al. "Thyroid Hormone and the TRH Stimulation Test in Refractory Depression." *Journal of Clinical Psychiatry,* 45:8 (1984), pp. 345–46.

Thiessen, I., and L. Mills. "The Use of Megavitamin Treatment in Children with Learning Disabilities." *Journal of Orthomolecular Psychiatry,* 4:4 (1975), pp. 288–96.

Thomas, J., et al. "Magnesium-Inhibiting Factor of Crystallization in Calcium Oxalate and Reducing Factor in Experimentally Induced Oxalic Lithasis." *Magnesium in Health and Disease,* eds. M. Canten and M. Seelig. New York: Spectrum (1980), pp. 479–83.

Thomas, P., et al. "Effect of Social Support on Stress-Related Changes in Cholesterol Level, Uric Acid Level, and Immune Function in an Elderly Sample." *American Journal of Psychiatry,* 142 (1985), pp. 735–37.

Thompson, T.L., et al. "Psychotropic Drug Use in the Elderly (First of Two Parts)." *New England Journal of Medicine,* 308 (1983), pp. 134–38.

―――. "Psychotropic Drug Use in the Elderly (Second of Two Parts)." *New England Journal of Medicine,* 308 (1983), pp. 194–99.

Thompson, W.L., and T. L. Thompson. "Treating Depression in Asthmatic Patients." *Psychosomatics,* 25:11 (1984), pp. 809–12.

Thornton, W.E., and B. J. Pray. "Lowered Serum Folate and Alcohol-Withdrawal Syndromes." *Psychosomatics,* December (1977), pp. 32–36.

Truss, C.O. "Metabolic Abnormalities in Patients with Chronic Candidiasis." *Journal of Orthomolecular Psychiatry,* 13:2 (1984), pp. 66–93.

―――. *Missing Diagnosis.* Birmingham, AL: Missing Diagnosis, Inc., 1983.

―――. "Restoration of Immunologic Competence to Candida Albicans." *Journal of Orthomolecular Psychiatry,* 9:4 (1980), pp. 287–301.

"Tryptophan—An Amino Acid Which Has a Future in Treating Depression and Insomnia." *Western Academy Review,* 1:2 (1976), pp. 49–51.

Uhde, T.W. "Glucose Tolerance Testing in Panic Disorder." *American Journal of Psychiatry,* 141:11 (1984), pp. 1461–63.

―――, et al. "Caffeine and Behaviour: Relation to Psychopathology and Underlying Mechanisms. Caffeine: Relationship to Human Anxiety, Plasma MHPG and Cortisol." *Psychopharmacology Bulletin,* 20:3 (1984), pp. 426–30.

Ulwelling, W. " 'Pseudo-allergy': Treatment with an MAO Inhibitor." *Psychosomatics,* 26:6 (1985), pp. 535–36.

Ushakov, A.S., et al. "Effect of Vitamin and Amino Acid Supplements on Human Performance During Heavy Mental and Physical Work." *Aviation, Space and Environmental Medicine,* October, 1978, pp. 1184–87.

Van Baak, A. "Tryptophan—Natural Alternative to Tranquilizers." *Bestways,* October, 1981. (Bestways Magazine, P.O. Box 2028, Carson City, Nevada 89701.)

van Praag, H.M. "Depression, Suicide and the Metabolism of Serotonin in the Brain." *Journal of Affective Disorders,* 4 (1982), pp. 275–90.

———. "Management of Depression with Serotonin Precursors." *Biological Psychiatry,* 16 (1981), pp. 291–305.

———. "Neuroendocrine Disorders in Depressions and Their Significance for the Monoamine Hypothesis of Depression." *Acta Psychiatrica Scandinavica,* 57 (1978), p. 389.

———. "Studies in the Mechanism of Action of Serotonin Precursors in Depression." *Psychopharmacology Bulletin,* 20:3 (1984), pp. 599–602.

Van Tiggelen, C.J.M. "Alzheimer's Disease/Alcohol Dementia—Association with Zinc Deficiency and Cerebral Vitamin B_{12} Deficiency." *Journal of Orthomolecular Psychiatry,* 13:2 (1984), pp. 97–104.

———, et al. "Vitamin B_{12} Levels of Cerebrospinal Fluid in Patients with Organic Mental Disorder." *Journal of Orthomolecular Psychiatry,* 12:4 (1983), pp. 305–11.

"Vanadium, Vitamin C and Depression." *Nutrition Reviews,* 40:101 (1982), p. 293.

Vander, A.J. *Nutrition, Stress and Toxic Chemicals.* Ann Arbor: University of Michigan Press, 1981.

"Variety of Research on Genetic Markers for Alcoholism Now Under Way in U.S." *Psychiatric News,* May 17, 1985, pp. 40–42.

Vasant, G.J., et al. "Vitamins B_1, B_6, and B_{12} in the Adjunctive Treatment of Schizophrenia—Further Studies to Examine the Effect of Reduction of Chlorpromazine Dosage." *Journal of Orthomolecular Psychiatry,* 11:1 (1982), pp. 45–49.

Veith, R.C., et al. "Cardiovascular Effects of Tricyclic Antidepressants in Depressed Patients with Chronic Heart Disease." *New England Journal of Medicine,* 306 (1982), pp. 954–59.

Verzosa, P.L. "A Report on a Twelve-Month Period of Treating Metabolic Diseases Using Mainly Vitamins and Minerals on the Schizophrenias." *Journal of Orthomolecular Psychiatry,* 5:4 (1976), pp. 253–60.

Vogel, G.W. "The Relationship Between Endogenous Depression and REM Sleep." *Psychiatric Annals,* 11:12 (1981), pp. 423–28.

Von Ammon, S., and M. D. Cavanaugh. "Diagnosing Depression in the Hospitalized Patient with Chronic Medical Illness." *Journal of Clinical Psychiatry,* 45:3 (1984), pp. 13–16.

Vroulis, G.A., et al. "The Effects of Lecithin on Memory in Patients with Senile Dementia of the Alzheimer's Type." *Psychopharmacol Bulletin,* 17 (1981), pp. 127–28.

Waldstein, S.S. "Thyroid-Catecholamine Interrelations." *Annual Review of Medicine,* 17 (1966), pp. 123–32.

Waller, M.B., et al. "Intragastric Self-Infusion of Ethanol-Preferring and Nonpreferring Lines of Rats." *Science,* 225 (1984), pp. 78–80.

Walton, R.G. "Seizure and Mania after High Intake of Aspartame." *Psychosomatics,* 27:3 (1986), pp. 218–20.

Ward, N.G., et al. "The Effectiveness of Tricyclic Antidepressants in Chronic Depression." *Journal of Clinical Psychiatry,* 40 (1979), pp. 49–52.

Warnes, H., and C. Fitzpatrick. "Oral Contraceptives and Depression." *Psychosomatics*, 20:3 (1979), pp. 187–94.

Watkin, D.M. *Handbook of Nutrition, Health, and Aging*. Park Ridge, NJ: Noyes, 1983.

Watkins, L.M. "Premenstrual Distress Gains Notice as a Chronic Issue in the Workplace." *The Wall Street Journal*, January 22, 1986, p. 29.

Watts, C.A.H. "Depressive Disorders in the Community: The Scene in Great Britain, 1965." *Journal of Clinical Psychiatry*, 45:2 (1984), pp. 70–77.

Weinberg, N.A., et al. "Depression in Children Referred to an Educational Diagnostic Center: Diagnosis and Treatment." *Journal of Pediatrics*, 83:6 (1973), pp. 1065–72.

Weinsier, R.L., et al. "Nutrition Knowledge of Senior Medical Students: A Collaborative Study of Southeastern Medical Schools." *American Journal of Clinical Nutrition*, 43 (1986), pp. 959–68.

Weiss, B. "Behavioral Toxicology and Environmental Health Science." *American Psychologist*, November, 1983, pp. 1174–87.

Weller, E.B., and R. A. Weller. *Current Perspectives on Major Depressive Disorders in Children*. Washington, D.C.: American Psychiatric Press, 1984.

————, et al. "The Dexamethasone Suppression Test in Prepubertal Depressed Children." *Journal of Clinical Psychiatry*, 46:12 (1985), pp. 511–13.

Westenberg, H.G.M., et al. "Postsynaptic Serotonergic Activity in Depressive Patients: Evaluation of the Neuroendocrine Strategy." *Psychiatry Research*, 7 (1982), pp. 361–71.

White, A., et al. *Principles of Biochemistry*. New York: McGraw-Hill, 1978.

White, J. "The Role of Nutrition in Recovery from Alcoholism." *Alcohol, Health and Research World*. U.S. Department of Health and Human Services (1982), pp. 36–37.

White, K., et al. "Combined Monoamine Oxidase Inhibitor-Tricyclic Antidepressant Treatment: A Pilot Study." *American Journal of Psychiatry*, 137: 11 (1980), pp. 1422–25.

Whybrow, P.C., et al. *Toward a New Psychobiology*. New York: Plenum, 1984.

Williams, R.J. *The Prevention of Alcoholism Through Nutrition*. New York: Bantam Books, 1981.

Wold, P.M., et al. "Depressive Symptoms and the Diagnosis of Affective Disorder in a Clinic Population of Low Socioeconomic Status." *American Journal of Psychiatry*, 139:7 (1982), pp. 916–18.

Wood, K., et al. "Tryptophan Accumulation by Blood Platelets of Depressed Patients." *Journal of Neural Transmission*, Suppl. 15 (1979), pp. 161–63.

Woolf, P.D., and L. Lee. "Effect of the Serotonin Precursor, Tryptophan, on Pituitary Hormone Secretion." *Journal of Clinical Endocrinol. Metab.*, 45 (1977), pp. 123–33.

Wright, J.V. *Dr. Wright's Book of Nutritional Therapy*. Emmaus, PA: Rodale, 1979.

Wurtman, R.J. "Nutrients That Modify Brain Function." *Scientific American*, 246 (1982), pp. 50–59.

————. "When—and Why—Should Nutritional State Control Neurotransmitter Synthesis?" *Journal of Neural Transmission*, Suppl. 15 (1979), pp. 69–79.

————, et al. "Brain Catechol Synthesis: Control by Brain Tyrosine Concentration." *Science*, 185 (1974), pp. 183–84.

————. "Lecithin Consumption Raises Serum-Free-Choline Levels." *Lancet*, 2 (1977), pp. 68–69.

Wyatt, R.J., et al. "Effects of L-Tryptophan (A Natural Sedative) on Human Sleep." *Lancet*, 2 (1970), pp. 842–46.

Yaryura-Tobias, J.A. "Tryptophan May Be Adjuvant to Obsessive-Compulsive Therapy." *Clinical Psychiatry News*, 9:9 (1981), p. 16.

Yaryura-Tobias, J.A., and H. N. Bhabavan. "L-Tryptophan in Obsessive-Compulsive Disorders." *American Journal of Psychiatry*, 134:11 (1977), pp. 1298–99.

"Younger Depressed Patients Being Seen." *Clinical Psychiatry News*, 13:8 (1985), pp. 3, 27.

Zieve, C. "Influence of Magnesium Deficiency on the Utilization of Thiamine." *Annals of the New York Academy of Science*, 162 (1969), pp. 732–43.

Zisook, S., et al. "Factors in the Persistence of Unresolved Grief Among Psychiatric Outpatients." *Psychosomatics*, 26:6 (1985), pp. 497–503.

Zoler, M. "Diet Restriction: New Way to Slow the Aging Process." *Geriatrics*, 39 (1984), pp. 130–44.

Zung, W.W., et al. "Self-Rating Depression Scale in an Outpatient Clinic." *Archives of General Psychiatry*, 12 (1965), pp. 63–70.

————. "From Art to Science: The Diagnosis and Treatment of Depression." *Archives of General Psychiatry*, 29 (1973), pp. 328–37.

————., and R. E. King. "Identification and Treatment of Masked Depression in a General Medical Practice." *Journal of Clinical Psychiatry*, 44:10 (1983), pp. 365–68.

————, et al. "Symptom Perception by Nonpsychiatric Physicians in Evaluating for Depression." *Journal of Clinical Psychiatry*, 45:7 (1984) pp. 26–29.